Trotsky as Alternative

Trotsky as Alternative

ERNEST MANDEL

Translated by
Gus Fagan

VERSO

London · New York

To Jakob Moneta,
an unswerving fighter for the German working class
and an exemplary internationalist,
in honour of forty-seven years of close friendship
and common struggle.

First published by Verso 1995
This edition © Ernest Mandel 1995
Translation © Gus Fagan 1995
First published as *Trotzki als Alternative*
© Dietz Verlag Berlin 1992
All rights reserved

Verso
UK: 6 Meard Street, London W1V 3HR
USA: 180 Varick Street, New York, NY 10014

Verso is the imprint of New Left Books

ISBN 1 85984 995 4
ISBN 1 85984 085 X (pbk)

British Library Cataloguing in Publication Data
A catalogue record for this book is available from the British Library

Library of Congress Cataloging-in-Publication Data
Mandel, Ernest.
[Trotzki als Alternative. English]
Trotsky as alternative / Ernest Mandel ; translated by Gus Fagan.
p.   cm.
Translation of: Trotzki als Alternative.
Includes bibliographical references (p.   ) and index.
ISBN 1–85984–995–4 (hbk.). — ISBN 1–85984–085–X (pbk.)
1. Communist revisionism. 2. Trotsky, Leon, 1879–1940.
I. Title.
HX518.R4M25713 1995   94–48402
335.43'3—dc20 CIP

Typeset by Solidus (Bristol) Limited
Printed and bound in Great Britain by
Biddles Ltd, Guildford and King's Lynn

Contents

1

Trotsky's Place in the Twentieth Century

Of all the important socialists of the twentieth century, it was Trotsky who recognized most clearly the main tendencies of development and the principal contradictions of the epoch, and it was Trotsky also who gave the clearest formulation to an appropriate emancipatory strategy for the international labour movement. His contribution to the history of this century was a predominantly political one and not, as some have maintained, purely sociological.[1] It was also an eminently practical one and not purely analytic-theoretical. He developed a concept or model of the differentiated processes of class struggle on a global scale and drew from this the necessary practical, strategic, tactical and organizational conclusions.

These ideas, however, were rooted in a magnificent theoretical achievement, the discovery of the law of uneven and combined development, quite distinct from the law of uneven development familiar to all Marxists.[2] On the basis of a thoroughgoing application of the dialectical method to the analysis of the imperialist epoch, in particular to the period of its decline, Trotsky's theory brings to light the articulation of all the major elements (economic, political, class, psychological, ideological and organizational) of a historical mechanism at work:

1. In the imperialist epoch, the Marxist evolutionary schema, according to which the advanced nations hold up to the more underdeveloped the image of their own future, is turned into its opposite. Imperialism blocks the radical modernization and industrialization of the underdeveloped countries.[3]

2. This leads, in the imperialist countries themselves, to a contradictory economic dynamic. The imperialist countries can grow organically only to the extent that there is space for expansion into the colonies and semi-colonies. But, with imperialism dominating the whole world, this underdevelopment which imperialism itself has consolidated in the colonies and semi-colonies becomes a hindrance to

1

its own further growth. This will lead increasingly to inter-imperialist conflict. Once the expansion process of imperialism has come to an end, it is the struggle over the division of the world market that becomes decisive. At the same time, the system as a whole tends towards stagnation or decline in productive forces.

3. This reversal of capitalism's economic advance and the onset of stagnation, accompanied by a sharpening of periodic economic crises, increases the susceptibility of the system to general social and economic crisis. What was an exception in the nineteenth century becomes the rule in the twentieth. This applies to the social and political relations within the underdeveloped as well as within the imperialist countries; it also applies to the relations among the imperialist states and between the latter and the Third World. The twentieth century will be the century of wars and civil wars, of revolutions and counter-revolutions.

4. The combined effect of all these factors will lead to a strengthening of retrogressive movements in society, to a growing threat to the progressive gains of the bourgeois revolutions and to an increasing fusion of the 'old' pre-capitalist barbarism with 'new' forms of barbarism being created by capitalism's decline. Massive catastrophes threaten the human race.[4] The First World War is an example of such barbarism. There will be other examples, even worse than this one.

5. The modern class of wage-earners is the only social force able to bring this series of social catastrophes to an end. This is a consequence of its key position in economic life as well as of its social and socio-psychological make-up. The individual wage-earners, because of their subordination and their material weakness in the economic process vis-à-vis the employers, can defend their immediate day-to-day interests only by developing co-operation and solidarity with their fellow workers and by making this co-operation the driving force behind their social practice, rather than egoism and competition.[5] But this is precisely the kind of motivation and driving force that is essential for the reorganization of society as a whole, to lead society out of the dead end of capitalism and towards the only possible positive alternative, namely, socialism.

6. Because of the system's increasing susceptibility to crisis, in the imperialist countries as well as in the Third World, the state, especially in periods of severe crisis, will become a violently repressive instrument of force in the hands of the ruling classes. Without the overthrow of this state, without the seizure of power by the working class, this class will not be able to fulfil its historic tasks of preventing the regression to barbarism.[6]

7. In the imperialist countries the main obstacle to the seizure of state power is the growing conservatism of the leadership of the organized labour movement, concomitant with ideological weaknesses in the working class itself.[7] (Later, Trotsky was to provide a materialist explanation of this conservatism with his account of the development of a labour bureaucracy as a distinct social layer with its own special interests.) It would require time and new experiences in struggle before the working class of the industrialized countries would be able to overcome these ideological weaknesses.

8. In some less developed countries[8] the working class can achieve a much higher level of class-consciousness, of unity and militancy than in the more developed countries. It is therefore possible, if not probable, that the working class in these countries will be able to seize state power before workers in the West.

9. Self-activity and self-organization are the natural instruments for seizing as well as exercising state power. The soviets or councils are the form of proletarian power brought forward by history itself, in the industrialized as well as in the less developed countries.[9] Shortly after his imprisonment in 1906, Trotsky wrote his *History of the Soviet*, in which he summed up the role of the Petrograd Soviet:

> Urban Russia was too narrow a base for the struggle. The Soviet tried to wage the struggle on a national scale, but it remained above all a Petersburg institution ... there is no doubt that in the next upsurge of revolution, such Councils of Workers, will be formed all over the country. An All-Russian Soviet of Workers, organized by a national congress ... will assume the leadership: ... with revolutionary co-operation between the army, the peasantry and the plebian parts of the middle classes ...[10]

This is exactly what happened in 1917.

10. In the less developed countries, however, the working class constitutes only a minority of the population. Without an alliance with the working peasantry, the workers cannot win or maintain state power. The historic tasks of the revolution in these countries are those of the bourgeois or national-democratic revolution. In this respect Trotsky, like the Bolsheviks and Mensheviks, was stating the position of classical Marxism. What was new in Trotsky's position, his strategy of permanent revolution, was his assertion that these historic tasks of the bourgeois revolution could only be achieved through the creation of a dictatorship of the proletariat in alliance with the working peasantry.[11]

11. It is only through self-activity and self-organization that the working class can conquer state power. For this precise reason it is

unrealistic to attempt to impose on the working class a self-limitation, whereby they restrict themselves, for historical-theoretical reasons, to achieving national-democratic goals (the classical tasks of the bourgeois revolution). A politically successful, self-activating, self-conscious, well-organized working class will not continue to allow itself to be commanded and exploited by the employers.[12] In a very practical way the working class, as soon as it has conquered state power, will begin to address the tasks of the socialist revolution. Without stages or interruptions, the revolution will combine the achievement of national-democratic goals with the beginning of the achievement of socialist goals.[13]

12. But precisely this same law of uneven and combined development, which made it possible for the working class in Russia to conquer state power before the workers in Germany, made it impossible for the workers in Russia alone to hold on to this power over a long period. (Trotsky later qualified this: what would be impossible in such circumstances would be the long-term direct exercise of state power by the workers.)

The construction of socialism is dependent on the existence of material preconditions which can be ignored only at the price of severe disillusionment (we would add today: of severe excesses). On this point Trotsky was firmly within the tradition of Marx, who wrote in *The German Ideology*:

> This 'alienation', to use a term which the philosophers will understand, can be abolished only on the basis of two practical premisses. To become an 'intolerable' power, that is, a power against which men make a revolution, it must have made the great mass of humanity 'propertyless' and this at the same time in contradiction to an existing world of wealth and culture, both of which presuppose a great increase in productive power and a high degree of its development. On the other hand, this development of productive forces (which already implies the actual empirical existence of men on a world-historical rather than local scale) is an absolutely necessary practical premiss because, without it, want is merely made more general, and with destitution the struggle for necessities and all the old muck would necessarily be reproduced; and furthermore, because only with this universal development of productive forces is a universal commerce among men established which produces in all nations simultaneously the phenomenon of a 'propertyless' mass (universal competition), makes each nation dependent on the revolutions of the others, and finally replaces local individuals with world-historical, empirically universal individuals. Without this, (1) communism could only exist locally; (2) the forces of interaction themselves could not have developed as universal and thus intolerable powers, but would have remained homebred, superstitious

'conditions'; (3) any extension of interaction would abolish local communism. Empirically, communism is only possible as the act of dominant
peoples 'all at once' and simultaneously, which presupposes the universal
development of productive power and worldwide interaction linked with
communism. Besides, the mass of propertyless workers – labour-power on
a mass scale cut off from capital or even limited satisfaction, and hence no
longer just temporarily deprived of work as a secure source of life –
presupposes a world market through competition. The proletariat thus can
only exist world-historically, just as communism, its activity, can only have
a world-historical existence. World-historical existence of individuals
means existence of individuals which is directly bound up with world
history.[14]

Today, this reads like a tragic anticipation of what has happened in
the Soviet Union and in the Eastern Bloc since the 1950s, if not since
the 1930s. The victory of the working class in underdeveloped Russia
could only have been consolidated by means of an extension of the
successful revolution to at least some of the leading industrial nations
of the world. Isolated in a relatively backward country, the revolution
was vulnerable to the growing pressure of the imperialist world
market, not just militarily but also, and above all else, economically.[15]

13. This by no means implied that the victorious Russian revolution
was confronted with the dilemma, either capitulate to capitalism or
seek salvation in 'revolutionary war', in the artificial 'export of the
revolution'.[16] Quite the contrary.

In view of capitalist society's fundamental susceptibility to crisis on
a world scale, the realistic alternative was the temporary consolidation
of the achievements of the Russian revolution at an intermediate level
(post-capitalist but not yet socialist), with political support for the
communist parties outside Russia, in order to take advantage of the
more favourable conditions that would exist when the workers fought
for the conquest of state power in a number of different countries. This
required mature and independent cadres and leaders in these parties as
well as politically mature workers who were united and willing to
engage in the struggle for power. Such an alternative would mean a
radical rejection of the utopian attempt to construct socialism fully in
a single country, on the one hand, and, on the other hand, the attempt
to subordinate the international movement, by means of manipulation,
directives and adventures, to the (supposed and short-sighted) state
interests and diplomatic manoeuvres of the 'besieged fortress'. This
alternative presupposed an autonomous maturation process of the
revolutionary movement and of the working-class parties of each
country. It also presupposed, in the Soviet Union, an economic policy

which was directed towards a gradual strengthening of the overall weight of the working class in society.

This alternative strategy simply meant the extension of Trotsky's fundamental orientation of self-organization and self-liberation of the proletariat (an orientation he shared with Marx, Luxemburg and the Lenin of *State and Revolution*) to the global level of world politics.

14. In the epoch that began with the First World War, reformist gradualism showed itself to be as much a reactionary utopianism as the attempt to construct socialism fully in a single country.[17] In a period of successive severe economic, social and political crises, bourgeois society is periodically forced to overturn previously established reforms, to avail itself of more repressive forms of rule, including that of a terrorist dictatorship. In such situations, to rely on the support of liberal currents or to trust the liberal traditions of middle-class society as a way of fighting against this danger is unrealistic. Only the forceful intervention of a united proletariat, in mass mobilizations and mass organizations, is capable of meeting this threat. To put a brake on this extra-parliamentary mass mobilization, because it would antagonize capital and push the liberals and the petty bourgeoisie into the camp of reaction, could only lead to a victory of reactionary forces.[18] Therefore, the conquest of state power by the working class will be periodically on the agenda in the imperialist countries just as it is in the less developed countries.

15. The main obstacle to the development of an adequate strategy and tactics for the working class and mass movements in our century is the theory and practice (the practice came before the theory) of substitutionism, in other words, the replacement of the independent working class as the agent of social change and transformation by some other agency: party, state, government, parliament, and so on. These are all useful and, at times, indispensable instruments of working-class emancipation. But they must remain subordinate to the real movement of self-emancipation.

Every attempt to reverse this means–end dialectic is doomed to fail eventually and it makes the process of working-class emancipation more difficult. This implies a rejection of both Stalinism and Social Democracy. No working class and no nation can be made happy against its own will. If a rejection of all forms of substitutionism means that the emancipation process takes longer than had been programmed by the bureaucrats, then this is certainly the lesser evil, especially in the light of the long-term disastrous consequences that follow from such substitutionist practices.

16. Blocking the mass organizations of the working class from

going beyond what they have already achieved corresponds not to the interests of the class itself but rather to those of its conservative leadership, the labour bureaucracy. In the capitalist countries, but particularly in the Soviet Union, this labour bureaucracy becomes an autonomous social layer with its own interests, which are quite different from those of both the working class and the bourgeoisie. It does not constitute a new class and is incapable of reproducing itself but, over a prolonged historical period, it is capable of maintaining and extending its power and privileges; in other words, it is capable of reaching a certain degree of historical autonomy. In the final analysis, this autonomy is a result of the relative passivity of the working class and the absence of the international revolution.

17. To break out of this historical impasse, in which neither the international working class nor international capital is able to fight its way out of the crisis of civilization, the emergence once again of broad mass struggles, which is inevitable in any case, is not enough. The conquest of political power and the construction of socialism are tasks that can only be resolved consciously. A breakthrough in the direction of socialism will only occur when these periodically erupting mass struggles coincide with the existence of politically mature and tested working-class militants and working-class parties and a high level of consciousness in broad layers of workers. Marxism of the twentieth century will only succeed if it never loses sight of the subjective historical factor, in other words, if it rejects both mechanical-evolutionary fatalism and primitive voluntarism.

Trotsky was well aware of the world-historical problem which lay at the root of this socio-political stalemate. In his report on the Third Congress of the Communist International, delivered at the Second Congress of the Communist Youth International in 1921, he made this clear:

> The bourgeoisie and the working class are thus located on a soil which renders our victory inescapable – not in the astronomical sense of course, not inescapable like the setting or rising of the sun, but inescapable in the historical sense, in the sense that unless we gain victory all society and all human culture is doomed. History teaches us this. It was thus that the ancient Roman civilization perished. The class of slave owners proved incapable of leading towards further development. It became transformed into an absolutely parasitic and decomposing class. There was no other class to supersede it and the ancient civilization perished ... the possibility is not excluded that the bourgeoisie, armed with its state apparatus and its entire accumulated experience, may continue fighting the revolution until it has drained modern civilization of every atom of its vitality, until it has

7

plunged modern mankind into a state of collapse and decay for a long time to come. By all the foregoing, I simply want to say that the task of overthrowing the bourgeoisie which confronts the working class is not a mechanical one. It is a task which requires for its fulfilment: revolutionary energy, political sagacity, experience, broadness of vision, resoluteness, hot blood, but at the same time a sober head.[19]

Trotsky's overall assessment of the main tendencies of development in this century, which we have just summarized, was developed during the years between 1903 and 1923 and completed in the period 1930–33. He was also a political actor during this period, attempting to put into practice the political conclusions that flowed from this general world-view, initially in the Russian revolution of 1905, when he was leader of the Petrograd Soviet; in 1917 as leader of the Petrograd Soviet and organizer of the October Revolution; in the period 1918–20 as creator of the Red Army, which he then led to victory in the civil war; in 1923/24 as initiator of the Left Opposition against the Soviet bureaucracy and against the Stalin faction which represented it in the Russian Communist Party and in the Communist International; in the struggle for the united front of the German workers in the fight against fascism in the period 1930–33; in his efforts to promote the new upsurge of the international revolution in the years 1934–37. His significance in the history of the twentieth century cannot therefore be reduced to his role in the Russian Revolution between 1917 and 1920.

If we look at his theoretical and practical achievements in the light of the actual course of events this century, we would also have to point to significant theoretical and practical errors of judgement. The most important of these was his continued acceptance of the theory, which stemmed more from Zinoviev, the young Bukharin and Rosa Luxemburg than it did from Lenin, according to which the growth of productive forces was impossible under imperialism. Although this thesis was by and large correct for the period 1914–45, it was definitely shown to be incorrect by the long post-war boom which lasted until the end of the 1960s or the early 1970s.

This misjudgement on Trotsky's part becomes all the more remarkable when we realize that in 1921 he predicted quite an alternative scenario. In his report to the Third Congress of the Communist International on the world economic situation, this is how he described the possibility of a new capitalist revival:

Here we approach the question of social equilibrium. . . . If we grant – and let us grant it for the moment – that the working class fails to rise in revolutionary struggle, but allows the bourgeoisie the opportunity to rule the world's destiny for a long number of years, say, two or three decades, then assuredly some sort of new equilibrium will be established. Europe will be thrown violently into reverse gear. Millions of European workers will die from unemployment and malnutrition. The United States will be compelled to re-orient itself on the world market, reconvert its industry and suffer curtailment for a considerable period. Afterwards, after a new world division of labour is thus established in agony for fifteen or twenty or twenty-five years, a new epoch of capitalist upswing might perhaps occur.[20]

Twenty-five/thirty years after 1921 the post-war boom of 1948/49 began. Trotsky's prediction was uncannily correct.

Closely linked to this misjudgement was a second. This was in the period just before the Second World War when Trotsky believed that a new decisive test of world-historical importance would, in a very short time, decide the fate of the Soviet Union and indeed the fate of the international working class. In an article, 'The USSR in War' (September 1939), Trotsky wrote:

If this war provokes, as we firmly believe, a proletarian revolution, it must inevitably lead to the overthrow of the bureaucracy in the USSR and the regeneration of Soviet democracy on a far higher economic and cultural basis than in 1918. In that case the question as to whether the Stalinist bureaucracy was a 'class' or a growth on the workers' state will be automatically solved. To every single person it will become clear that in the process of development of the world revolution the Soviet bureaucracy was only an episodic relapse.

If, however, it is conceded that the present war will provoke not revolution but a decline of the proletariat, then there remains another alternative: the further decay of monopoly capitalism, its further fusion with the state and the replacement of democracy wherever it still remained by a totalitarian regime.... This would be, according to all indications, a regime of decline, signalling the eclipse of civilization.... The historic alternative, carried to the end, is as follows: either the Stalin regime is an abhorrent relapse in the process of transforming bourgeois society into a socialist society, or the Stalin regime is the first stage of a new exploiting society. If the second prognosis proves to be correct, then, of course, the bureaucracy will become a new exploiting class. However onerous the second perspective may be, if the world proletariat should actually prove itself incapable of fulfilling the mission placed on it by the course of development, nothing else would remain except only to recognize that the socialist programme, based on the international contradictions of capitalist society, ended as a Utopia.[21]

This assessment flowed logically from the assumption that a new growth in productive forces would be impossible, thus blocking the preconditions for a successful breakthrough to socialism.

Six months later, in his *Manifesto of the Conference of the Fourth International*, his real political testament, Trotsky corrected his earlier assessment of the time-scale involved:

> It is not a question of a single uprising. It is a question of an entire revolutionary epoch.... It is necessary to prepare for long years, if not decades, of wars, uprisings, brief interludes of truces, new wars, and new uprisings.... The question of tempos and time intervals is of enormous importance; but it alters neither the general historical perspective nor the direction of our policy. The conclusion is a simple one: it is necessary to carry on the work of educating and organizing the proletarian vanguard with tenfold energy.[22]

Once this assumption about the impossibility of growth in productive forces under imperialism is seen to be wrong, then, at the same time, it becomes clear that the material and human preconditions for socialism in our epoch are not in decline; on the contrary, human productive forces in particular – the number of wage-earners, their levels of skill and culture – are expanding rapidly. Socialism, the world revolution, remain a real possibility.

Finally, it was not until 1917 that Trotsky succeeded in synthesizing his rejection of substitutionism and his clear understanding of the need for a proletarian vanguard organization to ensure a successful outcome to the struggles that erupt during those periodically recurring revolutionary crises. In the period from 1907 to 1916, he defended the illusion that the mass pressure of a revolutionary proletariat would be adequate to force the different wings of the socialist labour movement into common action. This was what actually happened during the Russian revolution of 1905. But from 1916 at the latest, in Germany, Austria and Russia, even earlier in Italy and elsewhere, it was clear that this semi-spontaneist, semi-conciliatory assumption had no basis in reality.[23]

But even taking into account these misjudgements, Trotsky's theoretical and political achievements are without parallel this century. He will go down in history as the most important strategist of the socialist movement. And now even more so, when the clearly recognized bankruptcy of Stalinism and Social Democracy put the debate about socialism once again on the historical agenda, Trotsky's inheritance will assume even greater importance as the main historical alternative to both those currents in the modern labour movement.

Notes

1. Nicolas Krasso, for instance.

2. There is a suggestion of this law of uneven and combined development in Engels's comments on the French Revolution, just as there is in Marx's famous address to the Communist League in 1850. Trotsky's theory of permanent revolution, however, was quite distinct.

3. This does not mean that imperialism is an absolute obstacle to the industrialization/modernization of the Third World. This was the incorrect view of the defenders of the so-called *dependencia* theory in the 1960s. Semi-industrialized countries have emerged in the Third World. But it is precisely a semi-industrialization and nothing more. Germany, the USA and Japan were able to catch up with and overtake the level of industrialization of Britain, France and Belgium. But Brazil, South Korea and Mexico will not be able to overtake Germany, the USA and Japan.

4. Both Rosa Luxemburg and Jean Jaurès had the same intuition before 1914, expressed in their pacifist–anti-militarist positions.

5. Lenin, Rosa Luxemburg and Roland-Holst, but especially Gramsci and Karl Korsch, systematized this analysis.

6. The root of the fundamental differences in strategy between revolutionary socialists from Engels to Rosa Luxemburg, Trotsky and Lenin on the one hand, and, on the other hand, gradualists such as Bernstein, the older Kautsky, Hilferding and others lies in their different attitudes to the bourgeois state – later called the social state. These fundamentally different attitudes to the state were based on different assessments of the underlying tendencies of development of capitalist society. Bernstein and the others assumed a long-term weakening of the conflicts within capitalism, while Engels, Luxemburg and the revolutionary socialists predicted a sharpening of conflicts and an increasing susceptibility to crisis. Actual developments this century have proved which of these two currents was correct. Our century is not, as Bernstein thought it would be, a century of gradual peaceful progress. Much more so than the eighteenth or nineteenth centuries, it has been a century of wars, crises, revolutions and counter-revolutions.

7. In quite a few of his writings, Trotsky dealt with this phenomenon of the conservative aspects of mass proletarian consciousness. A good example is the chapter on the February Revolution in the first volume of his *History of the Russian Revolution*, London 1965.

8. Not in all underdeveloped countries and certainly not in the poorest ones.

9. Engels saw no contradiction between the commune/council system, with its direct democracy and general elections on the basis of universal suffrage in a multi-party system, in which the people had real electoral choices. The latter was the system of the Paris Commune, which Engels saw as the model for the dictatorship of the proletariat.

10. Quoted in Isaac Deutscher, *The Prophet Armed*, Oxford 1964, p. 149.

11. The historical precedent for this were the Jacobins in the French Revolution. They had to seize political power from the bourgeois leadership precisely in order to carry out fully the tasks of the bourgeois revolution.

12. Stalin's attempt in Spain, especially in Catalonia, to impose such a self-limitation on the Spanish proletariat against its will, in the period between August 1936 and July 1937, required bloody repression.

13. This is the difference between Trotsky's theory of permanent revolution and that of Parvus-Helphand. For Parvus, the projected 'workers' government' of Russia would remain completely within the confines of a bourgeois parliamentary regime, similar to the Australian Labour government of that period.

14. *The German Ideology*, Part I, London 1970, p. 56.

15. Trotsky's predictions, in the mid 1920s, concerning the pressure of the world market on the Soviet economy have been completely confirmed by events since the 1970s.

16. Bukharin and Georg Lukács, as well as some of the Mensheviks and Otto Bauer,

wrongly accused Trotsky of having this view.

17. For Trotsky, of course, the emphasis lay on the word 'fully'. Trotsky never doubted, throughout his life, that it was essential, in those countries where the proletariat seized state power, to begin immediately with socialist construction.

18. This is an accusation which consistent gradualists, especially Bernstein, made against Marx's position at the time of the 1848 revolution.

19. In Leon Trotsky, *The First Five Years of the Communist International*, vol. 1, New York 1972, p. 299.

20. Ibid., p. 211.

21. Leon Trotsky, *In Defense of Marxism*, New York 1973, pp. 8–9.

22. *Writings of Leon Trotsky 1939–1940*, New York 1969, p. 218.

23. Like all great socialists of the twentieth century, Trotsky also lacked an adequate understanding of the ecological problem.

2

Trotsky's Internationalism

I

Trotsky's internationalism and its development in the theory of permanent revolution was the product of a dual concept of imperialism, as political and economic. Unlike Rudolf Hilferding, Rosa Luxemburg, Bukharin and Lenin, Trotsky did not develop a comprehensive theory of imperialism (monopoly capitalism, finance capital). But scattered throughout his many writings we find a rather precise insight into the specificity of the new epoch of capitalist production which began in the last decade of the nineteenth century, an insight which has been confirmed by history. He understood the crucial differences between this new epoch and the epoch of liberal, laissez faire capitalism.

More so than the others already mentioned, he correctly placed at the centre of his understanding of the economy of imperialism the fundamental contradiction between the nation-state and the development (increasing internationalization) of the productive forces. He saw the change from a predominantly progressive to a predominantly regressive tendency in the capitalist mode of production as an expression of the fact that not only private appropriation (the profit motive) but also the continued existence of the nation-state was increasingly becoming a threat to the further development of productive forces. This meant that the world market became an important if not decisive element in the analysis of imperialism. This was an insight he shared with Rosa Luxemburg, even though his starting point and method of analysis were different from hers.

The national element still predominated in Hilferding's and Bukharin's analyses of the economy of imperialism. Bukharin's contribution to Marxist economic analysis culminated in his concept of the state monopoly trust, from which the later theory of 'state monopoly capitalism' was only a shallow derivative. Lenin was more cautious on this issue, putting greater emphasis on the significance of international concerns and cartels independent of nation-state regulation. However, influenced by the experience of the German economy during the First World War, he tended, after 1916, to overemphasize the reality and long-term viability of such regulation.

Since Trotsky understood, from the late 1890s, that the world market constituted the decisive framework for the development of the capitalist economy, he had a much clearer understanding of the interplay between world trade (the operation of the law of value on the world market) on the one hand, and, on the other hand, state regulation of the economy within the national framework. When these two elements come into collision, as they clearly did after 1914 and again after 1929, then the world market breaks down, world trade declines, the investment and profit rates of all competitors fall, the economic crisis deepens, and this whole development then leads to a gigantic explosion, in other words, to world war and to national revolutions and counter-revolutions. State monopoly trusts are not strong enough to withstand the pressure of the world market over an extended period. The attempt by certain imperialist powers to achieve world domination is nothing but the attempt to overcome this contradiction within the framework of capitalism itself.[1]

In the course of time, productive forces were internationalized on a scale even greater than Trotsky had predicted. State monopoly trusts gave way not so much to international cartels as to multinational (transnational) concerns which, with respect to production facilities and, to a lesser extent, property, are no longer tied to particular countries of origin and are beyond the control of even the most powerful imperialist states. This is the main feature of that phase of imperialism which we have described as late capitalism.

The operation of the law of value is determined, in the final analysis, by differences in the average levels of labour productivity, or more precisely, by deviations (above and below) from this average. In the long term, no imperialist power can keep its place in the world market and its share of capital accumulation on a world scale if a competing power has a higher level of labour productivity in many of the most important industries. The prediction that 'rentier imperialism' would become hegemonic has been shown to be wrong by the events themselves, first in England and France, and in recent years in the USA as well.

This decisive role of the world market for the economic development of the twentieth century means also that, in the long term, the superiority of post-capitalist economies (regardless of whether we describe them as socialist or as transitional economies) would depend on their reaching a higher level of labour productivity than that attained by the leading imperialist economies. On this issue Lenin and Trotsky shared the same view. And it is precisely for this reason that any prospect of fully constructing socialism in a single country (or in a group of countries) was, right from the start, completely utopian. It was impossible, either in Russia or in the 'socialist camp', to achieve a higher average productivity of labour than the leading industrial nations of the world, which, in addition, were able to make use of the division of labour on the world market to their own advantage (and against the interests of the Third World).

The theory and strategy of permanent revolution thus had a sound economic basis. The world market, determined by an increasing internationalization of productive forces and by a growing international concentration and centralization of capital, produced not only differences in levels of labour productivity among the imperialist states. It also produced massive differences in productivity levels between these imperialist nations as a whole and the colonies and semi-colonies. It led, in other words, to a stalling of development at a very low level and on a massive scale in the Third World.

Trotsky was convinced that the people in these countries would rebel against this enforced misery. He emphasized from very early on that the Russian Revolution of 1905 would find its echo not only in the West (for instance, the franchise movement in Austria) but also in the East (the Persian and then the Chinese Revolution, pre-revolutionary unrest in Turkey). In a little known letter to the Central Committee of the Russian Communist Party in 1919, he predicted that the road from Moscow to London and Paris would lead through the urban centres of Afghanistan, Punjab and Bengal.[2]

One of the principal contradictions of imperialism and one of the most important features of this century, namely the dynamic of the anti-colonial revolution and the liberation movements of the Third World, was already a key element of Trotsky's concept of imperialism. It was this that gave his internationalism a solid materialist foundation. World revolution, for Trotsky, meant both the objective process of emancipation of the masses in the Third World who were the victims of exploitation by imperialism and by their own ruling classes, and also the objective emancipation process of the wage-earners in the imperialist nations. From 1932/33 he added the process of emancipation of the exploited and oppressed wage-earners of the Soviet Union.

His understanding of the world market as an increasing concentration and centralization of capital led to a conception of the growing internationalization of the class struggle. It wasn't just a matter of emphasizing the common interests of the wage-earners of all countries. What was at issue was the necessity to counter the international operations of capital with the international action of the working class. This was the only way to ensure that working-class actions against international capital were not divided by 'national' interests, weakened and paralysed.

II

Trotsky's political concept of imperialism is based on an understanding of the increasingly sharp economic, social, inter-state and political-ideological contradictions and conflicts of the imperialist epoch (the epoch of monopoly capitalism). This leads inevitably to a change in the relationship between the bourgeoisie and the state.

In the epoch of laissez faire capitalism big business by and large favoured a weak state. This by no means implied a questioning of the most severe repression in the colonies and in the imperialist centres in an age of increasingly bitter class struggles. What big business objected to was what it saw as unproductive and unnecessarily wasteful expenditure by the state, the use of resources which were thus not available for accumulation and valorization by productive capital.

The epoch of imperialism is not characterized by shortage of capital but rather by a relative surplus of capital. Military expenditure now plays a useful and increasingly essential role as a 'replacement market'. (This was Rosa Luxemburg's most important contribution to Marxist economic theory.) The imperialist epoch is characterized by the production of arms and by the arms race. It is the epoch of generalized militarism and of ideologies which justify and glorify militarism. It is the epoch of 'the strong state'.

But the armaments race and militarism are not goals in themselves. They have a precise social-political function in capitalist society. The 'strong state' is an instrument in the hands of each imperialist power by means of which it seeks to consolidate and extend its share of the world market. It is an instrument, in the final analysis, for the forceful resolution of inter-imperialist conflicts. It makes possible the conquest and maintenance of colonies. It makes possible a division of the world between imperialist states on the one side and colonies and semi-colonies on the other. It makes it possible for monopoly capital, in an epoch of increasingly radical class conflicts, to employ brute force to break, when necessary, the strength of the organized labour movement.

There is no contradiction between this political concept of imperialism and an understanding of the creeping crisis of the state, in other words, of the tendency towards a weakening of state monopoly trusts.

The increasing susceptibility of imperialism/monopoly capitalism to crisis forces monopoly capital to seek a way out of this crisis through counter-revolution and war. This is a universal tendency, even though it manifests itself, in a particular period, mainly in those imperialist states disadvantaged by the existing division of the world; at that time Germany, Japan and Italy. Later, it would manifest itself in US imperialism as well as in the weaker imperialist states, Britain and France.

This conception of imperialism as a political phenomenon leads to an internationalism which is, of necessity, revolutionary. It is revolutionary not because of the emphasis placed on the use of force but because it stresses the absolute necessity to overcome the repressive state apparatus of monopoly capital. That has been, in practice, the pivotal point of all revolutions of the twentieth century, in the imperialist countries, in the countries of the Third World and also in the conflicts between the imperialist countries and the national liberation movements of the Third World.

Revolutionary internationalism means first and foremost the duty of international solidarity with the oppressed and exploited popular masses in rebellion throughout the world, regardless of the ideological posture of these rebellions. There's no simple pattern here. The ideological mask can be very confusing and, in the long term, can lead to appalling consequences. But the refusal to give solidarity for ideological reasons has, in every case, a ten times more devastating effect on the possibility of achieving the necessary world-wide unity in action of the wage-earners and the oppressed.

At the basis of revolutionary internationalism, understood in this way, lies an objective concept of class which is one of the main elements of Marxism. Classes are objective categories irrespective of their degree of class-consciousness. Class-consciousness, in other words, the self-understanding of a particular class, is an essential element for the successful outcome of any class struggle. However, it is not essential for the definition of a particular economic and political conflict as a class conflict. Otherwise Marx's statement that history is the history of class struggles would be meaningless.

The slaves who revolted against their inhuman existence in the Roman Empire, and who later played a decisive role in bringing about the disintegration of the Empire through their massive flight from the cities and landed estates, certainly didn't have a 'slave class-consciousness' (although the slave-owners certainly did have a class-consciousness). None the less, the slaves were objectively a social class and carried out an objective class struggle. Any other definition of class can only lead to absurd conclusions and to practices quite inimical to the 'really existing' working class. This applies in particular to the late Stalinist, Maoist and semi-Maoist ideological definitions of class. One of the consequences of this definition was the fact that millions of real wage-earners who rebelled against the bureaucratic dictatorship were branded as 'counter-revolutionary bourgeoisie' and the violent suppression of workers' strikes and uprisings was described as the suppression of the bourgeoisie.

Revolutionary internationalism, however, goes beyond the stage of necessary international solidarity. It also includes the systematic and long-term attempt to co-ordinate real movements of emancipation and to alter the relation of forces in the medium and long term (sometimes even in the short term) between international capital and the oppressed and exploited. It can be summed up in the Marxist formula: counterpose to the global foreign policy of capital a global foreign policy of the working class.

Marx saw this as one of the essential features of the First International. It is important to emphasize that, even in the pre-imperialist epoch, Marx considered the successful action of the English workers and trade union movement against British intervention in the American civil war on the side of the slave-owning South to be the most important achievement of active global internationalism. In his Inaugural Address to the International Working Men's Association in October 1864, Marx wrote:

> If the emancipation of the working class requires their fraternal concurrence, how are they to fulfil that great mission with a foreign policy in pursuit of criminal designs, playing upon national prejudices, and squandering in piratical wars the people's blood and treasures? It was not the wisdom of the ruling classes, but the heroic resistance to their criminal folly by the working classes of England, that saved the west of Europe from plunging headlong into an infamous crusade for the perpetuation and propagation of slavery on the other side of the Atlantic. The shameless approval, mock sympathy, or idiotic indifference, with which the upper classes of Europe have witnessed the mountain fortress of the Caucasus falling a prey to, and heroic Poland being assassinated by, Russia; the immense and unresisted encroachments of that barbarous power, whose head is at St Petersburg, and whose hands are in every cabinet in Europe, have taught the working classes the duty to master themselves the mysteries of international politics; to watch the diplomatic acts of their respective

governments; to counteract them, if necessary, by all means in their power; when unable to prevent, to combine in simultaneous denunciations, and to vindicate the simple laws of morals and justice, which ought to govern the relations of private individuals, as the rules paramount of the intercourse of nations. The fight for such a foreign policy forms part of the general struggle for the emancipation of the working classes.[3]

To the end of his life, Trotsky remained true to this activist global conception of internationalism of Karl Marx and Friedrich Engels. It is true, of course, that Trotsky, like Marx, Engels, Luxemburg and Lenin, understood internationalism primarily as proletarian internationalism and placed the main emphasis on the common interests, solidarity and unity of action of the wage-earners. Like all other great socialists of the nineteenth and twentieth centuries, he took for granted that the objective position of the class of wage-earners in bourgeois society gave this class a certain potential for international struggle which no other class could achieve, neither the independent peasantry of the Third World nor the urban petty bourgeoisie and intelligentsia. History has confirmed that this judgement was basically correct although, of course, it needs to be qualified in certain ways. The ideological confusion created by Stalinism and Social Democracy includes a large dose of historical amnesia which time and the reconstruction of historical truth will gradually overcome.

Let us recall, in this respect, some of the principal examples of international solidarity in this century: the young German Social Democracy's courageous rejection of Bismarck's annexation of Alsace-Lorraine; the solidarity of Russian and Japanese Social Democracy during the Russo-Japanese war of 1904; Swedish Social Democracy's threat of a general strike in 1905 which prevented Sweden from intervening against Norway in its struggle for independence; the general strike in Italy and the refusal of the Italian workers to transport troops during Italy's war of aggression against Turkey in 1913; the massive anti-war demonstrations in Basle, Paris, Berlin, Brussels and Vienna, as well as in numerous German cities, which continued throughout 1913 and 1914 right up to the end of July 1914; the strikes of Berlin and Viennese workers in solidarity with the Russian Revolution and against Ludendorff's predatory peace of Brest-Litovsk in 1918; the British workers' active preparation for a general strike against Britain's threatened military intervention in the Russian–Polish war of 1920, an action which halted the intervention and probably saved Soviet Russia from defeat in what was a decisive moment of the international class struggle after the First World War; the courageous actions of the French Communist Party in the war of the French Colonial Empire against the Rif Kabylians in 1925; the extensive solidarity movement with the Spanish people against Franco in 1936–37; the no less impressive movement of solidarity by a section of the international proletariat with the Soviet Union and with the Soviet people in their struggle against Hitler's fascism in the years 1941–44; the impressive international solidarity movement with the Vietnamese revolution in its struggle against the barbaric attack by US imperialism in the 1960s (outside Italy and France, this involved students and working-class youth rather that the broader working class itself).

A historical balance sheet of this kind, however, should also point to the obvious failures of international solidarity: the lack of any response among broad sections of the working classes to the scandalous capitulation of the mainstream Social Democracy to war in the first months of the First World War (with the honourable exception of Italy and Spain, but these were also neutral states at the time, which obviously made it easier for them to respond as they did); the low level of reaction to the crimes of Japanese imperialism in China in the 1930s; the absence of solidarity in the European working classes with the European Jews who were the victims of Nazi genocide (with the famous exception of the Amsterdam and Copenhagen workers and, although to a lesser extent, the people of Italy and Greece); the failure to show solidarity with the Indian liberation struggle between 1942 and 1944; the inadequate support for the Algerian liberation struggle between 1954 and 1962; the lack of solidarity with the Hungarians in 1956, with the Czechoslovaks in 1968, with the Polish workers in 1980 and, above all, with the Nicaraguan revolution which was economically and militarily crushed by US imperialism after 1979.

In the long term, proletarian internationalism can only be effective if it radically rejects all 'superpower' or 'main fortress' concepts. Proletarian internationalism is credible only as solidarity among equals, in which the interests of the working people of no nation, no matter how small or weak, are sacrificed to some kind of 'higher interest'. With the single exception of the year 1921, Trotsky tried all his life to remain true to this principle. Alongside Rosa Luxemburg and Lenin (with the exception of the period 1921–22) he incorporated this proletarian internationalism in a most exemplary way.[4]

It is no accident that proletarian internationalism in the imperialist epoch takes the form of a political concentration on the struggle against militarism and war, for it is in militarism and war that the barbaric tendencies of capitalist society manifest themselves most clearly. The great socialist anti-war agitators, Rosa Luxemburg,

Trotsky, Lenin, Jean Jaurès, Karl Liebknecht, Martov and Fritz Adler recognized this very early on and fought passionately against it. The march into war was, for them, the march into barbarism. The full extent of the historic guilt of mainstream social democracy in Germany, France, Britain and Austria, when they broke with this tradition in a most cowardly manner in August 1914, has to be recognized. It was this, and not Lenin's 'sectarianism', which lay at the root of the split in the international labour movement and which put a question mark over the historical credibility of socialism in the eyes of the people.

For it wasn't only the essential unity of the international working class which collapsed on 14 August 1914 in the face of an imperialist predatory war. What was also destroyed on that day, for a long time to come, was the identification of the socialist labour movement with the unconditional defence of human rights, of democratic rights and freedoms. It was this identification which had been one of the main factors behind the growth of the labour movement in the decades before the war.

A truce with monopoly capital, support for war and for the warring imperialist bourgeois state, for militarism and for the military – it was inevitable that this would lead to support for censorship, states of emergency, limitation of the right to strike, to an apologia for arrest and condemnation of anti-militarists, even in one's own trade union or political party, and even to the denunciation of anti-war activists to the authorities. The fruits of this poisonous plant fell fully ripened into the lap of the counter-revolution, particularly in Germany after 1918. The fruits of this policy included not only Noske and the Kapp putsch, not only the murder of Rosa Luxemburg and Karl Liebknecht, Leo Jogiches, Hugo Haase, Kurt Eisner, Eugene Lewine and thousands of German workers. It also included the Free Corps (*Freikorps*), von Seeckt and led in a straight line from the Free Corps to the SA and SS, from von Seeckt to Hitler's appointment as Reich Chancellor on 30 January 1933.

III

Practical, active internationalism requires an international organization. Active internationalism, which is directed, in the first instance, against militarism, the arms race, war and its supporting ideologies (chauvinism, nationalism, racism and other forms of contempt such as Social Darwinism, idolization of the state and of state security, etc.) requires a *political* international organization. During the years of the

Second International before 1914, and even more so during the early years of the Comintern after the Russian Revolution, Rosa Luxemburg's slogan, 'The International is our fatherland', was a lived reality for hundreds of thousands if not millions of socialists in numerous countries.[5]

Trotsky's internationalism developed rapidly during the period of his involvement with the Socialist Buro, the organizational centre of the Second International. He was an active participant in many of the congresses of the Second International. But this activity was also marked by his conciliatory position in the internal struggles of the Russian Social Democracy during the period 1908–14. During the period of his second exile in Vienna he worked closely with the 'centre' of the German party leadership around Kautsky and the editorial board of *Neue Zeit*. There was an element of opportunism in Trotsky's position at that time, which culminated in his refusal to support Rosa Luxemburg against Kautsky in her campaign on the issue of the mass strike. Lenin also adopted a negative and hesitant attitude in this dispute and for similar reasons.[6]

Trotsky's role in the International changed completely, however, with the outbreak of the First World War and the capitulation of the social-democratic majority in most countries to the war efforts of their respective states. Having moved from Vienna to Paris, Trotsky, a radical opponent of the war, became an active organizer of both Russian and French internationalists. He was one of the most important initiators and participants in the Zimmerwald Conference. It was Trotsky who wrote the Zimmerwald Manifesto. He was also one of the most active builders of the Third International. It was Trotsky who drafted the Appeal for the Convocation of the First Comintern Congress. He was part of the 'hard core' of the Bolshevik leadership that was delegated to the executive committee of the Comintern (ECCI). In spite of the demands made on his time by his role as leader of the Red Army, he played an active role in the first four congresses of the Comintern and participated in many of the sessions of its executive committee.

Like no other socialist, Trotsky had the ability to recognize mass popular mood, with all its contradictions and dissonances, in times of pre-revolutionary or revolutionary unrest. This empathy was manifested in his activities as mass agitator, as politician and as theoretician, in his elaboration of tactics and strategy. He recognized much earlier and in a much clearer manner than his fellow internationalists the explosive effect which the slogans 'Peace', 'Immediate Peace', 'Peace without Annexations or Reparations' would have on the masses as soon as their enthusiasm for the war gave way to a clearer recognition of its material effect on their own lives. In war, the struggle for peace is the concrete form of internationalism. (In his criticism of the 'democratic peace plan', Lenin at first criticized the slogan 'Peace without Annexations or Reparations'. He changed his mind on this after his return to Russia.)

Trotsky's ideas were confirmed unambiguously by the outbreak of the February Revolution – both in Russia itself as well as internationally. The popular enthusiasm for the revolution was inextricably linked with the hope that the revolution would bring the war to an end. The Mensheviks and Social Revolutionaries began to lose their hegemony in the working class as soon as they began to hesitate on this question of peace. It was Bolshevik agitation for an immediate end to the war, much more so than their call for an immediate agrarian revolution, which won them the majority in the Soviets and in the Second All-Russian Soviet Congress. The October Revolution is largely a product of the fact that the Russian workers identified the Bolsheviks with soviet power and an immediate end to the war. Trotsky's agitation for peace, in the period between Zimmerwald and Brest-Litovsk, was the first highpoint in his role as the personification of active internationalism. What was true for Russia then became true to an even greater extent for the whole of Europe.

Trotsky's bold and defiant agitation for peace when confronting the representatives of German and Austrian militarism at the conference table of Brest-Litovsk gave expression to the interests, feelings and dreams of millions of European workers. For the first time in history, it was not just agitators and theoreticians but state leaders who were demanding 'An end to the war, without conditions, without exceptions, and immediately'. The surprise of the workers, their enthusiasm and their identification with the Russian leadership were boundless.

The prophet was still unarmed. Militarily, the revolution was still vulnerable. It was in danger of being defeated by arrogant and power-hungry German militarists. But the unarmed revolution had a secret weapon with a remarkably explosive potential – the war-weariness of the European people and of an increasing number of soldiers in all armies. Trotsky used this secret weapon at the negotiating table of Brest-Litovsk with all the rare agitational, rhetorical and dialectical ability he possessed. Over the heads of the negotiators, he spoke daily to the soldiers in the trenches on the eastern and the western fronts, to the workers in the munitions factories of Berlin, Paris, Glasgow and Turin, to the working people of Vienna, Stockholm, Barcelona, Amsterdam and Zurich.

The outrage of the traditional politicians and generals was as immense as was the enthusiasm of the people: 'Herr Trotsky flies in the face of all civilized rules of behaviour.' But their civilized chagrin was really the grimace of war, of human slaughter, of contempt for humanity, of mounting barbarism. The response of the people was a spontaneous sympathy for the new civilization which was represented at Brest-Litovsk by Trotsky: the civilization of peace, of fraternity among peoples, of self-determination and of popular power.[7]

There were spontaneous mass strikes in Berlin, Glasgow and Vienna. There were mutinies in the French army. Austrian sailors mutinied at Cattaro. Although there was no mutiny among German soldiers and sailors, they heard what Trotsky said and it would be remembered later. Ludendorff recognized too late that the real victor at Brest-Litovsk had been Trotsky.[8] The price Ludendorff had to pay for the predatory peace of Brest-Litovsk was Kiel and Berlin in October/November 1918.

But now the dialectic of history was at work and, within months, the passionate agitator for peace became the creator and leader of the Red Army, which was to emerge victorious from a bloody civil war. Was this a tragic reversal, the expression of an inner contradiction in his own ideas, if not a fundamental contradiction inherent in (his) Marxist socialism? Such an interpretation would be possible only on the basis of a linear, mechanical and fatalistic determinism, which Marxism has been wrongly accused of.

Trotsky's agitation for peace in Brest-Litovsk was to bear fruit only nine months later. The question of time was therefore decisive. During these nine months the counter-revolution in Russia would be able to organize, gather its forces and arm itself. In these nine months the German, British, French, American and Japanese militarists and their clients would be able to pounce like predators on the unarmed Russian Revolution and tear the country apart. It was not a matter of abstract principles. What was at stake was the protection of human life, self-protection and self-defence in the narrowest sense of the word. To be the hammer or anvil: German socialists confronted the same choice in November 1918. They didn't arm themselves, and the result was Hitler and the Second World War. The outcome was a great deal bloodier than was the case in Russia after 1918.

But this serious loss of nine months was neither fatal nor the consequence of some miscalculation on the part of the revolutionary socialists. We know today, partly as a result of available police archives, that a general strike against the war and against Ludendorff's predatory peace of Brest-Litovsk was a real possibility in Berlin and

Vienna.[9] Trotsky was more realistic at the time than the historians are willing to admit. It was only the manoeuvres of Ebert and Co. – objectively treacherous and, in the light of history, suicidal – as well as the inability of the emerging workers vanguard to fight these manoeuvres efficiently, that prevented the flames of an Austrian–German revolution from breaking out immediately, as it did later in the autumn of 1918. On this first occasion, the fate of Europe was decided negatively. But a positive outcome was an objective possibility.

Was the decision by Lenin and Trotsky to establish the Communist International a mistake? Was it premature, as Rosa Luxemburg believed? This question also cannot be answered on the basis of some fatalism of history.

Many things were still open at the beginning of 1919. If Rosa Luxemburg had not been murdered; if the German working class had not had a long year of retreats behind it when it launched its general strike against the Kapp putsch and reached the highest point of its fighting ability as a class; if the Austrian Social Democracy had not left the Hungarian Revolution of 1919 in the lurch; if the North Italian working class had reached such levels of combativity during the general strike of 1919 as it did later in 1920 – then in 1919 or 1920 the establishment of a Third International in Berlin would have been a possibility, an International built around the leadership of the Spartacist League led by Rosa Luxemburg and incorporating the most important workers' leaders from the left wing of the USPD (the Independent Socialists), with an openness for a genuine united front policy, an International which would have been a genuine pole of attraction for the whole left wing of the international Social Democracy and the international trade union movement.

Such an international, not dependent on the apparatus of the Russian party/state, was what Lenin and Trotsky would have liked. After the outbreak of the German–Austrian–Hungarian Revolution, it was a possibility. That this didn't happen was the second fateful turn of events in the period after the Russian Revolution. Under the circumstances, an international based in Moscow and too strongly tied in to the Russian party and state apparatus was, without doubt, a lesser evil. Like the Soviet Union itself, it was a holding operation, an attempt to improve the possibilities of a renewed explosion of the international revolution. And this is what it actually did, by and large, until 1924/25.

This was how Trotsky assessed his role and the role of his comrades in this transitional period. At every crucial point he made concrete tactical proposals to this end – at the time of the Kapp putsch, the

March action, the fascist seizure of power in Italy, the German uprising of October 1923, the British general strike, the beginning of the Chinese Revolution. These proposals were soon accompanied by an increasingly sharp critique of the wrong assessments and tactical errors being made as a result of pressure from the Stalin faction, errors which were later theoretically and strategically generalized in the theory of socialism in one country and the Comintern Programme.

Something qualitatively new now emerged: the transformation of the Comintern from an instrument of world revolution into an instrument for the bureaucratic 'defence of the Soviet Union', later into an instrument for the defence of the special interests of the Soviet bureaucracy. Trotsky's battle for a genuine international working-class organization of struggle, for a real Communist International, now fused with his struggle against the Stalinist bureaucracy.

IV

Before he was murdered by Stalin's assassin, Trotsky said that, of all his contributions to the working-class movement, it was his activity after 1933, in other words, the founding of the Fourth International, which he considered most important, even more important than his leadership of the October uprising or his formulation of the theory of permanent revolution, the theoretical preparation for the October Revolution.[10] This is the statement of Trotsky which today arouses the most vociferous objection, the greatest lack of understanding. I am convinced, however, that in time to come this statement of Trotsky's will be confirmed by history. His statement that the bureaucratic dictatorship in the Soviet Union would collapse and that a political revolution would be necessary to save the inheritance of the October Revolution and socialism also met with the same objections and the same disbelief.

The impotence of short-sighted pseudo-realpolitik, in other words, unprincipled opportunism and pragmatism, is nowhere so unequivo-cally demonstrated as on the issue of an appropriate political response to the long-term secular development of capitalism. Development in the second half of the twentieth century is dominated by the immanent logic of internationalization, of increasing globalization of the economy, of politics and of consciousness, within the framework of a capitalist society. Determined by competition, by the drive for enrich-ment and profit, this process is taking on an increasingly contradictory form and is developing, to an ever greater extent, a self-destructive dynamic. This destructive potential cannot be tamed without putting an end to the capitalist mode of production and the repressive bourgeois state which supports it. This destructive logic will continue to unfold, as was clearly demonstrated by the Gulf War of 1991, a blow to all the illusions of those who had been convinced by Gorbachev's 'new thinking'.[11] The central problems of our epoch can only be solved on a world scale. A new world order is unavoidable. This means an end of national sovereignty, which is, in any case, taking place spontaneously on an ever-increasing scale.

This spontaneous decline of the decision-making power of the nation-state brings advantages for certain social forces, disadvantages for others: advantages for multinational concerns and the most powerful imperialist states, disadvantages for the weaker ones. The spontaneous process of globalization will therefore not take place without resistance. Its potential victims will not accept their designated roles. Their protest, outrage, resistance and rebellion are inevitable; inevitable also will be the inclination of the powerful imperialist states to respond to this outrage with repression and violence.

But the growing use of force, given the present level of weapons technology, implies a growing threat of physical extinction for humanity. The capitalist solution to the problem of globalization is therefore no solution at all. The only possible solution is not a spontaneous but a voluntary and conscious limitation of national sovereignty. But a voluntary relinquishing of even part of national decision-making is only possible on the basis of the strictest equality of rights among all states, nations and nationalities – the small as well as the big, the rich as well as the poor, the weak as well as the powerful. It is completely utopian to assume that the weaker nations, which constitute the overwhelming majority of the world's population, will accept any other form of limitation of national sovereignty over a longer period. The choice is therefore not either the realpolitik of a 'new world order' dictated and enforced by the most powerful, or growing chaos which will threaten all mankind. The real choice is a growing chaos which will engulf all mankind, including the chaos that would result from a violently imposed 'new world order', or a genuinely new world order based on the voluntary co-operation of all nations as equals.

With the experience of the Gulf War behind us, we can illustrate this world-historical dilemma in the functioning of the United Nations. The Gulf War was fought on the basis of a unanimous decision of the Security Council of the United Nations. This so-called 'world community of nations' gives a right of veto to the five victorious powers of the

Second World War: the USA, the Soviet Union (now Russia), Britain, France and China. We are thus already a long way from equal rights of all nations. We have to add to this the fact that the weakening of the Soviet Union as a superpower, the decline in the power of Britain and France, the systemic crisis in China and the failure of the European Community to create a genuine political federation has given the USA, as military hegemonic power, a dominant position among these 'big five' in the Security Council. The veto power of the permanent members of the Security Council has therefore become in practice a veto power of the USA. This means concretely that the United Nations can act militarily against nations that violate UN decisions only if this does not conflict with the interests of the USA. We're all aware of Grenada, Panama, Cyprus, the right of the Palestinians to their own state; the clearest case of all is that of East Timor.

The repressive military dictatorship of Indonesia, which murdered almost a million people in its own country, has given the world the only real example of genocide since Nazi Germany: one third of the entire population of this unfortunate country has been killed. This mass murder has been severely condemned by the United Nations on many occasions, at least as severely as Saddam Hussein's invasion of Kuwait. But no practical measures were taken against the Indonesian dictatorship, neither boycott, blockade, nor military intervention, because this did not correspond to the interests of the United States.

It is unrealistic to assume that, over a longer period of time, the majority of the world's population will tolerate such an arrogant special status for the USA. The immediate demand which has to be raised here is for the immediate abolition of the right of veto in the UN Security Council. One nation one vote – not votes in proportion to dollars and fighter jets. Any other course will lead to human catastrophe. This is, of course, a transitional propagandistic demand; it will not be achieved without a radical transformation in the USA itself.

The only social force that can guarantee and consolidate such a genuinely new world order based on the voluntary co-operation of equal nations is the class of wage-earners. But the class of wage-earners can only achieve this on a global scale if it has already begun to acquire the necessary experience. The developing practical experience of workers' co-operation on an international scale will be an absolutely necessary school and practical apprenticeship for the creation of this new world order which is indispensable for the physical survival of humanity, a new world order which we describe as a world socialist federation. Without a new mass international there can be no genuinely new world order.

The road to this world socialist federation is a difficult one. There are obstacles to overcome, not the least of which is the catastrophic experience that can result from 'international' organizations that are actually subordinated to the interests of particular states. It will be a long time before national parties voluntarily relinquish the right of decision with respect to certain central questions of international politics.[12] But is it utopian to hope that this might happen? In any case, it is less utopian than the assumption that the questions of nuclear weapons, global warming or hunger in the Third World will be solved by simple co-operation of capitalist states.

But a genuine growing together of real mass movements and real mass struggles into a genuine mass international is only possible if such an international addresses itself to the most important goals and demands of all sections of the world proletariat. There are, in the world today, numerous new and not so new radical currents in the mass movements. But outside the Fourth International founded by Trotsky, there isn't a single one which unconditionally supports the demands and the struggles of the exploited and oppressed in the Third World, in the imperialist states and in the post-capitalist societies. That is its greatest strength; it is founded on the theoretical and strategic inheritance of Leon Trotsky and on the 'categorical imperative' of Karl Marx.

The struggle for the mass international of tomorrow is today, and probably for a very long time to come, linked to the struggle to build the Fourth International, although it is not reduced to this and includes numerous forms of international action and co-operation with broader forces in the framework of a united front. In this concrete sense, Trotsky's initiative in founding the Fourth International was actually his most important achievement. It ensured not only a continuity of the Marxist programme and the struggle for socialism, a continuity threatened by the crimes of Stalinism and reformism; it also created an organizational framework within which an ongoing common activity, based on voluntary co-operation and a common programme, welded together a genuine international political group of cadres that practises an exemplary, lively and uninhibited internationalism in many areas of political life far beyond the borders of its own still numerically weak organization.

Its numerical weakness is a reproach often levelled at the Fourth International. Nowhere in the world, it is said, has the Fourth International been able to establish mass parties. Paradoxically, however, this weakness, which is often exaggerated anyway, has been the source of a growing political strength. The Second and Third

Internationals numerically were incomparably stronger than the Fourth International. They had a massive material base in the trade unions, the mass parties and in a number of states. But this powerful material base also contained a dangerous tendency: the subordination of the real interests of the international proletariat to the special interests of the developing bureaucratic apparatuses in these organizations. This subordination was an enforced one, a product of opportunism and realpolitik, and it became increasingly unprincipled and even fundamentally non-political.

In the weaker Fourth International, the subordination of the individual members and sections to the International as a whole is voluntary and is based exclusively on common principles and a shared moral commitment – it is not based on any kind of material incentive. No one joins the Fourth International to make a career. This kind of homogeneity is more solid and more permanent than that of the other two Internationals, which is based on power and even on money. For members and sympathizers of the Fourth International, the voluntary relinquishing of national organizational sovereignty is something taken for granted. The International is their true motherland, in a much deeper sense than it was for members of the other two Internationals. Today it is 'only' tens of thousands who share this conviction and commitment. Tomorrow, in the broader mass international, it will be, must be, millions, if humanity is not to be destroyed.

Notes

1. It is characteristic of this imperialist grab for the world market that the coveted imperium by no means included a harmonization of the levels of development and living standards between the imperialist state and the other countries involved. On the contrary, it entails a stagnation if not a further widening of the development and welfare gap. This was clear at a very early stage in the case of the British and Japanese colonial empires, and was always present in the relations between the United States and the countries of South America. The world empire envisaged by Nazi imperialism was based right from the start on the transformation of whole nations into literally pauperised slaves.

2. *The Trotsky Papers*, ed. Jan M. Meijer, The Hague 1964, vol. 1, p. 625.

3. In *The First International and After*, London 1974, p. 81.

4. The section in Lenin's Testament in which he supports the Georgian communists against Great Russian chauvinism and his prophetic words concerning the terrible consequences of this chauvinism for the future relations between the Soviet Union and the peoples of Asia, are characteristic of Lenin's profound internationalism. These texts are to be found in Moshe Lewin, *Lenin's Last Struggle*, London 1975.

5. This does not imply a negation or an underestimation of the national specificity of the class struggle and the labour movement in each country. It implies only that,

alongside the specifically national goals and forms of struggle, it is essential to recognize forms and goals which are international and which, as such, have a specific and independent dynamic.

6. With hindsight, it is at least an open question whether Lenin, Rosa Luxemburg and Trotsky were mistaken, at the time of the Copenhagen Congress of the Second International, when they did not support the Hardie/Vaillant proposal for a general strike in the armaments industry, mining and transport, at the outbreak of war. It is certainly true that such a strike was not likely to succeed. But mass agitation during a period of intensive war preparation would have given a more concrete form to the later mass resistance to the war. In practice, this resistance took the form of mass strikes. Mass agitation of this kind would also have strengthened Rosa's own campaign for a political general strike.

7. Numerous authors have spoken of the 'myth of world revolution'. They ignore the simple fact that, in the period between 1916 and 1940, in dozens of countries, there were pre-revolutionary and revolutionary mass struggles. Does this not justify the conclusion that this period, unlike the period between the Paris Commune and the Russian Revolution of 1905, was an epoch of international revolution and counter-revolution? The real mystification consists in denying these facts or playing down their importance.

8. See General Erich Ludendorff, *Meine Kriegserinnerungen*, Berlin 1919.

9. See Roman Rosdolsky, 'Die revolutionäre Situation in Österreich im Jahre 1918 und die Politik der Sozialdemokraten. Der Österreichische Januarstreik 1918', in Roman Rosdolsky, *Studen über revolutionäre Taktik*, Berlin 1973.

10. See Trotsky's *Diary in Exile*, Cambridge, MA 1958.

11. My polemic with Gorbachev's 'new thinking' can be read in chapter 7 of my *Beyond Perestroika, The Future of Gorbachev's USSR*, London 1989.

12. This does not imply 'Cominternism', in other words, decisions made by international 'leaders' or 'organs' about the tactics and leadership of national parties. The statutes and the practice of the Fourth International combine an absolute autonomy of national sections in such areas with a duty of international discipline in key questions of international policy, for instance, the question of war.

3

Trotsky's Struggle against the
Stalinist Bureaucracy

I

In October 1923 the Left Opposition within the Russian Communist Party made its first appearance with the 'Platform of the Forty-Six'.[1] This was then followed by Trotsky's articles in *Pravda* in December 1923, published as a separate pamphlet in 1924 under the title *The New Course*.[2] Both publications attacked the suppression of inner-party democracy in the party and condemned the growing institutionalized power of the party apparatus. This party apparatus had grown, over a short period of time, from fewer than 800 to 18,000 full-time functionaries, in a party of something over half a million members. It was controlled centrally by the Central Committee Secretariat under Stalin and was being used systematically to stifle any criticism, expression of opinion or free discussion inside the party. The Politburo met once a week; the Secretariat under Stalin met daily and made most of the decisions, especially those concerning personnel.

The 'Platform of the Forty-Six' reads like an anticipation of the radical assessment made by the CPSU at its Nineteenth Congress in 1988, which stated that, from 1924, the Soviets in the USSR had lost all power and democracy no longer existed inside the party. The Left Opposition had recognized this as early as 1923 and stated it in unambiguous terms in the 'Platform':

> In the domain of internal party relations we see the same incorrect leadership paralysing and breaking up the party; this appears particularly clearly in the period of crisis through which we are passing ...
>
> We explain it by the fact that beneath the external form of official unity we have in practice a one-sided recruitment of individuals, and a direction of affairs which is one-sided and adapted to the views and sympathies of a narrow circle. As a result of a party leadership distorted by such narrow considerations, the party is to a considerable extent ceasing to be that living

independent collectivity which sensitively seizes living reality because it is bound to this reality with a thousand threads. Instead of this we observe the ever-increasing, and now scarcely concealed, division of the party between a secretarial hierarchy and 'quiet folk', between professional party officials recruited from above and the general mass of the party which does not participate in the common life.

This is a fact which is known to every member of the party. Members of the party who are dissatisfied with this or that decision of the Central Committee or even of the provincial committee, who have this or that doubt on their minds, who privately note this or that error, irregularity or disorder, are afraid to speak about it at party meetings, and are even afraid to talk about it in conversation, unless the partner in the conversation is thoroughly reliable from the point of view of 'discretion'; free discussion inside the party has practically vanished; the public opinion of the party is stifled. Nowadays it is not the party, not its broad masses, who promote and choose members of the provincial committees and of the Central Committee of the Russian Communist Party. On the contrary, the secretarial hierarchy of the party to an ever greater extent recruits the membership of the conferences and congresses, which are becoming to an ever greater extent the executive assemblies of this hierarchy.

The regime established within the party is completely intolerable; it destroys the independence of the party, replacing the party by a recruited bureaucratic apparatus which acts without objection in normal times, but which inevitably fails in moments of crisis, and which threatens to become completely ineffective in the face of the serious events now impending.

'The Platform of the Forty-six' p. 7

The majority of the Politburo – the troika of Zinoviev, Kamenev and Stalin, supported by Bukharin – reacted officially with embarrassment. They affirmed the need for a 'new course' and more party democracy.[3] But at the same time they started a campaign against Trotsky and the other representatives of the opposition,[4] which they first accused of 'factionalism' and later of 'Trotskyism', an allegedly 'petty-bourgeois semi-Menshevik' deviation.[5] One of the main instigators of this campaign on the ideological/political level was Zinoviev. His motive appears to have been the party leadership, as Lenin's successor, and thus the exclusion of Trotsky, who was the public's choice and also Lenin's own choice, from the Politburo. But behind closed doors it was Stalin who was already master of the situation and it was he who was to defeat the opposition,[6] using methods which were administrative-repressive as well as criminal.[7]

The situation in the party leadership had become acute after the Twelfth Party Congress at the beginning of 1923, when Lenin's 'Testament' became known, with its sharp attack on Stalin and his recommendation that Stalin should be dismissed as party secretary. Lenin's break with Stalin was not motivated by personal considerations (for instance, Stalin's crude behaviour towards Lenin's companion, Nadezhda Krupskaia). It arose from a deep concern about the process of bureaucratization in the party and state, a worry which clouded Lenin's last year.[8] Stalin used every means and manoeuvre at his disposal to prevent the party congress from acting on Lenin's advice. He didn't even hesitate to make personal attacks on Lenin himself. (In numerous speeches, Stalin described Lenin's letters to the Twelfth Congress as 'the product of a sick man' and not representing the 'true Lenin'.)

The counter-offensive being prepared by Lenin for the Twelfth Party Congress was based on a bloc with Trotsky. He asked Trotsky to raise the Georgian question at the Congress. In spite of his friendship with the Georgian opposition, Trotsky didn't comply.[9] The defence of the principle of equality of national republics was left to Rakovsky.[10] Trotsky's silence at the Twelfth Congress remains one of the biggest mysteries of his political life. The triumvirate of Zinoviev, Kamenev and Stalin was profoundly shocked by Lenin's letters and attempted to come to some understanding with Trotsky. Trotsky agreed. Why? Was this the greatest 'missed opportunity' of his life?

His most important biographers – Isaac Deutscher, Pierre Broué, Ronald Segal, Knei-Paz, Viktor Serge, Tony Cliff, Volkogonov – give a variety of explanations: He didn't want to appear as a contender for Lenin's successor as long as Lenin was still alive. He thought he was already the victor and wanted to be generous in victory. He underestimated Stalin, a product of his own sense of superiority. He preferred to concentrate on what seemed to him to be more important, the question of economic policy (the relationship between NEP, market and plan). He didn't want to threaten the unity of the party, including its leadership. He was too conciliatory and never fought in a hard and uncompromising manner for his own correct views, an accusation made by his close personal friend, Yoffe, in his well-known farewell letter of 1927. He was afraid of seeming to confirm the existing strong prejudices against him among the 'old Bolsheviks'. And so on.

It is difficult to decide among these competing explanations. Perhaps it would be reasonable to suggest that Trotsky's motives at the time were complex and contradictory. He never offered an explanation later in his life for this 'rotten compromise' with Kamenev and Stalin. My own opinion is that it was less decisive than his biographers assume. I am inclined to think that the 'sociological/psychological' analysis which Trotsky offers in his own autobiography, *My Life*,[11] is by and large correct, although it doesn't explain the reasons for his passivity:

I have already said that Lenin, from his death-bed, was preparing a blow at Stalin and his allies, Dzerzhinsky and Ordzhonikidze. Lenin valued Dzerzhinsky highly. The estrangement began when Dzerzhinsky realized that Lenin did not think him capable of directing economic work. It was this that threw Dzerzhinsky into Stalin's arms, and then Lenin decided to strike at him as one of Stalin's supports. As for Ordzhonikidze, Lenin wanted to expel him from the party for his ways of a governor general. Lenin's note promising the Georgian Bolsheviks his full support against Stalin, Dzerzhinsky and Ordzhonikidze was addressed to Mdivani. The fates of the four reveal most vividly the sweeping change in the party engineered by the Stalin faction. After Lenin's death, Dzerzhinsky was put at the head of the Supreme Economic Council, that is, in charge of all state industries. Ordzhonikidze, who had been slated for expulsion, has been made the head of the Central Control Commission. Stalin has not only remained the General Secretary, contrary to Lenin's wish, but has been given unheard-of powers by the apparatus. Finally, Budu Mdivani, whom Lenin supported against Stalin, is now in the Tobolsk prison. A similar 'regrouping' has been effected in the entire directing personnel of the party and in all the parties of the International without exception. The epoch of the epigones is separated from that of Lenin not only by a gulf of ideas, but also by a sweeping overturn in the organization of the party.

Stalin has been the chief instrument in carrying out this overturn. He is gifted with practicality, a strong will and persistence in carrying out his aims.... His mind is stubbornly empirical and devoid of creative imagination. To the leading group of the party (in the wide circles he was not known at all) he always seemed a man destined to play second and third fiddle. And the fact that today he is playing first is not so much a summing up of the man as it is of this transitional period of political backsliding in the country ... Stalinism is above all else the automatic work of the impersonal apparatus on the decline of the revolution. (p. 506)

... I say to myself that we are passing through a period of reaction. A political shifting of the classes is going on, as well as a change in class consciousness. After the great effort there is the recoil.... The deep molecular processes of reaction are emerging to the surface.... They have as their object the eradicating, or at least the weakening, of the dependence of the public consciousness on the ideas, the slogans and the living figures of October.

My Life, p. 517

In other words, in spite of his massive authority, Lenin's 'bombshell' to the Twelfth Congress, even if boldly supported by Trotsky, would not have succeeded, given the social relation of forces at the time, in decisively weakening the bureaucratic party apparatus led by Stalin and the 'secret' Politburo. Lenin's widow summed up the situation quite aptly in 1926 when she said: 'If Lenin were still alive today, he'd be in jail.' One shouldn't understand this interpretation in too fatalistic a manner. It remains an open question whether a bolder intervention by Trotsky at the Twelfth Congress would have had an effect on developments.

Lenin's death and its immediate consequences increased the tensions within the party leadership. In a move that was completely unexpected, Stalin delivered the oration at Lenin's graveside, putting himself forward for the first time in the public eye as one of the contenders for Lenin's succession. (Trotsky was absent from Moscow at the time owing to illness. The date of Lenin's funeral was deliberately kept from him and he was therefore not able to attend.) But, above all, it was the decision to allow a large number of politically uneducated and inexperienced workers into the party (the so-called 'Lenin levy') which made it possible for the party bureaucracy to suppress any serious discussion by means of manipulation of a largely passive party membership. At the same time, the campaign against the opposition increased in intensity; it was officially condemned and silenced. At the Thirteenth Party Congress and at the Fifth Comintern Congress the opposition was condemned as a 'right-wing petty-bourgeois deviation'.

II

This first battle between the ruling apparatus and the Left Opposition did not come out of the blue. For the middle ranks and for the worker Bolsheviks this was seen as the continuation of a conflict which had existed in the party and in society for some years and which was the expression of a pressing problem confronting Soviet Communists as well as the broader working-class and labour movement in Russia. But this continuity had a very contradictory effect on the response to the Left Opposition within the party.

The struggle of the Left Opposition appeared to be the continuation of the struggle of similar oppositional groupings from previous years, especially that of the Democratic Centralists around Ivan Smirnov[12] and of the Workers' Opposition around Shlyapnikov and Alexandra Kollontai.[13] These groupings had also opposed the growing power of the party apparatus, the break with the Bolshevik tradition of internal party democracy and the freedom of tendencies, the increasingly repressive tendencies, the transformation of democratic into bureaucratic centralism and, above all, the party's growing collision with the immediate as well as the historic interests of the working class.

In both these conflicts, however, the most important leaders of the Left Opposition, especially Trotsky and Preobrazhensky, had opposed the opposition. They totally supported the condemnation of these groups by the party leadership under Lenin, and in many cases even led the way in formulating these condemnations. It was therefore easy for Stalin to use against the Left Opposition leaders their own previous pronouncements on 'factionalism' and 'syndicalist deviations'. It was a manoeuvre that Stalin was to repeat when Zinoviev and Kamenev, and then later Bukharin, Tomsky and Rykov, went into the opposition.

Among party members as well there was some doubt about the meaning, if not the sincerity, of the democratic-proletarian orientation of the Left Opposition. Why is it only now that they are coming forward with their complaints and proposals? Why didn't they support the earlier Workers' Opposition? Is this really a struggle over principles, or is it, as the malicious rumours suggested, simply a struggle for power? What was even more negative, from the point of view of the Left Opposition, was the fact that between the struggle against the Workers' Opposition and the confrontations of 1923, there had been another struggle – the debate around the trade union question which had reached its peak at the Eleventh Congress. This debate about the unions had seen the last sharp clash between Lenin and Trotsky before Lenin proposed the bloc with Trotsky against Stalin. In the debate about the unions, Trotsky seemed to have defended the 'command-administrative' position while Stalin gave the appearance of supporting Lenin's more worker-friendly conception.

Even today many aspects of this debate are still unclear.[14] Historians have been quite unfair to Trotsky by identifying his attitude to the unions with his alleged 'militarization of labour'. We find this not only among the historians who accepted Stalin's falsifications but also among bourgeois, social-democratic and socialist critics of Trotsky. Most of these critics overlook the fact that the decision concerning the 'militarization of labour' adopted at the Ninth Congress had been approved by the whole party, including the leaders of the Workers' Opposition. They also ignore the fact that Trotsky's theses clearly emphasize that the 'militarization of labour' would only be possible if it had the *voluntary* support of the majority of the workers.

It remains a fact, none the less, that Trotsky was wrong on the trade union question and this mistake, shared by Preobrazhensky and Bukharin, raised a question mark over the credibility of the Left Opposition leaders as defenders of the workers' interests in the party. These continuities and discontinuities in the internal party conflicts became increasingly linked, as time passed, with the question of the fate of the Russian Revolution itself: can the Russian workers hold on to power if the revolution does not spread to Central and Western Europe? It wasn't just the Mensheviks and Western social democrats who posed this question; it was a question that the Russian socialists, especially the Bolsheviks, Lenin and Trotsky, never evaded. Their answer was usually negative. For the Bolsheviks and for Trotsky this answer applied not in a short-term but in a wider historical sense. Herein, after 1917, was the decisive difference between the Bolsheviks on the one hand, and the Mensheviks and the 'ultra-left' on the other.

Temporary retreats, setbacks and compromises were seen as possible in order to gain time, to hold out, to preserve state power until they were rescued by the next upturn in the international revolution. It was in this sense that Lenin saw the NEP as an unavoidable but limited retreat. But simultaneously the question was posed: What happens to the Soviet working class and Soviet power during such retreats? Can the workers really exercise power in an economically and culturally backward country, isolated and surrounded by a hostile capitalist environment? As in the French Revolution, is a Russian Thermidor possible? Would such a Thermidor lead to Bonapartism? Who could play the role of a Soviet Bonaparte? Isn't it likely to be Trotsky, the popular leader of the Red Army? These were questions actively discussed in private by leading party circles. In answering these questions, most of the party's leaders and middle ranks themselves became the victims of their wrong judgement.

With his political attitudes and theoretical convictions, Trotsky was absolutely not prepared to take on the role of a Russian Bonaparte in the Soviet Union of the 1920s. Most of the party's leading ranks were blind to the reality of what Stalin was doing in creating, to a great extent with their active co-operation, all the practical preconditions which would enable him to step into this role. The tragedy of this party was that nearly all its leaders, even those within the Stalin faction itself, recognized this eventually, but not together, not early enough and not to the extent that they could stop him. They paid for this mistake with their lives.

III

The problem of a Soviet Thermidor has many dimensions: political, economic, social and ideological. It was a great historical achievement of Trotsky that he was able to bring all these dimensions together into a coherent explanatory theory. Alongside his theory of permanent revolution, this was his second major contribution to Marxism.

The ebb in the Russian Revolution was directly linked to the ebb in the political activity of the Russian proletariat. The latter was a result of the economic misery as well as the numerical and social weakness of the working class, the failure of the international revolution and, as time passed, a certain exhaustion of militant energy and the temptation to live a quiet life as soon as this was materially possible (thanks to NEP). But this was not a linear development, predetermined in some fatalistic manner to lead inevitably to Stalinist dictatorship. The decisive stages along this road have to be recognized and the right conclusions drawn for the sake of political action as well as for theoretical clarity.

A long-term retreat of the international revolution and the growing scepticism of the Russian workers and its vanguard vis-à-vis the chances of the spread of the revolution were not historically inevitable. As Trotsky saw it, new possibilities of revolutionary triumph would emerge in the East as well as in the West. This would arouse the political attentiveness of the workers and could even give rise to a new level of commitment and revolutionary enthusiasm among the Soviet vanguard. The events of the decades following the Russian Revolution show that Trotsky was right: Germany 1923, China 1925–27, Spain in 1936.[15] Therefore, the struggle for correct strategy and tactics on the part of the communist parties outside Russia and for the kind of Russian intervention in the Comintern that would promote the international revolution and not hinder it, also played a crucial role in the fight against a Soviet Thermidor.[16] The wrong policy on the part of the Comintern, which was at least partly determined by the special social interests of the Soviet bureaucracy, helped to turn these pre-revolutionary and revolutionary mass struggles into an unbroken chain of defeats. It was only at the end of this process, and not at the beginning, that the consolidation of a Soviet Thermidor became unavoidable.

Scepticism about the spread of international revolution and the temptation to go back to a 'quiet life' were stronger in the ranks of the apparatus (after 1923) than among the ordinary workers. For the apparatus this had a firm material basis in the very real material privileges increasingly at its disposal, something the ordinary workers didn't have. For the worker, return to private life meant a return to privation. For the apparatchik it was a retreat into a 'happy life'. Stalin's sudden proclamation of the theory of 'socialism in one country', which meant a total break with the Marxist tradition as well as with the inheritance of Lenin, was an almost perfect expression of the psychological-ideological needs of the bureaucratic apparatus. (I say 'sudden' because, as can be easily documented, the official line of the party up to 1924 said the exact opposite.)

But even here we cannot close our eyes to the contradictory character of this sudden turn in official policy. Stalin's and Bukharin's theory of 'socialism in one country' corresponded not only to the conservative inclinations of the Soviet bureaucracy. For the mass of Soviet communists it seemed to give an acceptable and credible answer to the question 'What is to be done now?' Instead of waiting for the increasingly unlikely success of the international revolution, shouldn't we concentrate on the construction of our own society? This was Stalin's proposal and to many it seemed a realistic alternative.

However, it was by no means the case that the Left Opposition simply proposed to 'wait for the international revolution'. It was even less true that they saw themselves as confronted with the dilemma, 'either capitalist restoration or revolutionary war', something Georg Lukács accused Trotsky of until into the late 1960s. On the contrary: Trotsky and the Left Opposition argued *simultaneously* for a correct Comintern policy which would take advantages of the very real possibilities of international revolution and for an accelerated industrialization and modernization of Russia. It was the Stalin–Bukharin bloc that rejected both coherent aspects of the approach of Trotsky and the Left Opposition. In so doing, they were giving expression to the conservative character of the theory of 'socialism in one country'.

We are dealing here not just with rational political alternatives but with social and social-psychological processes. And the way that certain social groups interpret projects, proposals or platforms plays a not insignificant role in history, quite independently of the objective contents of such platforms.[17]

In socio-political terms, the democratic and economic proposals of Trotsky and the Left Opposition (dealt with in chapter 4), later also the United Opposition, represented an attempt to create more favourable material and institutional conditions to enable the Soviet working class to intervene in developments once again in an active and independent manner. This was the second decisive element in the struggle against a Soviet Thermidor. And once again it is essential to emphasize: the outcome of this struggle was not predetermined. The growing attack on the powers and rights of the workers met with resistance.[18] The Communist Party could have supported this resistance instead of attempting to put a brake on it, preventing it and finally drowning it in terror. It was only at the end of this series of events that the victory of the counter-revolution was inevitable. At the beginning it was still possible to slow it down if not prevent it altogether.

The fact that this did not happen was due, first and foremost, to the fact that the large majority of the party leadership did not understand the social character of this problem. They never went beyond seeing it as a purely power-political, institutional, in other words, as a bureaucratic-administrative problem, a viewpoint rooted in a sub-stitutionist concept of the party–worker relationship: the dictatorship of the proletariat is exercised by the party under the leadership of its Leninist Central Committee. To question this party leadership is thus to question the dictatorship of the proletariat: 'the party leaders decide everything.' What is decisive is not the interplay of the party and the self-active working class and even less so the self-activity of the workers; what alone is decisive is the omniscient party leadership (later, the omniscient General Secretary).

It was Trotsky's great theoretical achievement that he cut through this Gordian knot practically right from the beginning, from 1923, by recognizing the social degeneration of the Soviet bureaucracy, in other words, the transformation of this bureaucracy into a specific social layer with its own particular material interests. The party apparatus defended its monopoly of political power as a means of defending and extending its own material interests. This was something which, apart from Trotsky, even the most competent Marxists in the leadership of the Russian Communist Party either did not recognize or did not recognize adequately.

A proper understanding of this social transformation was essential in order to mount a consistent struggle against the Soviet bureaucracy. Right to the end, they did not grasp the extent of the social transformation in their own party.[19] To the last they hung on to the illusion that the party leadership or Stalin himself would return to a correct policy. As they were dragged into the whirlpool of the mass purges, they were psychologically and politically helpless because they didn't understand what was really happening.[20]

This tragic failure to understand the process of degeneration of the party reflects one of the fundamental features of the Soviet Thermidor, analogous to the French Thermidor. Thermidor is not simply counter-revolution. It is a political counter-revolution following a powerful revolution that was driven by the enthusiasm of millions of people. The revolution lives on in the consciousness of many of these millions. They identify with its achievements, with its spirit and its new values. Political reaction cannot triumph, or its triumph would be very difficult, if it breaks openly and completely with the revolutionary tradition.

Thermidor, therefore, presents itself initially as the heir of the revolution and not as its gravedigger. This specific combination of continuity and discontinuity makes it very difficult even for the cleverest of the *dramatis personae* to recognize clearly what is happening. It is only gradually that the elements of discontinuity, of break with the revolutionary tradition, of counter-revolution, begin to predominate over revolutionary continuity. Trotsky's historical achievement was that he recognized this earlier than the great majority of communists and provided a theoretical explanation of it.

IV

Trotsky's activity on this question was not just theoretical but also political and, to an increasing degree, organizational. It is this which explains the growing hostility and later the paranoid hatred which the bureaucracy and Stalin personally had for Trotsky and Trotskyism.

The bureaucracy, in its own manner, understood the significance of Trotsky's analysis and proposals. Many of them, particularly Stalin, studied his writings with great care. But this bureaucracy was profoundly pragmatic and had very little interest in theory; to a growing degree it was intellectually and culturally a backward layer.[21] What they were afraid of was Trotsky's readiness – and with him the 'hard core' of the Left Opposition – to fight for his ideas, to organize for this purpose first inside the party, among working-class communists and youth, later among all potentially oppositional workers and youth in Soviet society.

The bureaucracy and Stalin knew that they were dealing with experienced Bolshevik militants. Many had been steeled in the civil war, many were 'old Bolsheviks' from the period of illegality. They were capable of establishing links with critical workers in the factories, with critical students, with critical officials in the administration. Rejecting any form of adventurism, not to mention terrorism, their goal was to become a pole of attraction for broader layers of communists in the event that the working class, at some future date, were to become active again. The bureaucracy saw this as the main danger which threatened them.[22] Their fear was not totally unfounded. It was this fear which explains to a great extent Stalin's and the Stalinists' obsession with Trotskyism.

In his struggle against the Stalinist bureaucracy, extending his activity outside of the ranks of the party was not a decision he took lightly. Up to the time of his exclusion from the party, it was something he had hardly even considered. The reason for this self-limitation had nothing to do with any underestimation of the extent of bureaucratic repression inside the party. It had to do with his conviction, confirmed by experience, that the party was still made up of tens of thousands of honest communists and not just corrupt careerists. Sooner or later these communists would recognize the true character of the Stalin faction, the Soviet bureaucracy and the Soviet Thermidor.[23] History confirmed the correctness of Trotsky's view but not to the extent that he had assumed.

This decision to work only inside the party flowed mainly from an objective analysis of the situation in the Soviet working class. Trotsky was convinced that the decline in mass activity was profound and would last for a long time. Only a correct intervention of the communist vanguard into this process could halt this general decline in the short or medium term. The concentration on political activity inside the party followed logically from this analysis. Trotsky also did not exclude the possibility that, in spite of the suppression of party democracy, even a limited acceptance of some of the proposals of the Left Opposition could bring about changes in the official party line which would protect the Soviet state, the existence of which Trotsky continued fully to defend, from serious dangers.

Because of this, the Left Opposition was prepared to make tactical retreats in order to be able to remain in the party. They were also prepared, for principled reasons, to accept the rules of democratic centralism in a Leninist sense, in other words, to implement the majority decisions of party congresses loyally, without giving up their own views and without giving up the right to defend these ideas in the next round of discussion.

It is this overall viewpoint which explains why Trotsky strictly opposed any means of 'struggle for power' other than that of influencing and organizing the working class. In the 1920s, there were many who didn't understand this and saw in Trotsky only the potential candidate for the role of Bonaparte. In the 1930s and after the beginning of Glasnost there were some who saw Trotsky's refusal to countenance any other means as a mistake (for instance, Professor Demitchev at the Wuppertal Trotsky Symposium). Trotsky explained his own position on this quite clearly:

The question – it is very current (and very naive) – 'Why did Trotsky at the time not use the military apparatus against Stalin?' is the clearest evidence in the world that the questioner cannot or does not wish to reflect on the general historical reasons for the victory of the Soviet bureaucracy over the revolutionary vanguard of the proletariat . . .

As for the military apparatus, it is part of the bureaucratic apparatus, in no way distinguished in qualities from it. It is enough to say that in the years of the civil war, the Red Army absorbed tens of thousands of former Czarist officers. . . . These cadres of officers and functionaries carried out their work in the first years under the direct pressure and surveillance of the advanced workers. In the fire of the cruel struggle, there could not be even a question of a privileged position for officers: the very word was scrubbed out of the vocabulary. But precisely after the victories had been won and the passage made to a peaceful situation, the military apparatus tried to become the most influential and the most privileged part of the whole bureaucratic apparatus. The only person who would have relied on the officers for the purpose of seizing power would have been someone who was prepared to go further than the appetites of the officer caste, that is to say, who would have ensured for them a superior position, given them ranks and decorations, in a word, would have done in one single act what the Stalinist bureaucracy has done gradually over the succeeding ten to twelve years. There is no doubt that it would have been possible to carry out a military coup d'état against the faction of Zinoviev, Kamenev, Stalin, etc. without any difficulty and even without the shedding of any blood; but the result of any coup d'état would have been to accelerate the rhythm of this very bureaucratization and the Bonapartism against which the Left Opposition had engaged in struggle.

The task of the Bolshevik-Leninists was by its very essence not to rely on the military bureaucracy against that of the party but to rely on the proletarian vanguard and through it on the popular masses, and to master the bureaucracy in its entirety, to purge it of its alien elements, to ensure the vigilant control of the workers over it, and to set its policy back on the rails of revolutionary internationalism. . . . To be sure, the banner of the Bolshevik-Leninists gathered tens of thousands of the best revolutionary fighters, including some military men. The advanced workers were sympathetic to the opposition, but that sympathy remained passive; the masses no longer believed that the situation could be seriously changed by struggle.[24]

The extent of sympathy and support for Trotsky among the workers and soldiers at this time, shortly before his expulsion from the party, is indicated in the following report of the Moscow correspondent of the Associated Press, William Reswick:

In the autumn of 1926 the Moscow Soviet called for a demonstration against the British threat to boycott Soviet harbours. . . . The most prominent leaders of the party and state were assembled on the platform, all except Trotsky. But his name was on everyone's lips and it was clear that this massive gathering had come to greet the one-time Commissar of War who, since his demotion to Commissar for Foreign Concessions, had not made a public appearance . . .

Around five o'clock on a very sunny afternoon the public assembly was officially opened in Trotsky's absence. . . . One after another the speakers came to the podium, spoke their lines and received unenthusiastic applause. Among the leading figures on the platform were Rykov, Stalin, Yenukidze, Kamenev, Zinoviev, Lunacharsky and Bukharin. Everyone had spoken except Stalin and Zinoviev. . . . But the audience remained strangely quiet . . .

Then, in the middle of Kamenev's speech, the sound of a distant roar came in through the open windows. It grew louder and louder like the thunder of an approaching storm. Kamenev's speech was completely drowned out. While he stood there, gesticulating hopelessly, Trotsky walked on to the platform. The auditorium was transformed immediately into a howling, surging and screaming mass. People stood up on their chairs, soldiers and sailors threw their caps into the air. For more than fifteen minutes they shouted, laughed and threw kisses to their idol.[25]

A year later the number of people who were willing to demonstrate their support openly for the opposition in Moscow was much smaller, but it was still significant. Trotsky and the Left Opposition abandoned the restriction of their struggle to within the party only when the qualitative increase in bureaucratic repression made the continuation of this internal struggle impossible.[26] The opposition staged a public demonstration in Moscow on the tenth anniversary of the October Revolution and there was a mass rally at the funeral of Adolf Yoffe, whom Stalin had driven to suicide.[27] When Stalin violated the Leninist norms concerning the publication of oppositional platforms, the opposition attempted to print their views using an illegal press. In all this activity they strictly observed the borderline between a political campaign against the bureaucracy and activities hostile to the state. And they completely rejected any recourse to terrorism in their struggle against the bureaucracy.[28]

The organizational pressure which led the opposition to extend its political activity outside of the party was only one of the factors that brought about this change of course; the other was a political decision concerning the dangers facing Soviet society.[29] The Soviet bureaucracy was in the process of liquidating essential gains of the October Revolution, particularly in the superstructure but not only there. Repression was on the increase and was being directed not only against the opposition but also against the mass of the workers and peasants. The overthrow of the bureaucracy was becoming increasingly a question of life or death for the Soviet Union. It could not be achieved by means of reform; a new revolution was needed. But a new revolution required a new revolutionary party. From the spring of 1933, Trotsky abandoned the view that the opposition was only building a faction inside the old party.[30] The new course was now directed towards constructing a new Bolshevik-Leninist party. Whether this change in course came too late is something that anti-Stalinist historians disagree on.

V

The French Thermidor threw light on a more general law about the relationship between revolution and counter-revolution. It is not, as Vico and other pessimists have argued, a circular movement in which society, like the planet, returns to its original position. (Originally the term 'revolution' did have this astronomical meaning but the experience of real revolutions and counter-revolutions gave rise to the modern concept of radical transformation without a return to the status quo.) A counter-revolution can be regarded as *political* to the previous extent that it does not involve a return to the social starting point. The restoration of the monarchy after the English Revolution of 1640 did not mean the restoration of semi-feudal society. The restoration of the monarchy, first under Napoleon and then under the Bourbons, after the Great French Revolution, did not entail a return to the *ancien régime*. Racial segregation of the blacks in the southern states of the United States, shortly after their political emancipation at the end of the American civil war, did not mean the re-introduction of slavery.[31] Trotsky and other Marxist opponents of the Stalin dictatorship asked themselves the question: Does this apply also to the Soviet Thermidor?

Trotsky never deviated from an affirmative answer to this question. Soviet Thermidor, for him, was an increasingly severe regression in all areas of social life but without a return to capitalism, either private or state capitalism. The new socio-economic foundation created by the October Revolution would, by and large, be maintained. This socio-economic foundation has a historically progressive character and has to be unconditionally defended by the Soviet and international working class against any attempt at capitalist restoration, especially in the case of war with an imperialist state.[32] Trotsky was also convinced that this would be the attitude of the Soviet working class, in spite of their hatred of bureaucratic privilege, if the Soviet Union were drawn into a world war. History confirmed this prognosis of Trotsky, as it did his judgement that a war of the Soviet Union against an imperialist aggressor would be a just war.[33]

This did not mean that Trotsky was unaware of similar regressive tendencies in the relations of production. The massive repression directed against the workers and peasants that began in the early 1930s also had catastrophic consequences for economic growth. This also had to be fought. Trotsky's concept of 'political revolution' was not, in this sense, purely political, in other words, directed only at the superstructure. It also contained for him numerous socio-economic elements.[34] The term 'political revolution' was justified in this sense, and in this sense alone, that the coming 'second revolution', far from replacing the new socio-economic foundation created by the October Revolution, would historically consolidate it once and for all and would, for the first time, allow it to fully develop in a positive way.[35]

Numerous non-bourgeois critics of the Stalin dictatorship, as well as a not insignificant number of his own supporters,[36] have criticized this judgement of Trotsky's. Alternative positions – state capitalism, 'new class' and 'bureaucratic collectivism' – still attract support.[37] These latter theories are, of course, the only ones acceptable in petty-bourgeois and social-democratic circles. In the light of the collapse of the Stalinist regimes in Eastern Europe, with its tendency towards the restoration of classical private capitalism, these theories have lost a lot of their attraction. This is not the case, however, with Trotsky's theory of a bureaucratized workers' state, in other words, the theory of transitional society between capitalism and socialism, which explicitly included the danger of capitalist restoration.[38]

Trotsky regarded the dictatorship of the bureaucracy as a historically transitional phenomenon which would, at least in the long term, lead unavoidably to a restoration of capitalism if it were not replaced before this by a restoration of workers' power, of soviet democracy. Council (soviet) democracy, however, could not be won by means of a self-reform of the bureaucracy but only by means of a real revolution from below. (Trotsky described in *The Revolution Betrayed* the actual programme of such a revolution.) The relation of forces between the Soviet proletariat, in escalating mass action, and the bureaucracy would be such that this revolution would not require armed insurrection but would rather resemble a surgical action, 'the removal of a malignant growth'.[39]

As has been pointed out in the previous chapter, the question of the class nature of the Soviet Union was linked for Trotsky with the question of the international class struggle. His hesitation to answer the question 'What is this Soviet Union?' with a simple 'either yes or no, either 100 per cent red or 100 per cent black' had to do with the stalemate in the international class struggle. Only when this stalemate, in one way or another, was resolved, would the fate of the Soviet Union itself be resolved. In rejecting the characterization of the Soviet bureaucracy as a new class, Trotsky was emphasizing the parasitic nature of this caste and saying that, unlike every other ruling class for at least a period of its existence, it had no progressive role to play in history. On this point, the overwhelming majority of the Soviet people today share Trotsky's view.

VI

Trotsky's struggle against Stalinism and against the bureaucratic dictatorship increased in intensity after 1934, when Stalin's crimes took on a truly monstrous character. The murder of Kirov in that year unleashed the mass terror in Soviet society known as the Yezhovsh-china (after the then head of the secret police, Nikolai Yezhov, who was himself a victim of the same terror and was replaced by the equally monstrous Lavrenty Beria).

The reason for the mass purge lay not only in Stalin's lust for power or his pathological jealousy vis-à-vis all real or potential rivals. These features of his personality were already apparent in 1932/33 when, unexpectedly, a proposal was put to the Politburo to recall Trotsky from exile, also when, at the Seventeenth Party Congress, Kirov got more votes than he did in the election of the Central Committee. A proper explanation has to place those facts in the context of the concrete social situation in the Soviet Union at the time.

To an ever-increasing extent, Soviet society at this time was characterized by large-scale unrest among the population, first among the peasants, the victims of forced collectivization and mass deporta-tions, but also among the urban workers, whose levels of consumption had been radically reduced. The terror and the fear did not give rise to open resistance, but the dissatisfaction was there. Through his vast network of informers in the secret police, Stalin was well informed about the mood of the population. There was also a growing unrest inside the party and the first signs of criticism, however extremely cautious. The Soviet Union's international position was also much worse following the victory of Hitlerite fascism in Germany, and this added to the unease.

Stalin was aware that any attempt to come to some agreement with French or German imperialism would meet with hostility in the party. With his usual pragmatism, Stalin came to the conclusion that he wouldn't be able to achieve the goals of his cynical realpolitik with this party, no matter how bureaucratized, and certainly not with its core of communists from the period before 1930. He would have to destroy the party in order to consolidate his power once and for all. A river of blood would have to separate the party from classical socialism and communism. This decision of Stalin's corresponded politically to the particular interests of the Soviet bureaucracy as a consolidated social layer above the workers and peasants.

The terror unleashed by Stalin was one of the most gruesome crimes in modern history. Millions of workers, peasants, intellectuals and communists lost their lives. More than a million communists, among them practically the whole of Lenin's Central Committee and a large part of the leadership of party and state between 1924 and 1933, became victims of the murder machine.[40] The victims were slandered and accused as enemies of the people, terrorists, agents of foreign imperialism and supporters of capitalist restoration. Confessions were forced from them by means of the most gruesome methods of torture. This perfected machinery of murder and deceit, the scale of which is barely conceivable, met with hardly any resistance. In the Soviet Union itself the people were paralysed by fear and outrage.[41] In the international labour movement and in liberal bourgeois circles, Stalin was accepted as the 'lesser evil', partly for opportunist reasons, partly from demoralization. International capital regarded the 'realpolitiker' Stalin, especially after the signing of the Stalin–Lavel Pact, as less dangerous than Trotsky, who was still promoting world revolution.

The Stalinized communist parties defended the terror practically without exception. Comintern leaders such as Togliatti and Pieck delivered leading members of their parties who happened to be in Moscow to the executioner, content to try to save a few. Herbert Wehner, already affected by self-doubt, wrote in 1938:

> Trotskyism is growing like a poison in the soil of a decaying capitalist social order ... and is being used by those fascist and imperialist forces ... who want to restore capitalism on the territory of the USSR and annex parts of the Soviet Union. It is no accident, but rather corresponds completely to the corrupting function of Trotskyism, that Trotsky and many of his accomplices have been paid spies for many years.[42]

In the Communist Party press of this period one can find numerous such quotations. The French Communist Party press, during the Moscow trials, used the phrase, 'Shoot the rabid dogs!'

International Social Democracy behaved in a most cowardly manner.[43] The Otto Bauer–Zyromsky wing condemned Trotsky and the other victims as more guilty than their hangmen. The 'left Social

Democratic' government of Norway tried to stop Trotsky from revealing the lies of the Moscow trials. (He was interned, forbidden to undertake any journalistic activity and even prohibited from taking any legal action.) The 'humanist' Leon Blum refused to condemn Stalin's crimes because he didn't want to risk his alliance with the French Communist Party. Numerous left-wing intellectuals, including the French League of Human Rights, degraded themselves before Stalin and tried to justify the Moscow show trials and Stalin's slanders by pointing to the forced confessions of the unfortunate 'old Bolsheviks'. At that historic moment, it was Friedrich Adler, Secretary of the Socialist International, who, almost alone, rescued the honour of international Social Democracy.

The question of the Moscow trials also puts a serious blot on the record of the Brandler–Thalheimer grouping. Probably as the result of a congenital hostility to Zinoviev (related to the controversy about Brandler's alleged responsibility for the defeat of the German October 1923), they refused to condemn the first and second trials. Only when their friend Bukharin was put on trial in 1938 (third Moscow trial) did they revise their attitude.

Gerhard Rosenthal has recalled a little-known fact; the main French ideologue of the far right, Charles Maurras, saw in the Moscow trials the proof that the Trotskyists were in the pay of Germany.[44] Churchill accepted as good coin the story of Tukhachevsky's treason, passed on by the Czechoslovak president, Beneš. (De Gaulle, however, was not fooled by this.) In this sinister intrigue, which led to the decapitation of the Red Army, it is not known who was manipulating whom: Was the GPU manipulating the Nazi secret service or were the latter manipulating the GPU and Stalin? The incredible blindness of intellectuals in the West was manifested in a most striking manner in the case of the English writer H. G. Wells, who wrote in 1929 about Stalin: 'I never met a man more candid, fair and honest. No one is afraid of him and everybody trusts him.' If unengaged intellectuals could write such nauseating nonsense, what wonder that 'sincere' Stalinists (but were they really sincere, or just cynical?) such as the leaders of the American Communist Party, William Foster, Elizabeth Gurley Flinn and Pettis Perry, could call the mass butcher Stalin, at the time of his death, 'the best-loved man on earth, enshrined in the hearts of people everywhere' (*Political Affairs*, April 1953).

Stalin's murder machine also attempted to act against critics of the Stalin course and of the purges outside the borders of the Soviet Union. This happened first in Spain. The leader of the POUM, Andres Nin, who only months previously had sat with representatives of the

Spanish Communist Party in the government of Catalonia, was literally tortured to death.[45] Numerous foreign revolutionaries, among them Trotsky's secretary, Erwin Wolf, were murdered. The GPU killers then struck in Switzerland and France. The head of the Soviet secret service in Western Europe, Ignaz Reiss, who broke with Stalin because of the Moscow trials and joined the Fourth International, was murdered in Geneva. The dismembered body of Rudolf Klement, administrative secretary of the Fourth International, who was working on the preparation of its founding conference, was found floating in the Seine. Trotsky's son, Leon Sedov, died in mysterious circumstances in a Russian clinic in Paris.

Trotsky and Sedov, practically alone, stood out against the Stalin campaign of murder and slander. When Trotsky was silenced by the Norwegian Social Democracy, so that he could not expose the lies of the Moscow trials, Sedov published his *Livre rouge sur le procès de Moscou*, a factual refutation of the main Stalinist charges.[46] There was very little public response, but it did make it possible for those left-wing circles that had not capitulated to Stalinism to give voice to their outrage over the witch-hunt. In this way, the terrain was prepared for an international campaign to expose Stalin's lies and to rescue the honour of the slandered and murdered leaders of the Russian Revolution. In many cities of the world local or national committees were established.[47] The international campaign culminated in the counter-trial in Mexico chaired by the American liberal philosopher, John Dewey. On 17 April 1937 it reached its verdict on Trotsky and the others accused in the Moscow trials: Not guilty![48] The response was not insignificant in the Anglo-Saxon countries.

Trotsky summarized his response to the Moscow lies and slanders in his book, *Stalins Verbrechen* (Stalin's Crimes). His speech before an audience of six thousand at a mass meeting organized by the New York Committee in Defence of Trotsky, on 9 February 1937, is still today the best exposure and explanation of the show trials.[49]

VII

Trotsky's fight against Stalin's crimes was not based on personal animosity. What was at stake for Trotsky was the honour of the Russian Revolution and Lenin. Logically, such a frontal attack on the 'old Bolsheviks' implied a judgement on the revolution, the Bolshevik Party and Lenin.[50] What was at stake also was a political defence of what was for Trotsky, right to the end of his life, his Soviet homeland, in both the social and national sense of the word.

Trotsky was profoundly convinced that Stalin's crimes would weaken the Soviet Union and Soviet society more than any of his own oppositional activities since 1923. When the purges extended into the Red Army and when, after the execution of General Tukhachevsky, two-thirds of the commanders of the Red Army were executed by Stalin, Trotsky was literally possessed by the thought, expressed in the title of his famous Appeal of 1918 which led to the formation of the Red Army: 'The Fatherland is in Danger!' As events were to demonstrate, Trotsky's fears were well grounded. The crippling of the Red Army leadership contributed significantly to its defeats in 1941, defeats that brought the Soviet Union to the brink of collapse.[51]

If, as a Marxist, one looks at the conflicts between the oppositional groups, mainly the Left Opposition, on the one hand, and the 'hard core' of the Stalinist faction (the big majority of whom were also victims of the terror) on the other hand, and if we take into account the massive scale of the terror (we repeat: one million communists murdered), then there can be very little doubt about the civil war-like character of the terror.[52]

Supporters of the Marxist theory of historical materialism do not explain civil wars as inter-personal conflicts but as conflicts between social classes or major sections of social classes. In this sense, the bloody mass purges in the Soviet Union were the civil war-like end-phase of the political counter-revolution in that country. Trotsky's struggle against the counter-revolution expressed historically the socio-political conflict between the Soviet proletariat and the Soviet bureaucracy. For Stalin to win this bloody civil war, it was essential for him to exercise political power. This assessment of the nature of the Yezhovshchina enables us also to come to a conclusion on the question of the beginning of the Soviet Thermidor, a question that occupied Trotsky for more than fifteen years and on which he changed his mind a number of times.

When did the Soviet Thermidor begin? The answer is: in 1923. At the Trotsky Symposium held in Wuppertal, Germany, in 1990, Professor Pechekoldin, who had access to secret Soviet archives, stated that in 1923 the standard of life of a top functionary at the regional level was nine times higher, of a top functionary at Central Committee level thirty times higher than that of the average skilled worker.[53]

For the Soviet bureaucracy and for its political representative, Stalin, Trotsky's campaign against the Moscow trials was the final proof that the founder of the Red Army was their most important political enemy. In their eyes, there was no political solution to this conflict. It could only be resolved by the physical elimination of Trotsky. The decision, already taken some years earlier, to murder Trotsky, presented itself now with even greater urgency.[54] The murder machine established itself in North America, from where it could reach more easily into Mexico. On 20 August 1940, it finally succeeded.[55]

As in many other cases, the Soviet bureaucracy was mistaken in its belief in the power of administrative repression. To the surprise of everyone, both his greatest enemies and his closest friends, Trotsky's funeral turned out to be an impressive demonstration of the spontaneous sympathy of the Mexican people for the murdered revolutionary. Tens of thousands mourned him and followed the funeral procession. It was a sign of what was to come. His ideas and his role as symbol of the revolution remained alive. In the years and decades to come his ideas were to spread, though not to the extent that he had anticipated.

And then, with Glasnost, came the next decisive turn in the Soviet Union. Trotsky's speech, written for the rally in New York in 1937, contained the words:

> But all those for whom socialism is not an empty word but the real contents of an ethical life – forward! Neither threats nor persecution nor violence will stop us. Perhaps we will be defeated, but the truth will triumph. We will clear the path for it. It will win.[56]

In the meantime, the truth has indeed triumphed in the Soviet Union. The accused of the Moscow trials have been officially rehabilitated by a decision of the Soviet court. The judgments of the show trials have themselves been judged as unfounded and untrue. Stalin's whole network of lies has been officially exposed. Trotsky himself was politically rehabilitated when, on the eve of the fiftieth anniversary of his murder, *Izvestia* wrote that Trotsky had been 'a great and honest revolutionary, second only to Lenin as leader of the party [after joining the Bolsheviks in 1917 (author's addition)] and of the state'. And, what is more important, the struggle for the truth, especially for the truth about history, is seen as a decisive element in the struggle for democratization, against the profound crisis of the system and for a proper political solution.

In August 1937, Trotsky wrote:

> The memory of mankind is magnanimous as regards the application of harsh measures in the service of great historical goals. But history will not pardon a single drop of blood if it is shed in sacrifice to the new Moloch of arbitrary rule and privilege. Moral sensibility finds its highest satisfaction

in the immutable conviction that historical retribution will correspond to the scope of the crime. Revolution will unlock all the secret compartments, review all the trials, rehabilitate the slandered, raise memorials to the victims of wantonness, and cover with eternal infamy the names of the executioners.[57]

All these predictions have, in the meantime, been fulfilled. Nothing manifests Trotsky's human, moral and political greatness better than the fact that, in the face of death at the hands of Stalin's assassins, which he himself expected, he was filled with confidence in a better future for all of humanity.

Notes

1. 'Declaration of the Forty-Six', in Leon Trotsky, *Challenge of the Left Opposition*, New York 1975, pp. 397–403.

2. In *Challenge of the Left Opposition*, New York 1975, pp. 64ff.

3. 'The New Course Resolution', in *Challenge of the Left Opposition*, pp. 404–13.

4. It was well known to the Troika that hostility to the apparatus of functionaries was widespread in the party. Hence their caution. On the sixth anniversary of the revolution, Zinoviev promised to restore (!) democracy in the party (*Pravda*, 2 November 1923).

5. '[T]he All-Union Party Conference comes to the conclusion that in the person of the present opposition we have before us not only an attempt at the revision of Bolshevism, not only a direct departure from Leninism, but also a clearly expressed petty-bourgeois deviation' (Resolution of the Thirteenth Party Conference of January 1924, in Robert V. Daniels, *A Documentary History of Communism*, vol. 1, London 1987, p. 165).

6. At the Trotsky Symposium in Wuppertal, Germany, in March 1990, the Yugoslav historian, Marjan Britovsek, presented a detailed analysis of the manoeuvres of the Troika in relation to Trotsky's New Course. See Marjan Britovsek, 'Das Dilemmata des "Neuen Kurses"', in Theodor Bergmann and Gert Schäfer, eds, *Leo Trotsky – Kritiker und Verteidiger der Sovjetgesellschaft*, Mainz 1993.

7. Stalin falsified the result of the vote in the Moscow party organization, in which the opposition had won a majority.

8. In Lenin's 'Testament', he pointed out the dangers to the party of the conflict between Stalin and Trotsky. He recommended that Stalin be removed from the post of general secretary. He also insisted that some hundreds of workers and peasants should be brought into the Central Committee, but only those still involved in production and not those already part of the bureaucratized Soviet apparatus. At the same time, he called on Trotsky to join in a bloc with him against Stalin. See the text of his letter to Trotsky in Trotsky's *My Life*, New York 1960, chapters 38–40. Moshe Lewin's *Lenin's Last Struggle* (London 1975) also deals with the Testament and with the relationship between Lenin and Trotsky.

9. Within the party leadership, however, Trotsky defended his and Lenin's position on the 'Georgian question' and he was the only one to call for the publication of Lenin's Testament.

10. Rakovsky's 'Speech to the Twelfth Party Congress' is in Christian Rakovsky, *Selected Writings on Opposition in the USSR 1923–1930*, ed. Gus Fagan, London 1980.

11. *My Life*, New York 1970.

12. On the Democratic Centralists, see Robert Daniels, *The Conscience of the Revolution*, Harcord 1960.

13. Selection of documents from the Workers' Opposition and Democratic Centralists in Daniels, *A Documentary History of Communism*.

14. In the historical accounts of this period, what tends to be overlooked is Trotsky's proposal that the trade unions should train workers to take the place of the factory directors in the running of the big enterprises, which would be an obvious step in the direction of workers' self-management, a demand enthusiastically supported by Bukharin.

15. The Soviet workers followed with great interest and enthusiasm the rising tide of revolution in Germany in 1923. The successful resistance to the fascist putsch in Spain had a similar effect. In a remarkable book (*Staline et la révolution – le cas espagnol*, Paris 1993), Pierre Broué sheds new light on the mechanisms through which Stalin and his henchmen throttled the Spanish Revolution.

16. The assertion by many historians that Lenin himself had subordinated the interests of the international revolution to the interests of the Russian state has no empirical support. It was not until the 1930s that this actually began to happen, although it was already implied by the theory of 'socialism in one country'.

17. In the case of both Stalinism and fascism, Trotsky pointed out that completely absurd and irrational myths can play a real role in history.

18. See Charles Bettelheim, *Luttes de classe en URSS*, 2 vols, Paris 1972–74.

19. Leopold Trepper, head of the Red Orchestra, paid tribute to the Trotskyists, the only communists who did not capitulate to Stalin and who went to their deaths unbroken. Trepper explains this through the fact that they were the only ones who clearly understood the nature of Stalinism, while Stalin's other communist victims were completely demoralized because they never understood the fate that befell them. Tukhachevsky was also such an exception. See Leopold Trepper, *The Great Game*, London 1977.

20. Right to the end, Bukharin had the illusion that 'comrade Stalin' would save him. For an account of Bukharin's last letter to Stalin, recently uncovered in Soviet archives, see the article by Alec Nove, 'Compliant to the Last', in *The New Statesman*, 21 January 1994.

21. This was obviously no longer the case for the 'modern technocrats' whose political representative was Mikhail Gorbachev.

22. One such example is M. Ryutin. At first he was an enthusiastic supporter of the Stalin faction in its fight against Trotskyism and against other opposition groupings. In the spring of 1928, however, he changed course. He was not elected to the Central Committee, he lost his post as party secretary in the Moscow area and in the autumn of 1930 he was expelled from the party. He then organized an 'illegal' communist organization, the League of Soviet Marxist-Leninists. He produced an extensive manifesto in which he accused Stalin of having already prepared his 'Eighteenth Brumaire' in 1923–24. Although the manifesto was critical of Trotsky, it contained a very generous tribute to him as a person and of the role that he was playing. At the same time, it contained a bitter attack on the bureaucratic apparatus and its privileges. Stalin's response was to demand the death sentence. See the account of Ryutin's case in *Nouvelles de Moscou*, 27 May 1990. Pierre Broué has published a series of interesting documents about the activities of Rekovsky in exile in Siberia (*Cahiers Léon Trotsky* No. 52, January 1944 and No. 53, April 1994).

23 In the procedure to expel Trotsky from the ECCI on 27 September 1927, the reasons given were not only breach of discipline (the 'illegal press' set up with the help of 'anti-Soviet agents') but also explicitly his views and the views of the Left Opposition on the Soviet Thermidor, the degeneration of the apparatus and the practice of 'appointing Comintern leaders'. The text of the expulsion resolution was first published in the West by Octavio Rodriguez Araujo and Paulina Fernandez in the Mexican newspaper, *Perfil de la Jornada*, 20 August 1990. It was taken from *Pravda* of 1 October 1927.

24. 'How Did Stalin Defeat the Opposition?' (12 November 1935), in *Writings of Leon Trotsky 1935–36*, New York 1977, pp. 172, 175.

25. Quoted from *Leo Trotski 1879–1940. In den Augen von Zeitgenossen*, Hamburg 1979, pp. 112–13.

26. At the plenum of the Central Committee and Central Control Commission on 1 August 1927, Stalin proclaimed: 'These cadres can only be swept away by means of civil war.' Couldn't they be simply 'swept away' by free elections at a Party Congress? At the Fifteenth Party Congress it was demanded (in a completely undemocratic and non-Leninist manner) that the opposition should not only submit to party discipline but also declare, against their own convictions, that their views were false. Trotsky, at this time, had already been expelled from the party (on 14 November 1927).

27. On Yoffe and the rally at his funeral, see Isaac Deutscher, *The Prophet Unarmed*, Oxford 1970, pp. 380–84.

28. Trotsky wrote, in his article 'The Stalinist Bureaucracy and the Kirov Assassination', 28 December 1934:

> Only political fakers who bank on imbeciles would endeavour to link Nikolaev with the Left Opposition, even if only in the guise of the Zinoviev group as it existed in 1926–27. The terrorist organization of the Communist youth was fostered not by the Left Opposition but by the bureaucracy, by its internal corruption. *Individual terrorism is in its very essence bureaucratism turned inside out.* For Marxists this law was not discovered yesterday. Bureaucratism has no confidence in the masses and endeavours to substitute itself for the masses. Terrorism works in the same manner; it seeks to make the masses happy without asking their participation.
>
> *Writings of Leon Trotsky 1934–35*, p. 124

Today it is almost universally agreed in the Soviet Union that the Kirov murder was not organized by any youth group but was organized personally by Stalin, both as a provocation to justify the mass purges and as a revenge for the fact that Kirov had received more votes than he in the election to the Central Committee at the Seventeenth Party Congress. As Roy Medvedev has reported, Kaganovich, at Stalin's command, falsified the official results. See Roy Medvedev, *Let History Judge*, Oxford 1989, p. 332.

29. Inside the leadership of the Left Opposition there was one grouping (Preobrazhensky, Radek, Smilga, Pyatakov) that did not agree with this judgement. They later capitulated to Stalin.

30. Trotsky's secretary for many years, Jean Van Heyenoort, recalls Trotsky saying at the beginning of July 1933:

> Until April we were for a reform of the Communist Parties in all countries except Germany, where we were for a new party. Now we can take a symmetrical position, in other words, we are for a new party in all countries except the USSR, where we still favour a reform of the Bolshevik Party.
>
> Jean Van Heyenoort, *With Trotsky in Exile, from Prinkipo to Coyoacan*, Cambridge, MA 1978

On 20 July 1933, Trotsky wrote an article, using the pseudonym Gussev, in which he also called for a new party in the USSR. ('It is Impossible to Remain in the Same International with Manuilsky, Lozovsky and Company', in *Writings of Leon Trotsky 1933–34*, New York 1972, pp. 17ff.

31. See *A Documentary History of the Negro People of the United States*, ed. Herbert Aptheker, New York 1968, vol. 2.

32. Trotsky's proposed tactics for the workers in countries allied with or hostile to the USSR are described in his article, 'War and the Fourth International' (10 June 1934), in *Writings of Leon Trotsky 1933–34*, pp. 315–16.

33. The mass murder which the Nazis planned for Eastern Europe (the *Generalplan Ost* implying 100 million deaths) was to justify this policy later in a way that was not even imagined in 1933.

34. The 'social aspects' of the political revolution are discussed by Trotsky in *The Revolution Betrayed*, New York 1972, pp. 288–90. The revolution would change

> the methods of administering the economy.... The bringing of democracy into industry means a radical revision of plans in the interests of the toilers. Free discussion of economic problems will decrease the overhead expense of bureaucratic mistakes and zigzags.... 'Bourgeois norms of distribution' will be confined within the limits of strict necessity...
>
> *The Revolution Betrayed*, p. 289

35. Gorbachev also defended this view in his book, *Perestroika*. The sociologist, Tatyana Zaslavskaya, titled her book *The Second Socialist Revolution* (London 1990).

36. In particular, Viktor Serge and the Americans, Carter and Burnham, from 1937, Schachtman from 1941, and the English Trotskyist, Tony Cliff, from 1947.

37. The best known supporter of the theory of 'new class' is the Yugoslav Milovan Djilas. A critique of those theories can be found in my book, *Power and Money. A General Theory of Bureaucracy*, London 1992.

38. Trotsky wrote in October 1933:

> The further unhindered development of bureaucratism must lead inevitably to the cessation of economic and cultural growth, to a terrible social crisis and to a downward plunge of the entire society. But this would imply the collapse not only of the proletarian dictatorship but also the end of bureaucratic domination. In place of the workers' state would come not 'social bureaucratic' but capitalist relations.

Quoted from 'The Class Nature of the Soviet State', in *Writings of Leon Trotsky 1933–34*, p. 115. The thesis of self-reform of the bureaucracy was defended by Isaac Deutscher and Moshe Lewin. Trotsky had a conception of a dialectical interaction of 'pressure from below – differentiation and reform from above – political revolution'. I deal extensively with this in my book *Beyond Perestroika* (London 1989), especially in chapter 12, 'The Dialectic of Reform and Social Movement'.

39. *Writings of Leon Trotsky 1933–34*, p. 118.

40. On the scale of the purges, see Medvedev, *Let History Judge*.

41. The Soviet people, however, demonstrated their attitude to the terror indirectly in the humane and sometimes moving way they cared for the children of the victims, when these children themselves were not killed or interned.

42. On the fate of German communists and anti-fascists in the Soviet Union, see Hermann Weber, *Weisse Flecken in der Geschichte*, Frankfurt/M 1989.

43. Among them the British Fabians, Sidney and Beatrice Webb, the British lawyer, Pritt, the German writer, Leon Feuchtwanger, important French intellectuals such as Romain Rolland, Henry Barbusse and André Malraux. The London Buro of the Left Socialists, which included the ILP and the German SAP (with Willy Brandt), refused to participate in the committee to investigate the Moscow trials.

44. The writers André Gide, André Breton and Ignacio Silone were honourable exceptions.

45. There was later a trial of the POUM leaders, who were sentenced to long prison terms. The accusation however was not that they were 'counter-revolutionaries', or that they had 'co-operated with the Fascists', etc. On the contrary, the accusation was that they had prepared for a dictatorship of the proletariat. The documents of the POUM trial have been published by Victor Alba and Marisa Arderol: *El Proceso del P.O.U.M.*, Barcelona 1989.

46. Sedov's *Livre Rouge* has recently been published in Germany (ISP Verlag, Frankfurt/M). The Norwegian police under Norway's Social Democratic government threatened Trotsky's secretaries Jean Van Heyenoort and Jan Frankel that they would be handed over to the Nazis if they did not stop helping Trotsky and leave Norway immediately.

47. I would like to register here a more personal anecdote. It was under the influence of the Committee to Defend Trotsky in Antwerp, as well as the influence of the Spanish Civil War, that I first began, at the age of thirteen, to sympathize with Trotskyism.

48. *The Case of Leon Trotsky. Report of the Hearings on the Charges made against him in the Moscow Trials*, New York 1968.

49. *Stalins Verbrechen* was first published in Zurich in 1937. His speech for the New York rally is in *Leon Trotsky Speaks*, New York 1972.

50. What can one think of a revolution that was led by counter-revolutionaries? How should we assess the political and organizational abilities of Lenin if the majority of leaders in his party were bandits? The argument cannot be made that it was only later that they became counter-revolutionaries, since the third Moscow trial concluded that they had been engaged in their criminal activities from as early as 1918. Lenin, of course, wasn't aware of this. It took a great man like Stalin to discover it.

51. Tukhachevsky was probably the best military strategist in Europe in the 1930s. He had foreseen the German plan of attack and was preparing the right response.

52. Figures published in the Soviet Union recently name four to four and a half million victims of the terror in 1937–38, among them almost a million executed. Stalin murdered more than three times the number of senior officers in the Red Army than were later to fall at the front.

53. Quoted in the *Frankfurter Rundschau*, 31 March 1990.

54. There is an extensive literature in the Soviet Union today about the preparation for Trotsky's murder. Stalin's responsibility was known long before Glasnost. The murderer was posthumously granted the Lenin Order and was given an 'official' grave in Moscow. Recently opened archive material suggests that Stalin personally ordered Trotsky's murder as early as 1931 and had it organized by the highest officials in the GPU.

55. See Isaac Don Levine, *The Mind of the Assassin*, London 1959.

56. In *Leon Trotsky Speaks*.

57. 'The Beginning of the End', in *Writings of Leon Trotsky 1936–37*, New York 1970, p. 382.

4

Trotsky's Alternative Economic Strategy

The old slanders against Trotsky have been officially rejected. But now new myths and accusations are being produced, both in party circles and among the liberal intelligentsia.[1] One of the most important of these accusations says that it was really Trotsky's ideas that were implemented in Stalin's adventurous economic policy after 1928, in other words, the forced collectivization of the peasantry, the mass deportation of the so-called kulaks, the breakneck pace of industrialization, economic autarky and a hierarchical command economy. It is claimed that Trotsky was historically responsible for this policy. Stalin is said to have put Trotsky's programme into practice, even if with a brutality Trotsky himself would not have approved.

The conclusion is clear: had Trotsky and the Left Opposition been victorious, little would have been different in the social and economic development of the Soviet Union after 1928. The political regime that corresponded to this development would, in all major respects, be similar to that created by Stalin, although possible without the mass repression and the terror of the Yezhovshchina after 1934.

In the light of the documents from the period 1923–40, this legend can be completely demolished. There are already quite a few Soviet writers who reject these accusations. The Leningrad historian, Vladimir Billik, for instance, has pointed out that it was Trotsky who first called for the introduction of NEP and rejected any extension of War Communism. Leonid Radzikhovsky has admitted that Trotsky, in his fight against the NEP men and the kulaks on the one hand, and the bureaucracy on the other, had developed a programme for the reorganization of the Soviet Union based on the twin pillars of democratic self-management and the market. Bordyugov and Koslov, one-time members of the Institute for Marxism-Leninism, published a study in *Pravda* which said that many of the warnings of the United Opposition of 1926–27 on the question of economic policy were very relevant. Yevgeny Dainov has argued energetically that Trotsky's economic policy was completely consistent with NEP. According to Dainov, Trotsky's struggle against the bureaucracy was a battle for the democratization of social relations in the Soviet Union. Trotsky defended a 'civilized Bolshevik model'.[2]

The Historical Background

The economic policy proposed by Trotsky and the Left Opposition undoubtedly underwent many changes in the period 1923–35. We have to distinguish between the proposals of the Left Opposition in 1923; the proposals of the United Opposition of 1926–27; the alternative strategy developed by Trotsky in *The Revolution Betrayed* (1936), in the 'Transitional Programme' (1938), in *In The Defence of Marxism* (1939–40) and in his Stalin biography (1940). But all these successive economic policy proposals had a common thread; they were based on a common strategy that related to certain historical premisses:

1. It is impossible to complete the construction of socialism, of a classless society, in one country. As long as the socialist revolution has not spread to at least the leading industrialized nations of the world, the non-capitalist economy and society of the USSR remains threatened both militarily and through the pressure of the world market.

2. It is none the less possible to begin the construction of socialism in the USSR, in other words, to industrialize and modernize the country and gradually to reduce social conflicts and inequalities.

3. Long-term economic and foreign policy, as well as the long-term construction of public institutions, must be directed primarily towards the goal of *increasing the social weight of the working class in both Soviet society and in the world*. This requires a gradual change in the relationships between the town and the countryside, between the working class and the peasantry, between industry and agriculture, between the immediate producers in industry and agriculture and the administrators of the state and society. It required a rapid reduction in unemployment,[3] as well as a gradual restructuring of the relations of production in the enterprises in the direction of an increasing participation of the workforce in enterprise management. Socialist democracy has to be promoted and developed because without this the whole strategy will fail. This presupposes that overall social conflicts and tensions are reduced, not intensified. This, once again, requires a

consolidation of the *smychka*, the alliance between the workers and peasants. The growing polarization in the countryside between the poor peasants and the richer peasants (kulaks) has to be decreased and the concentration of agricultural surplus in the hands of the richer peasants has to be reversed.

The only significant change that Trotsky made to these basic historical premisses was after 1932–33, when his model of a basically bipolar social conflict (between petty-bourgeois pre-capitalist and semi-capitalist forces and, at the other pole, proletarian forces) was replaced by a three-sided model, in which the increasingly autonomous bureaucracy, developing into a social caste, is seen as having a much greater degree of independence and also the ability to pursue an economic policy which is both anti-socialist (anti-proletarian) and anti-capitalist, over a certain historical period, as a means of increasing its power and privilege. This new model was also linked with a re-evaluation of the role of the market in the transitional period.

The Economic Platform of the 1923 Left Opposition

As has already been described in chapter 2, the 'Forty-Six' opposition group of October 1923 concentrated its attention on political issues, particularly internal party matters. This group, however, had very definite economic policies. Preobrazhensky, in his speech to the Moscow Conference on 10–11 January 1924, emphasized the historical significance of economic planning for the further development of the USSR. But this was a general historical tendency and did not imply any particular conclusions about day-to-day economic policies:

> In the sphere of economic and social relations we have the following process: our state economy is developing but our capitalist economy is also developing in parallel to this. . . . The line must be towards the development of the state economy, the transition to an organized system of accumulation and to the formation of another basic form of organization to counterpose to NEP [the peasant bloc]. . . . Following a period of lack of planning, during which NEP has developed with gigantic success, the Central Committee is making a turn towards the line of the greater planning, the socialist organization and the socialist accumulation that we have been speaking of. But if this turn is inadequate, if our party's recognition of the importance of this turning point is not sufficiently full . . . then we shall have many dangers along this road.[4]

Pyatakov's speech at the Thirteenth Party Conference (16–18

January 1924) raised the issue of the 'price scissors' which Trotsky had already raised in his 'New Course' articles in *Pravda*.[5] Development of prices had been negative in two respects. First, agrarian production had grown more rapidly than industrial production, which produced mainly consumer goods for the countryside. From the point of view of the peasantry, the terms of trade between the city and the countryside had deteriorated. For the same amount of agricultural products, the peasants received a smaller amount of industrial consumer goods. So the peasants felt at a disadvantage.

Small-scale trade, however, was dominated by private traders (the so-called NEP men). These small traders had, for instance, a quasi-monopoly in the sale of products such as refined sugar and sold these products at much higher prices than did the state outlets. The poorer sections of the urban population were therefore largely unable to buy these products. So the workers also felt at a disadvantage.

In 1923–24 the Left Opposition made concrete proposals on how to overcome the price scissors, in order to prevent it from damaging the relationship between the workers and the peasants. Priority should be given to an increased production of industrial consumer goods and agricultural implements for the countryside. As a means of increasing industrial production, the Left Opposition proposed a progressive income tax on the richer sections of the population, on the NEP men and the kulaks. At the same time, the opposition proposed that the state should abandon the goal of a positive trade balance, i.e. the accumulation of gold and foreign currencies. The goal should be an equilibrium of import and export and the use of some of the accumulated reserves to purchase machinery from abroad to speed up the process of industrialization.

It is clear that these are indeed very moderate proposals. There is no question here of any 'hostility to the peasantry'. On the contrary, these proposals corresponded entirely to the interests of the overwhelming majority of the peasants. The claim that the opposition wanted an increase in industrial prices, at the expense of the peasantry, is simply not true. None the less, Bukharin condemned this policy as 'liquidation of the NEP' and 'super-industrialization'. In the light of the Stalin course after 1928, and of his own proposals in 1928–29, this judgement of Bukharin was a tragic error.

The proposals of the Left Opposition in the period 1923–24 were, in no sense, an attempt to abolish the market mechanism in the Soviet economy. What they represented was an attempt to use price and market mechanisms in such a way as to promote what Preobrazhensky later called 'primitive socialist accumulation'.[6] In his popular brochure published in 1922, *From NEP to Socialism: A Glance into the Future of Russia and Europe*,[7] Preobrazhensky emphasized that market mechanisms would continue to exist for decades. But he also advocated measures that would diminish social inequality in the town and countryside, promote socialist democracy and allow the workers gradually to increase their direct participation in the management enterprises.

Bukharin and Preobrazhensky were close friends for many years. Together they had written a popular edition of the party's programme, published under the title *The ABC of Communism*.[8] The polemic between them began in 1924 and concerned the long-term dynamic of the contradictions unleashed by the NEP, contradictions which Lenin himself had emphasized on many occasions.[9] Bukharin obstinately refused to deal with economic problems that went beyond considerations of short- or middle-term economic policy. Any long-term analysis signified 'doubt about the inner strengths of the Russian Revolution', tantamount to a sliding into Menshevik positions. Trotsky and Preobrazhensky, however, addressed the long-term problems: Which economic and social processes would foster a restoration of capitalism? Which would foster a development towards socialism? Which of the party's economic policies promotes the first trend and which the second?

Basically, it was a question of the form and the distribution of the social surplus product. What had to be prevented was the growing concentration of this social surplus in private hands in the form of private money capital. An increasing part of the social surplus should flow into the state sector.

This problem was linked to the problem of long-term developments in agriculture. What Bukharin had in mind was at best a two-sector agricultural economy; what existed in reality was a dominant private agriculture and weak agricultural co-operatives. Bukharin underestimated completely the objective process of social differentiation that was already in full swing.[10] Preobrazhensky and Trotsky, on the other hand, based themselves on Lenin's project of an accelerated formation of agriculatural co-operatives[11] and a gradual but limited increase in the number of state farms which would make the towns (and the workers) less dependent on the fluctuations in private deliveries from the countryside.[12]

There was no element whatever of repression in Preobrazhensky's proposals. The co-operative and state sectors in agriculture were to develop with the voluntary co-operation of the poor peasants. Their entry into the co-operatives was not to be achieved mainly by the use of educational and propaganda measures but was to develop out of the material interests of the poor peasants themselves. Therefore, it was clear that the voluntary and gradual collectivization of agriculture would have to be preceded by the mass production of agricultural machinery and equipment. The co-operatives and state farms that possessed a higher level of technology than the farms of the rich peasants would guarantee a higher standard of living for the peasants that joined them. They would be able to sell their produce at lower prices with higher levels of profit. There was no question of forced deliveries. All Preobrazhensky's proprosals assumed the use of the price mechanism in trade and were based consciously on the material interests of the small and medium peasantry. Hence the proposal of the opposition, made in 1923, to construct a major tractor factory in Tsaritsyin, later Stalingrad.

In other words, from 1923 there were three fundamentally different agricultural policies:

1. The policy of Bukharin, which denied that there was a historic conflict between, on the one hand, private production, private exchange and private accumulation of wealth (capital) and, on the other hand, the long-term trend of socialist construction, a historical conflict in which either the one or the other tendency would win out in the end.

2. The line of the Stalin faction, which recognized this conflict later and wanted to resolve it by breaking with the logic of the NEP,[13] but mainly by using bureaucratic-administrative and terrorist means and without regard for the social and economic consequences of these methods. This line in the long run proved itself to be ineffective and inhuman.

3. The line of Trotsky and the Left Opposition, which understood the historic conflict and wanted to resolve it gradually with economic and political means. It wanted to increase the participation of the majority of the population (mainly the workers and poor peasants and youth, but also, to a certain degree, the middle peasants and the intelligentsia) in strengthening the public sector and limiting the private sector. This would not be possible without an extension of socialist democracy.

The Economic Proposals of the United Opposition, 1926–27

The United Opposition of 1926–27 was mainly a bloc of the Left Opposition and the group around Zinoviev and Kamenev (supported by Krupskaya). Members of the older opposition groups, the Democratic Centralists and the Workers Opposition, also joined. On questions of economic policy the United Opposition adopted most of the critical analysis and practical proposals of the Left Opposition of 1926–27.

The United Opposition was sharply critical of the low level of accumulation in the state sector (in industry it was lower than at certain times under Czarism). The planned rate of growth under the first five-year-plan (4–9 per cent annually) was rejected as too low. It proposed that an increased rate of industrialization and a greater investment in the state sector should be financed from two sources: a progressive tax on the richer sector of the population and a radical reduction in unproductive expenditure, especially in the state administration.

Of some interest today, in the light of the anti-alcohol campaign of the 1980s, is the fact that the United Opposition campaigned against the terrible consequences of the state monopoly in vodka, and the public promotion of sales of vodka, with arguments that anticipated those of the Gorbachev leadership more than fifty years later:

> The state sale of vodka was originally introduced as an experiment and with the proviso that the bulk of the income derived should be used for industrialization, especially for the development of the metal industry. In reality, the state sale of alcohol has only damaged industry. This experiment should be regarded as a complete failure. The state sale of vodka has had negative effects not only in the private economy, as was already the case under Czarism, but mainly in the state sector itself.[14]
>
> The increase in absenteeism, shoddy work and waste, the damage to machinery, the increase in accidents, fires, brawls, etc. cost hundreds of millions of roubles annually.... The abolition of the state sale of vodka would automatically improve the material and cultural resources for industrialization.[15]

The economic policy proposed by the United Opposition of 1926–27 contained no rejection of money–price relations or market mechanisms, no transition to 'barracks Communism' or 'command economy'. On the contrary, like the policy of the Left Opposition of 1923, it was based on a use of these mechanisms in the interests of the workers and in the interests of a more rapid but by no means forced industrialization:

> The necessary acceleration in industrialization is impossible without a systematic and determined lowering of the costs of production and of wholesale and retail prices of industrial goods, nor is it possible without an

adaptation to world market prices. This is the only way to develop our technological infrastructure and to respond in a better way to the needs of the working masses.[16]

Under NEP, a certain growth of hostile forces, of kulaks, NEP men and bureaucrats is unavoidable. These forces cannot be destroyed simply by administrative order or economic pressure. In creating and carrying through the NEP, we created a certain space for capitalist relations in our country, and we should regard this as unavoidable for a considerable time to come.... But we can win out against them, we can fight them by means of a correct, well-considered and systematic working-class policy, relying on the small peasant and an alliance with the middle peasant.[17]

At the centre of the platform of the United Opposition was the defence of the interests of the Soviet working class. It is clear to anyone who reads the platform that the claim to the contrary, a claim still made today, is nothing but slander. The platform contained a detailed list of demands for the defence of workers' interests: against unemployment and against any decrease in real wages, for an immediate improvement in housing conditions for workers, against bureaucratic misuse of the rationalization campaign, for real worker control over wages and norms, for real independence of the trade unions from the factory leadership, for a guaranteed right to strike. The opposition wanted a decisive increase in the participation of the workers in the leadership of the economy.[18] The platform culminated in the statement:

> The decisive factor in judging the progress of our country on the road to socialism must be, alongside the growth in productive forces and the dominance of the socialist over the capitalist elements, above all else the decisive improvement in the living conditions of the working class.[19]

Trotsky's Struggle against the Adventurous Course of the Stalin Faction from 1929 to 1933

When Stalin introduced his turn to the forced collectivization of agriculture and to a super-accelerated, disproportionate and wasteful industrialization, Trotsky and most of the opposition were very critical. It was their view that this adventurous course would be extremely damaging to the interests of the working class. We could quote numerous articles from the *Bulletin of the Opposition*. The most important documents are Trotsky's article of 1932, 'The Soviet Economy in Danger', and the articles of Christian Rakovsky published between 1929 and 1931. In his 'Declaration of 1930', Rakovsky wrote:

> The slogan of complete collectivization is itself the greatest economic nonsense. We are Marxists and we know that new forms of property can be founded only on the basis of new productive relations. But these new productive relations still do not exist.... The decree abolishing NEP and the kulaks as a class is another economic absurdity.... No charter or decree can abolish the contradictions which are still at work in the economy and in everyday life, contradictions which besiege the collective farms or already operate within them. Attempts to ignore this economic truth have led to the systematic use of violence.... Intensive collectivization was launched in breach of the Party Programme, in breach of the most basic principles of Marxism, and with contempt for Lenin's most elementary warnings about collectivization, the middle peasantry and NEP.... The decrease in the number of food products on the market and the rapid rise in prices lead to a fall in real wages.... The decrees on discipline are in direct breach of the Party Congress resolutions of 1921 on trade unions.... [This is accompanied by] the introduction, not even as an exceptional measure and without the consent of the workers, of socialist competition (with methods similar to those used in the countryside for the introduction of intensive collectivization), a reduction in wage rates, an increase in norms ... and a deterioration in the legal and material situation of the working class.[20]

In his article 'The Soviet Economy in Danger', Trotsky later wrote on the fundamental question of economic policy in the whole historic period of the transition from capitalism to socialism:

> If a universal mind existed, of the kind that projected itself into the scientific fancy of Laplace – a mind that could register simultaneously all the processes of nature and society, that could measure the dynamics of their motions, that could forecast the results of their interactions – such a mind, of course, could a priori draw up a faultless and exhaustive economic plan, beginning with the number of acres of wheat down to the last button for a vest. The bureaucracy often imagines that just such a mind is at its disposal; that is why it so easily frees itself from the control of the market and of Soviet democracy. But in reality, the bureaucracy errs frightfully in its estimate of its spiritual resources ...
>
> The innumerable living participants in the economy, state and private, collective and individual, must serve notice of their needs and of their relative strength not only through the statistical determinations of the plan commission but by the direct pressure of supply and demand. The plan is checked and to a considerable degree, realized through the market. The regulation of the market itself must depend on the tendencies that are brought out through its mechanism. The blueprints produced by the

departments must demonstrate their economic efficacy through commercial calculation. The system of the transitional economy is unthinkable without the control of the rouble. This presupposes, in its turn, that the rouble is at par. Without a firm monetary unit, commercial accounting can only increase the chaos ...

Only through the interaction of these three elements, state planning, the market and Soviet democracy, can the correct direction of the economy of the transitional epoch be attained. Only thus can be assured, not the complete surmounting of contradictions and disproportions within a few years (this is utopian!), but their mitigation, and through that the strengthening of the material bases of the dictatorship of the proletariat until the moment when a new and victorious revolution will widen the arena of socialist planning and will reconstruct the system.[21]

And even more clearly:

The economic foundation of the dictatorship of the proletariat can be considered fully assured only from that moment when the state is not forced to resort to administrative measures of compulsion against the majority of the peasantry in order to obtain agricultural products; that is, when in return for machines, tools and objects for personal use, the peasants voluntarily supply the state with the necessary quantity of grain and raw material. Only on this basis – along with other necessary conditions, nationally and internationally – can collectivization acquire a true socialist character.[22]

One year later, in his article 'Planned Economy in the USSR: Success or Failure' (7 September 1933), Trotsky repeated this argument in an even more systematic manner.[23] There were two further problems to which Trotsky devoted particular attention: the stability of the rouble, which he thought could only be achieved if the rouble were based on the gold standard, and the problem of autarky of the Soviet economy, which he rejected. Both problems are obviously linked, which is why Trotsky placed so much emphasis on the monopoly of foreign trade. The link with the world market is one thing; domination by the world market is something quite different.

It is true that some of the leaders of the United Opposition around Zinoviev and Kamenev, and later some of the Left Opposition leaders (Preobrazhensky, Pyatakov, Radek and Smilga), had a different view. They capitulated to Stalin because they thought that his adventurous course represented basically a decisive blow against the bourgeois and petty-bourgeois forces in Soviet society.[24] The defence of this position logically meant that they had to break with the opposition, a capitulation the theoretical and economic premises of which Trotsky and the other opposition leaders condemned totally.

Trotsky and the other opposition leaders regarded the bureaucratically planned economy, the forced collectivization of agriculture and the adventurist pace of industrialization with its massive disproportions as a third variant of development, which corresponded neither to the interests of the medium-sized bourgeoisie and petty bourgeoisie, nor those of the workers and small peasants, but rather to the interests of the bureaucracy which was on the road to consolidating itself as a special caste in Soviet society. This policy therefore did not represent 'the realization of the programme of the opposition with barbarous means'.

Trotsky's Economic Policy in the Period 1934–40

We really do not need to look in great detail at Trotsky's economic proposals between 1934 and 1940. Basically, these represented a continuation of the policies advocated between 1932 and 1934. The sections on economic policy in the last chapter of *The Revolution Betrayed* sound today like an anticipation of what numerous Soviet economists and public figures have been saying in recent years since the introduction of Glasnost under Gorbachev:

> The growth of power and independence in a bureaucracy, however, is not unlimited. There are historical factors stronger than marshals, and even than general secretaries. A rationalization of economy is unthinkable without accurate accounts. Accounts are irreconcilable with the caprice of a bureaucracy. Concern for the restoration of a stable rouble, which means a rouble independent of the 'leaders', is imposed on the bureaucracy by the fact that their autocratic rule is coming into greater and greater contradiction with the development of the productive forces of the country – just as absolute monarchy became in its time irreconcilable with the development of the bourgeois market. Money accounting, however, cannot fail to give a more open character to the struggle of the different strata for the distribution of the national income. The question of the wage-scale, almost a matter of indifference during the epoch of the food-card system, is now decisive for the workers, and with it the question of the trade unions. The designation of trade union officials from above is destined to meet more and more resistance. More than that, under piecework payment the worker is directly interested in a correct ordering of the factory management. The Stakhanovists are complaining more and more loudly of the faults of organization in production. Bureaucratic nepotism in the matter of appointing directors, engineers, etc., is becoming more and more intolerable. The co-operatives and the state trade are coming much more than

formerly into dependence upon the buyer. The collective farms and the individual collective farmers are learning to translate their dealings with the state into the language of figures. They are growing unwilling to endure submissively the naming from above of leaders whose sole merit is frequently their closeness to the local bureaucratic clique. And, finally, the rouble promises to cast a light into that most mysterious region: the legal and illegal incomes of the bureaucracy. Thus, in a politically strangled country, money circulation becomes an important lever for the mobilization of oppositional forces, and foretells the beginning of the end of 'enlight-ened' absolutism.

While the growth of industry and the bringing of agriculture into the sphere of state planning vastly complicates the task of leadership, bringing to the front the problem of *quality*, bureaucratism destroys the creative initiative and the feeling of responsibility without which there is not, and cannot be, qualitative progress. The ulcers of bureaucratism are perhaps not so obvious in the big industries, but they are devouring, together with the co-operatives, the light and food-producing industries, the collective farms, the small local industries – that is, all those branches of economy that stand nearest to the people.

The progressive role of the Soviet bureaucracy coincides with the period devoted to introducing into the Soviet Union the most important elements of capitalist technique. The rough work of borrowing, imitating, trans-planting and grafting was accomplished on the bases laid down by the revolution. There was, thus far, no question of any new word in the sphere of technique, science or art. It is possible to build gigantic factories according to a ready-made Western pattern by bureaucratic command – although, to be sure, at triple the normal cost. But the further you go, the more the economy runs into the problem of quality, which slips out of the hands of a bureaucracy like a shadow. The Soviet products are as though branded with the grey label of indifference. Under a nationalized economy, *quality* demands a democracy of producers and consumers, freedom of criticism and initiative – conditions incompatible with a totalitarian regime of fear, lies and flattery.

Behind the question of quality stands a more complicated and grandiose problem which may be comprised in the concept of *independent, technical and cultural creation*. The ancient philosophers said that strife is the father of all things. No new values can be created where a free conflict of ideas is impossible. To be sure, a revolutionary dictatorship means by its very essence strict limitations of freedom. But for that very reason epochs of revolution have never been directly favourable to cultural creation: they have only cleared the arena for it. The dictatorship of the proletariat opens a wider scope to human genius the more it ceases to be a dictatorship. The socialist culture will flourish only in proportion to the dying away of the state. In that simple and unshakeable historic law is contained the death sentence of the present political regime in the Soviet Union. Soviet democracy is not the demand of an abstract policy, still less an abstract moral. It has become a life and death need of the country.[25]

Without doubt, Trotsky was mistaken about the rhythm of 'the mobilization of oppositional forces'. He underestimated the depoliticizing effects of the terror, the fear and the atomization of the working class. But the long-term tendencies of development are described in the passage just quoted in a masterly and prophetic manner. Sixty years later there is little that needs to be added to this analysis. It reads as a description of the systemic crisis of the Soviet Union, which today is so clear to everyone.

Notes

1. See, for example, Grigory Vololazov, 'L'Essence et les racines du stalinisme', *Science Sociales, Revue de l'Académie des Sciences d'URSS*, No. 3, 1990, p. 218.

2. Vladimir Billik's article is in a special edition of the French weekly *Rouge*, commemorating the fiftieth anniversary of Trotsky's murder. Leonid Radzikhovsky in *Les Nouvelles de Moscou*, 9 September 1990. Bordyugov and Koslov in the German edition of *Pravda*, 30 September 1988.

3. Unemployment was very high during the NEP, perhaps as high as 16–18 per cent of the urban proletariat. See E. H. Carr, *Foundations of a Planned Economy*, vol. I, 2, London 1969, p. 456.

4. *Documents of the 1923 Opposition*, London 1975, pp. 47–8.

5. *The New Course 1923*, London 1973. On the 'price scissors', see E. H. Carr, *The Interregnum 1923–1924*, London 1969, pp. 95ff.

6. See E. Preobrazhensky, *The New Economics*, Oxford 1965 (chapter 2, 'The Law of Primitive Socialist Accumulation').

7. Published by New Park Publications, London 1975.

8. Published by Penguin Books, Harmondsworth 1969, with an Introduction by E. H. Carr.

9. On this issue, Lenin expressed himself in much stronger terms than did the Left Opposition. Of many possible quotations here are just two:

The New Economic Policy means substituting a tax for the requisitioning of food; it means reverting to capitalism to a considerable extent – to what extent we do not know. Concessions to foreign capitalists, and leasing enterprises to private capitalists definitely means restoring capitalism, and this is part and parcel of the New Economic Policy; for the abolition of the surplus-food appropriation system means allowing the peasants to trade freely in their surplus agricultural produce, in whatever is left over after the tax is collected – and the tax takes only a small share of that produce. The peasants constitute a huge section of our population and of our entire economy, and that is why capitalism must grow out of this soil of free trading . . .

From the point of view of strategy the root question is: who will take advantage of the new system first? The whole question is – whom will the peasantry follow? The proletariat who wants to build a socialist society? Or the capitalist . . .?

Collected Works, vol. 33, Moscow 1966, p. 64

Peasant farming continues to be petty commodity production. Here we have an extremely broad and very sound, deep-rooted basis for capitalism, a basis on

which capitalism persists or arises anew in a bitter struggle against communism.
Collected Works, vol. 30, p. 109

10. Once again, I shall quote from Lenin:

What is free exchange? It is unrestricted trade and that means turning back towards capitalism. Free exchange and freedom of trade mean circulation of commodities between petty proprietors. All of us who have studied at least the elements of Marxism know that this exchange and freedom of trade inevitably lead to a division of commodity producers into owners of capital and owners of labour-power, a division into capitalists and wage-workers, i.e. a revival of capitalist wage slavery, which does not fall from the sky but springs the world over from the agricultural commodity economy.
Collected Works, vol. 32, p. 218

On social differences in the countryside in the mid 1920s, see E. H. Carr and R. W. Davies, *Foundations of the Planned Economy*, vol. I, 1, London 1969, pp. 18–26.

11. See Lenin, 'On Co-operation', in *Collected Works*, vol. 33, pp. 467–75.

12. The party leadership practically reduced the problem of co-operatives to consumer co-operatives. See, for example, Rykov's speech on the Soviet economy given to the Fifth Congress of the Comintern, in Ulf Wolter, *Die Linke Opposition in der Sovjetunion 1923–1928*, vol. 2, Berlin 1975, p. 170.

13. Stalin said this openly. He published an article in *Pravda* under the title 'To Hell with the NEP!' (27 December 1929).

14. Quotations from the 'Platform of the United Opposition' are from the German collection of opposition documents, *Die Linke Opposition in der Sovjetunion 1923–1928*, 5 volumes, ed. Ulf Wolter, Berlin 1976. The above quotation is from vol. 5, pp. 345 and 385.

15. Ibid., pp. 586–7.

16. Ibid., p. 474.

17. Ibid., pp. 336–7.

18. Ibid., pp. 349–59.

19. Ibid., pp. 344–5.

20. In Christian Rakovsky, *Selected Writings in Opposition in the USSR 1923–1930*, London 1980, pp. 167–8.

21. 'The Soviet Economy in Danger' (22 October 1932), in *Writings of Leon Trotsky 1932*, New York 1973, pp. 273–5.

22. Ibid., p. 271.

23. 'Planned Economy in the USSR: Success or Failure' (7 September 1933), in *Writings of Leon Trotsky. Supplement 1929–1933*, New York 1977, pp. 292–3, 296–7.

24. Isaac Deutscher also described the social and economic changes in the USSR from 1928 to 1932 as a 'third revolution'.

25. *The Revolution Betrayed*, New York 1972, pp. 274–6.

5

Class Self-organization and
Vanguard Party

The relation between self-organization of the masses and the vanguard party is one of the most complex problems of Marxism. It has never really been systematically dealt with. This applies also to the founders of scientific socialism, although Engels addressed the problem in numerous articles and letters, as did Marx, to a lesser extent.[1]

If we look at the best known works that deal with this problem – Lenin's *What Is To Be Done?*, Rosa Luxemburg's *Organizational Questions of Russian Social Democracy*, Kautsky's writings against Bernstein, Luxemburg and the Bolsheviks, Lenin's *Left-Wing Communism: An Infantile Disorder* and Otto Bauer's *The Illegal Party* – we find that they are all of a polemical nature. They do not set out to deal with the problem in a systematic way. Georg Lukács's early writings, *History and Class Consciousness* and *Lenin*, are of such a high level of abstraction that they cannot be regarded as a systematic treatment of the problem. Gramsci also deals with the problem in his writings of the early 1920s, but in his case what we have are basically a series of disconnected newspaper articles.[2]

The picture changes, however, when we look at the complete works of some of the classical Marxists. Lenin and Rosa Luxemburg thought about this central problem of Marxist theory and practice for over a quarter of a century. Their writings on this question are evidence of a maturation of their ideas, enriched by experience over many years, and, on the basis of these writings, we are able to construct an integrated theory. This does not mean, of course, that they would have agreed in every detail with such a reconstruction.

Trotsky, who lived much longer than either Lenin or Luxemburg, was able to base himself on a much richer international experience in his dealing with this problem of class and party, self-organization and vanguard organization. He was personally familiar with the working-class movement in ten countries and was able to study the experiences in others. He was able to analyse the new phenomena of fascism and Stalinism and the methods of struggle against them. Nevertheless, and perhaps precisely because of this wealth of experience, his contributions to this problem were much more heterogeneous than those of Lenin or Luxemburg.

Trotsky's basic position on the problem of party and class, self-organization and vanguard, changed at least five times, although there was undoubtedly some common 'red thread' in all of these positions. Whereas, for Lenin and Luxemburg, it is possible to create a synthesis of their views, in the case of Trotsky what has to be attempted is an assessment of how his ideas on this issue developed.

The Dangers of a Centralized Vanguard Party in the Absence of Class Self-organization

Trotsky, as we all know, completely supported Lenin, Martov and Plekhanov in their fight against the 'economists' in the first *Iskra*. Lenin valued Trotsky's contribution and referred to him as 'the pen'. It was due to Lenin's efforts that Trotsky joined the editorial group of *Iskra* as its youngest member.

What's more, during his Siberian exile in 1901, a year before Lenin, he stressed the necessity of a centralized party as a way of generalizing the fragmentary, local and immediate experiences of the working class and helping to build a political class-consciousness.[3] It was this political goal, and not some organizational concept, that was the principal element in Lenin's centralism. This was an insight which, unfortunately, Trotsky was to lose sight of in the years between 1902 and 1916. At the time of the first split between the majority (Bolsheviks) and minority (Mensheviks) of the Russian Social Democratic Labour Party (RSDLP), at its Second Congress, Trotsky sided with the Mensheviks.[4]

His polemic against Lenin led to the publication in 1904 of his pamphlet, *Our Political Tasks*, famous for the passage which was to acquire a somewhat dramatic and prophetic significance in the light of later developments in the Russian Communist Party and in the history of the Soviet Union:

> In the internal politics of the party, these methods will lead to a situation in which the party caucus substitutes itself for the party; then the Central Committee substitutes itself for the party caucus; and finally a dictator substitutes himself for the Central Committee.[5]

Innumerable political opponents of Lenin as well as historians saw the course of events in the Soviet Union as a confirmation of the correctness of Trotsky's early views and of the incorrectness of Lenin's.[6] Trotsky, it is said, changed his position after 1917 and regarded his earlier views as an error.[7] The reality is somewhat different: both Trotsky and Rosa Luxemburg were unfair to Lenin when they took the positions of *What Is To Be Done?* out of their concrete historical context and ascribed to them a universally valid character.[8]

Lenin's intention, in writing this pamphlet, was to deal with the immediate tasks of an illegal party and to help prepare a broad, independent, political mass movement of the working class. His aim was not to develop a general theory about the relationship between party and class, and it was certainly not his view that the class should be subordinate to the party. In this same pamphlet, Lenin wrote the following sentences, which could have come from the pen of Luxemburg or Trotsky:

> The organization of professional revolutionaries makes sense only in relation to a real revolutionary class that spontaneously begins to struggle. Everyone will agree that the 'comprehensive democratic principle' includes the following two essential preconditions: first of all, complete openness and, secondly, the election of all officials. We would describe the organization of the German Socialist Party as democratic, because everything that happens in the party is public, including its congresses.

After the experience of the February Revolution of 1905, he formulated it even more clearly:

> Take the whole pre-revolutionary period and the first two and a half years of the revolution (1905–1907). Compare our Social-Democratic Party during this whole period with the other parties in respect of unity, organizsation, and continuity of policy. You will have to admit that *in this* respect our party is unquestionably superior to all the others – the Cadets, the Socialist-Revolutionaries, etc. Before the revolution it drew up a programme which was formally accepted by all Social Democrats, and when changes were made in it there was no split over the programme. From 1903 to 1907 (formally from 1905 to 1906), the Social Democratic Party, despite the split in its ranks, gave the public the fullest information on the inner-party situation (minutes of the Second General Congress, the Third Bolshevik and the Fourth General, or Stockholm congresses). Despite the split, the Social Democratic Party, earlier than any of the other parties, was able to take advantage of the temporary spell of freedom to build a legal organization with an ideal democratic structure, an electoral system and representation at congresses according to the number of organized members.[9]

... It seems to me that Comrade Radin is wrong in raising the question: the Soviet of Workers' Deputies or the Party? I think that it is wrong to put the question in that way and that the decision must certainly be: *Both* the Soviet of Workers' Deputies *and* the Party...

It seems to me that the Soviet of Workers' Deputies, as an organization representing all occupations, should strive to include deputies from *all* industrial, professional and office workers, domestic servants, farm labourers, etc., from *all* who want and are able to fight in common for a better life for the whole working people, from *all* who have at least an elementary degree of political honesty, from all but the Black Hundreds.[10]

Lenin valued Trotsky's role in the Petrograd Soviet,[11] although Trotsky and he were in different currents. Concerning the relationships between the different currents in Russian Social Democracy, Lenin wrote shortly after the 1905 revolution:

We were all agreed on the principle of democratic centralism, on guarantees for the rights of all minorities and for all loyal opposition, on the autonomy of every party organization, on recognizing that all party functionaries must be elected, accountable to the party and subject to recall. We see the observance in practice of these principles of organization, their sincere and consistent application, as a guarantee against splits, a guarantee that the ideological struggle of the party can and must prove fully consistent with strict organizational unity, with the submission of all to the decisions of the Unity Congress.[12]

As these quotations make clear, the claim that Stalin's theory and practice of bureaucratic centralism were already present in Lenin's organizational model is completely unfounded and in no way corresponds to the actual course of development.

The Menshevik alternative completely underestimated the difficulties created by illegality, by the discontinuities in class action, by the efforts needed to bring together the fragmented experiences of struggle, by the struggle for the working class's political autonomy and later for its political hegemony.[13] The split at the Second Congress of the Russian Social Democracy already contained the core of what would later emerge as the decisive difference between the Bolsheviks and Mensheviks on the question of the role of the Russian bourgeoisie in the coming revolution.[14]

These Menshevik positions were not defended by either Luxemburg or Trotsky. With his views on the political independence of the working class in the Russian revolution, Trotsky actually stood to the left of the Bolsheviks. These views are summarized in his concept of 'permanent revolution' and were completely confirmed by the October

Revolution of 1917. Lenin developed practically the same views in his 'April Theses', probably without having read Trotsky's writings on this question from 1904 to 1906.[15]

Although Lenin rejected any form of 'substitutionism' in all phases of the revolutionary rise of mass activity, this was not the case for the majority of 'old Bolsheviks'. This explains why initially they adopted such a cautious if not explicitly hostile attitude to the creation of the Petrograd Soviet, only joining and fully supporting it later.

Trotsky was the first to recognize that the soviets were the form created by history itself for the self-organization of the working class and for its future exercise of power. What Lenin gave classical expression to in *State and Revolution*, and what was later developed in a sociological and theoretical manner by Gramsci, the Comintern and Karl Korsch, had already been anticipated by Trotsky in his *Results and Prospects* of 1906.[16]

Soviets (councils) are organs of proletarian revolution.[17] They cannot survive in non-revolutionary periods. This has been confirmed by the failure of the Dutch Left Communists, Pannekoek and Gorter, and of the German Communist Workers Party (KAPD). Mass trade unions can grow and flourish during periods of capitalist stability, but not soviets. Similarly, after the conquest of state power by the workers, any decline in the self-activity of the working class can limit and even end the role of the soviets as organs for the direct exercise of working-class power. Therefore the soviets, in and of themselves, are not a universal panacea and they can be effective as instruments of self-organization and self-liberation of the working class only when linked with other organizational forms – mass trade unions and vanguard parties.

The Dangers of a Decline in Mass Activity in the Absence of a Vanguard Party

These necessary preconditions for the existence of soviets give rise to a dialectical interaction between class self-organization (a very uneven process) and a permanent vanguard party. The size and degree of mass influence of a permanent vanguard party is also affected by the conjunctural ebb and flow, but the party is more stable, has greater continuity of action and is better able to resist the pressure of unfavourable circumstances. The disappearance of the vanguard party and the loss of its cadres with their roots in the working class would make a later revival of mass action more difficult.

This was something Trotsky failed to recognize at the Stockholm

Congress of the RSDLP. His underestimation of the danger from the 'liquidators' (those Mensheviks who did not want to continue the clandestine struggle after the defeat of the 1905 revolution); his unprincipled blocs with the Mensheviks in spite of major political differences; his conciliationism, which effectively separated the organizational question from its political content (partly under the influence of German 'centrism', i.e. Kautsky, although he understood Kautsky's political limitations better than Lenin did) – these errors from the period 1908 to 1914 were quite major ones and they were to have grave consequences later in the unfolding of events inside the Russian Communist Party because they nurtured the mistrust of the 'old Bolsheviks' towards Trotsky.

Underlying Trotsky's conciliationism of this period was an overestimation of the spontaneous ability of the working class to discover the correct and necessary solution to the problem of state power and to impose this in some manner on the Social Democracy which was itself divided on this very issue.[18] This was an inappropriate generalization of what actually happened, to some extent, in the period 1905–1906 and which, at the time, had led to a reunification of the Bolsheviks and Mensheviks. But certainly from 1912, and probably even earlier, the politically rightward movement of the Mensheviks made this impossible. It wasn't until after the outbreak of the February Revolution that Trotsky recognized this.

The struggle against the liquidators, in other words, Lenin's insistence on the continuity of the political vanguard party even in times of reaction, proved itself to be entirely correct and it made it easier to stimulate working class independence again after 1912. A Commission of Observers set up to look at the Russian question and chaired by Emile Vandervelde, a member of the Praesidium of the Second International, reported, after a trip to Russia in 1914, that in the newly emergent mass organizations of the Russian working class, the Bolsheviks almost without exception were playing the leading role.[19] This refuted Trotsky's view that the Bolsheviks were an isolated sectarian group – a view which he still defended as late as 1916.[20]

1917–19: The Synthesis of Soviet Power and Vanguard Organization

Immediately after the outbreak of the February Revolution, Lenin and Trotsky adopted identical views with respect to the tasks of the Russian proletariat, a viewpoint summed up in the slogan, 'All Power to the Soviets!' Lenin's 'April Theses' represented an important shift on his part and met at first with opposition from the 'old Bolsheviks'.[21] It was significant, however, that the worker Bolsheviks, in other words, the proletarian cadres, the worker vanguard, including those who were not members of any party, supported Lenin. This made it possible for him to overcome the resistance of the party leadership.

At the same time, Trotsky altered his view of the Bolshevik Party as an isolated sect. He recognized the vanguard role which the Bolshevik-trained workers had played in the February Revolution.[22] This shift led him logically to give up his conciliationist attitude towards the Mensheviks, all the more so since the strategic differences between them about the future course of the revolution were, for Trotsky as for Lenin, questions of life and death. This was no secondary issue; what was at stake was the victory or defeat of the revolution.[23]

Paradoxically, it was now some of the 'old Bolsheviks', Kamenev, Stalin and Molotov, who defended a conciliatory attitude towards the Mensheviks.[24] What followed was a very rapid fusion between the Bolsheviks and Trotsky's Inter-Regional Organization, the *Mezh-rayonka* (formed in 1913 and included Lunacharsky, Ryazanov, Yoffe and other later prominent Bolsheviks). Lenin's judgement on this, which he was never to change, was: 'Trotsky understood that unity with the Mensheviks is impossible and, since that moment, there is no better Bolshevik than Trotsky.'[25]

As president of the Petrograd Soviet, as tireless mass agitator, as leader of the Military Revolutionary Committee of the Soviet which organized the October uprising and which brought about its victory using political-agitational means, in that it convinced the Petrograd garrison to take its orders from the Soviet and not from the bourgeois general staff, Trotsky solved the problem of the self-organization–vanguard party relationship in practice before he mastered it in theory. This solution was expressed in the simultaneity of the uprising and the Second Soviet Congress. The uprising was neither a conspiracy nor a putsch by a small minority. The decision to establish Soviet power, the 'workers and peasants state', was a democratic decision of the majority of Russian workers and poor peasants.[26]

Winning over the majority of the Russian workers to the side of Soviet power was made possible only by the permanent, impressive and breathtaking work of the Bolshevik Party among the proletariat. Non-Bolshevik eye-witnesses have fully confirmed this.[27] The dialectical unity of class self-organization and vanguard party achieved here its classical maturity.

This is how Trotsky summed it up in his *History of the Russian Revolution*:

> The dynamic of revolutionary events is *directly* determined by swift, intense and passionate changes in the psychology of classes which have already formed themselves before the revolution . . .
>
> The masses go into a revolution not with a prepared plan of social reconstruction, but with a sharp feeling that they cannot endure the old regime. Only the guiding layers of a class have a political programme, and even this still requires the test of events and the approval of the masses. The fundamental political process of the revolution thus consists in the gradual comprehension by a class of the problems arising from the social crisis – the active orientation of the masses by a method of successive approximations . . .
>
> Only on the basis of a study of political processes in the masses themselves can we understand the role of parties and leaders, whom we least of all are inclined to ignore. They constitute not an independent, but nevertheless a very important element in the process. Without a guiding organization the energy of the masses would dissipate like steam not enclosed in a piston-box. But nevertheless what moves things is not the piston or the box but the steam.[28]

The dialectical unity and mutual enrichment of class self-organization and vanguard party activity was evident after 1917 in the development of the young Soviet system and in the construction of the Red Army. Contrary to the legends that are also widespread in the Soviet Union, the years 1918 and 1919 were highpoints of independent activity by the Russian working class, even more than 1917. There are numerous documentary, journalistic and literary sources that confirm this.[29] An unlikely witness here is Alexander Solzhenitsyn, someone quite hostile to the October Revolution. In his *Gulag Archipelago*, Solzhenitsyn reports how a prison wardens' soviet intervened on behalf of a conscientious objector who had been sentenced to death by a revolutionary tribunal and forced the tribunal to revise its sentence.[30] Where else in the history of modern states could one find such an example of popular democracy? Does it exist in any country today?

The problem of 'the leading role of the party' is described by Trotsky, in the above quotation, in classically Marxist fashion. Without this leading role the powerful potential of the volatile mass movement threatens to dissipate. But this leading role is not, as Plekhanov described it at the Second Congress of the RSDLP, a 'birthright'. It has to be continuously fought for politically and won democratically; the majority of the workers have to be convinced, they have to give their consent. It is only in the struggle for this majority that the party's leading role is realized. And the policies of the party, its programme, are neither infallible nor unalterable; they change through the test of practice, they are corrected by events. The party is an accompaniment to the self-activity of the masses.

The 'Dark Years' 1920–21: Trotsky's 'Substitutionism'

In order for this interplay between class self-organization and political leadership of the revolutionary vanguard party to be realized, there has to be a self-active working class or at least a self-active broad vanguard of the working class. As has already been pointed out, it is not possible to achieve this permanently under capitalism.

The experience of the Russian Revolution, and of all other socialist revolutions that followed, confirms that this continuous self-activity is also not automatic in a post-capitalist society. These societies too have their conjunctural ebb and flow. It reaches its highpoint in periods of great revolutionary upheaval (this is practically a tautology). It retreats when the revolutionary process has passed its highpoint. Russia reached such a turning-point at the end of the civil war, in the period 1920–21.

It would be of some interest to investigate the political-psychological sources of such a turning-point. People cannot live for years in an uninterrupted state of high tension and intense activity. The need for occasional rest is an almost physiological one. But much more important than this kind of generalization is the analysis of the concrete material and social living conditions which bring about this decline in political mass activity.

In the case of Russia in 1920 and 1921, these are well known and have been described many times: the massive numerical weakening of the proletariat following the decline in productive forces and the collapse of industries destroyed in the civil war; the qualitative weakening of the proletariat by the loss of its best forces into the Red Army and into the apparatus of the Soviet state; the sharp turn in the motivation of the workers, the concentration of their interests on immediate day-to-day needs, staying alive, finding food, and so on, all of this a consequence of the pressure from hunger and need; the growing disillusionment caused by the absence of a revolutionary victory abroad which could lead to a rapid improvement in their own situation; an inadequate level of culture, which limited the possibility of a direct exercise of power through the soviets.

There were two central links in this chain of causes which now reached breaking point. The backwardness of the country and the isolation of the revolution in a hostile capitalist environment severely limited the scope for self-activity of the Russian working class, in other words, for a real exercise of power by this class. Instead of leading the working class in the exercise of power, the party ruled increasingly in the name of the class.

For a certain crucial period during these difficult years, this change was perhaps unavoidable. The working class had shrunk to 35 per cent of its size in 1917. Even the one-time leader of the Workers' Opposition, the worker Bolshevik, Alexander Shlyapnikov, said to Lenin, half ironically, half seriously: 'I congratulate you, Comrade Lenin, that you exercise the dictatorship of the proletariat in the name of a non-existent proletariat.'[31]

But this setback was a conjunctural and not a structural phenomenon – something we can recognize more clearly today than was possible at the time. With the introduction of the NEP, industry and the working class began to grow again. According to the official history, in 1926 the working class reached and exceeded its numerical level of 1917. According to the Opposition, this point had in fact been reached much earlier. The precise figures, however, are not decisive. What is essential is that the predominant tendency was clearly towards a reconstruction and growth of class forces. The key question, in view of the quantitative and qualitative growth of the Russian working class from 1922, is whether the concrete political measures of the Bolshevik leadership, its medium-term and long-term strategy on this question of the exercise of power, promoted or hindered the self-activity of the working class.

Today, the answer to this question seems clear. From 1920–21 the strategy of the Bolshevik leadership hindered rather than promoted the self-activity of the Russian workers. What is more, the theoretical justification and the generalization of this 'substitution' made the situation even worse. This is certainly true of the practical measures: the prohibition of all Soviet parties except the CPSU and the prohibition of factions inside the party. In the final years of his life, Trotsky made an unmistakable self-criticism on this issue:

> The prohibition of oppositional parties brought after it the prohibition of factions. The prohibition of factions ended in a prohibition to think otherwise than the infallible leaders. The police-manufactured monolithism of the party resulted in a bureaucratic impunity which has become the source of all kinds of wantonness and corruption.[32]

Trotsky, like all the other leaders of the party, voted for these measures and defended them for many years. But these measures were indefensible, especially coming as they did *after* the end of the civil war. In the long term, the theoretical justification of this substitutionism was even more horrendous, although Trotsky didn't formulate it in such a radical manner as Lenin and, unlike Lenin, did not speak of déclassé workers or of their long-term inability to exercise power. In his speech to the Second Comintern Congress in 1920, Trotsky said:

> Today we have received a proposal from the Polish government to conclude peace. Who decides such questions? We have the Council of People's Commissars but it too must be subject to certain control. Whose control? The control of the working class as a formless, chaotic mass? No. The Central Committee of the party is convened in order to discuss the proposal and to decide whether it ought to be answered. And when we have to conduct war, organize new divisions and find the best elements for them – where do we turn? We turn to the party. To the Central Committee. And it issues directives to every local committee pertaining to the assignment of Communists to the front. The same thing applies to the agrarian question, the question of supplies and all other questions.[33]

Even worse, in his attack on the Workers' Opposition at the Tenth Party Congress, Trotsky argued:

> The Workers' Opposition has come out with dangerous slogans. They have made a fetish of democratic principles. They have placed the workers' right to elect representatives above the party, as it were, as if the party were not entitled to assert its [sic] dictatorship even if that dictatorship temporarily clashed with the passing moods of the workers' democracy.[34]

In the same way, he approved of the temporary right of the workers' state – the 'proletarian Sparta' – to use conscription and militarization of labour as an instrument for imposing labour discipline.[35] These incorrect views, however, had only a secondary influence on his proposals in the trade union debate (on this issue there is a widespread historical myth to which I shall return in chapter 8). Similarly, the violent conquest of Georgia, for which Stalin was directly responsible, cannot be attributed to any initiative of Trotsky or to his temporary 'substitutionist' aberration.

It is nevertheless a fact that in his statements made during the years 1920–21, and in his book *Terrorism and Communism* (certainly his worst book), Trotsky justified and defended the practice of substitutionism without considering its political and social consequences.[36]

There was no longer any talk of the independent role of the soviets or of the separation of party and state.

In some pseudo-orthodox (conservative and dogmatic) circles inside the various communist parties, the events of 1989–90 are seen as subsequent justification of the correctness of substitutionism. Didn't the 'undisciplined' discussion inside the party lead inevitably to political differences in the population which ultimately undermined the 'dictatorship of the proletariat'? Didn't political pluralism and free elections put wind in the sails of anti-socialist forces, leading to the overthrow of the power of the workers and peasants and to the restoration of capitalism? Has history not proved that only a mono-lithic communist party can maintain worker-and-peasant power, using the state apparatus consistently towards this end, and not distracted by any self-activity of a politically immature working class that is vulnerable to manipulation by counter-revolutionary forces?

This, however, is not the lesson to be learned from the collapse of the bureaucratic dictatorships. This collapse was unavoidable. What the events of 1989–90 in Eastern Europe and the severe crisis of the system in China have demonstrated is that it is impossible, in the long run, to realize the project of constructing socialism without the conscious support, co-operation and self-activity of the working class. The rebellion of a manipulated people is sooner or later unavoidable. To respond to this with repression is not only unsocialist but inhuman. It is also ineffective, as the examples of Albania and Romania have demonstrated. It simply pushes the masses into the arms of the bourgeois politicians. Stalinism and neo-Stalinism are no alternatives to restorationist tendencies. They can only lead to growing crises and explosions. They have no future.

Internal Party Democracy as a Bridge to Soviet Democracy

In 1923 Trotsky began to recognize the dangers of the bureau-cratization process, the beginnings of which he had theoretically defended in 1921. Later than Lenin, but more consistently, he began to fight it, and he began this fight where he thought he had the best chances of success, inside the party itself.

The fight for internal party democracy was seen by the Left Opposition as a necessary bridge to the struggle for soviet democracy. Trotsky and his supporters still hesitated to appeal simultaneously to the workers inside and outside the party. They were even more hesitant to appeal over the heads of the party leadership to the non-party workers. This was a step they were to take later. Their behaviour at this time was not an example of 'centrist' hesitancy. It was based on a fundamentally pessimistic assessment of the level of self-activity of the Russian working class. It was their assessment, in other words, that the Russian Revolution had entered a stage of retreat. Under such circumstances, the stimulus for a revival of workers' democracy (of soviet democracy) had to come from the party. Only the party was in a position to create the conditions for a gradual revitalisation of soviet democracy.

Trotsky's offensive, initiated by the 'Group of Forty-Six', the first Left Opposition of 1923, seemed to meet with success. The Politburo agreed to his proposals. In practice, however, the party apparatus around Stalin, supported by almost all the members of the Politburo, especially Zinoviev and Kamenev, but also Bukharin, Rykov, Tomsky and others, began a systematic campaign to silence the opposition, to prohibit discussion, to suppress independent thought among the cadres and ordinary party members, and to impose obedience and conformity under the cover of 'democratic centralism'.

This was in complete contradiction to the traditions of Bolshevism and the Russian Communist Party. For fifteen years (in spite of a historical myth propagated by Stalinists as well as by anti-Leninists) this party had allowed free and often public discussion and conflict of ideas. What happened in 1923 was a change from democratic to bureaucratic centralism.

The organizational instrument for the throttling of internal party democracy was the system of appointment of party officials from above instead of having them elected democratically by the membership. The sociological expression of this process was the rapid growth of the full-time apparatus. In the immediate aftermath of the revolution, there were fewer than one thousand full-time officials, but by 1922 there were ten times that many and soon one hundred times. This apparatus made itself independent and formed a particular social layer within Soviet society – the Soviet bureaucracy.[37]

In view of these circumstances, was it illusory for Trotsky and the Left Opposition to attempt to revive party democracy? It certainly had a better chance of success than any attempt to reactivate, with one blow, the disillusioned and largely passive working masses. What Trotsky and the Left Opposition did was to appeal to the conscience, the tradition and the character of the Bolshevik leadership, to its sensitivity and its theoretical understanding. This attempt failed. The tragedy of this failure was that this leadership eventually did come to understand the danger Trotsky was pointing to, but unfortunately they recognized this not simultaneously and in most cases too late. They paid for this with their lives. The Soviet workers and the international working class as well as the whole of Soviet society paid for this also with innumerable unnecessary sacrifices, including the sacrifice of many lives.

The Final Synthesis

For ten years, from 1923 to 1933, Trotsky grappled with the problem of the Soviet Thermidor, the problem of political counter-revolution in the USSR. He was also concerned to examine critically the relationship between class self-organization and vanguard party, especially in the light of the experience of the bureaucratic degeneration of the first workers' state. But he went even further than this. Following the rise of fascism in Germany, but beginning already with an assessment of the General Strike of 1926 in Britain, Trotsky came to certain conclusions about the relationship between class, mass trade unions, councils and workers' parties, which were finally confirmed for him by the tragic experience of the Spanish Revolution of 1936–37. These conclusions can be summarized in the following set of theses:

1. The working class is neither socially nor with respect to its consciousness homogeneous. Its relative heterogeneity implies the possibility, if not the inevitability, that a number of parties and currents will develop and will be supported by sections of the working class.

2. The success of the day-to-day struggle of the working class, for its immediate economic and political goals (for instance, against the fascist danger), requires a high degree of unity in action on the part of the whole class. It requires, therefore, organizations that are able to include workers with different political convictions and different organizational loyalties, in other words, organizations based on a united front of different political currents and parties. Mass trade unions and councils (soviets) are examples of such organizations. The militia committees in the Spanish Revolution, especially in Catalonia, played such a role.

3. Even if these mass organizations are partly or even, in the long term, completely led by apparatuses that are to a great extent integrated into the bourgeois state (into bourgeois society), this doesn't mean that they are simply forms of manipulation and control of the working class. These mass organizations have a contradictory character and they are, at least to a degree, potential instruments of

emancipation and self-activity of the working class. They are 'seeds of proletarian democracy within bourgeois democracy'.

4. The revolutionary vanguard party distinguished itself fundamentally from other workers' parties through the fact that, in its programme, its strategy and its practice, it defends and represents the immediate and historic interests of the working class by having as its goal the overthrow of the bourgeois state and of the capitalist mode of production and the construction of a socialist classless society. The classical formulation of this was already in the *Communist Manifesto* of Marx and Engels and it is still valid today:

> The Communists do not form a separate party opposed to other working class parties. They have no interests separate and apart from those of the proletariat as a whole. They do not set up any sectarian principles of their own, by which to shape and mould the proletarian movement. The Communists are distinguished from the other working-class parties by this only: (1) In the national struggles of the proletarian of different countries, they point out and bring to the front the common interests of the entire proletariat, independently of all nationality. (2) In the various stages of development which the struggle which the working class against the bourgeoisie has to pass through, they always and everywhere represent the interests of the movement as a whole. The Communists therefore are, on the one hand, practically the most advanced and resolute section of the working class parties of every country, that section which pushes forward all others; on the other hand, theoretically, they have over the great mass of the proletariat the advantage of clearly understanding the line of march, the conditions, and the ultimate general results of the proletarian movement.[38]

But in order to achieve this goal, the majority of the working class has to be convinced of the correctness of the party's programme, its strategy and its current political line. This can only be done using political and not administrative means. It requires, among other things, the correct application of the tactic of the proletarian united front.[39]

This in turn depends on whether or not the revolutionary socialists are able to combine a firmness of principle and resolute defence of their programme and political views – which also requires a sharp denunciation of theoretical and practical opportunism – with an openness to dialogue and a minimum of tolerance in their relations with the other parties and formations of the organized labour movement.

5. The same rules apply *mutatis mutandis* to the construction of the workers' state and to the forms in which power is exercised in the workers' state (with possible exception in the case of a threat of civil

war). The leading role of the party is realized by a process of political persuasion and not by means of administrative measures, certainly not by means of repression directed against sections of the working class. It can only be realized, as used to be said in the GDR, by the application of the 'rentability principle' (*Leistungsprinzip*) to politics. This means: strict separation of state and party; direct exercise of power by the democratically elected organs of the working people and not by the vanguard party; a multi-party system – the workers and peasants must be free to elect whomsoever they wish.

6. Socialist democracy, internal trade union democracy and internal party democracy (the right to form tendencies and factions) have a mutual effect on each other. They are not abstract norms but practical preconditions for an effective workers' struggle and for an effective construction of socialism. Without proletarian democracy, the proletarian united front and therefore success in the workers' struggle is at best made difficult, at worst made impossible.[40] Without socialist democracy, an efficient socialist planned economy is also impossible.

Nothing that has happened in the East and in the West since these theses were first formulated in the years between 1930 and 1936 has put a question mark over their validity.[41] On the contrary, later historical developments in the capitalist countries as well as in the so-called 'socialist countries' have completely confirmed their historical and theoretical relevance. Already in 1925 Trotsky had written:

> We must not build socialism by the bureaucratic road. We must not create a socialist society by administrative orders; only by way of the greatest initiative, individual activity, persistence, and resilience of the opinion and will of the many millioned masses, who sense and know that the matter is their own concern ... only in these conditions is it possible to build socialism.[42]

Notes

1. The important texts by Engels on this question are in vol. 22 of the *Marx Engels Werke* (*MEW*), which contains his articles from the period 1890 to 1895. See also his correspondence with numerous representatives of the European and North American socialist movement in the period 1882–95, in vols 35–38 of the *MEW*.

2. The most important articles by Gramsci on this subject are not his prison letters but his articles on *Ordine Nuovo* from the period 1919–21. Some of these are to be found in A. Gramsci, *Selections from Political Writings 1910–1920*, London 1977.

3. Trotsky wrote his 'Report of the Siberian Delegation' for the Second Congress of the RSDLP in 1903. It has been published in French (*Rapport de la Délégation Sibérienne*, Paris 1970, see pp. 87–8) and it is dealt with by Norman Geras in his article, 'Political Participation in the Revolutionary Thought of Leon Trotsky', in G. Parry, ed., *Participation in Politics*, Manchester 1972.

4. The first split in the RSDLP was a temporary one and was overcome at the

Stockholm Conference in 1906. The Bolsheviks and Mensheviks were really two 'public factions' of the RSDLP, rather than two different parties. They only became separate parties after 1912.

5. Quoted from Isaac Deutscher, *The Prophet Armed*, Oxford 1970, p. 90.

6. See Robert Daniels, *The Conscience of the Revolution*, Harvard 1960; and *The Prophet Armed*, vol. 1.

7. See *The Conscience of the Revolution*.

8. The much-quoted formula from Lenin's *What Is To be Done?* concerning the revolutionary intellectuals who have to bring socialist consciousness 'from the outside' into the workers' movement, actually stems from Kautsky and Victor Adler (in the so-called Hainsfelder Programme of the Austrian Social Democracy).

9. Preface to the collection 'Twelve Years', In *Collected Works*, vol. 13, p. 103.

10. From 'Our Tasks and the Soviet of Workers' Deputies', in *Collected Works*, vol. 10, pp. 19–20.

11. 'I remember someone saying in Lenin's presence: "Khrustalev's star is waning and now the strong man in the Soviet is Trotsky." Lenin's face darkened for a moment, then he said: "Well, Trotsky has earned it by his brilliant and unflagging work"' (Anatoly Lunacharsky, *Revolutionary Silhouettes*, London 1967, p. 60).

12. 'An Appeal to the Party by Delegates who Belonged to the Former Bolshevik Group', *Collected Works*, vol. 10, p. 314.

13. It is interesting to note that the Austrian Social Democracy, in its attempt to build an illegal party in the period 1934–38, used organizational principles similar to those developed by Lenin.

14. As is well known, there were three views in the Russian Social Democracy about the form of state (government) which could carry out the bourgeois-democratic tasks of the Russian revolution. The Mensheviks thought that these could be carried out by a bourgeois-democratic government which should have the support of the Social Democracy. This option of critical support was carried as far as coalition. The Bolsheviks supported the view that the workers, in an alliance with the peasants, should exercise state power in the framework of a bourgeois state (the 'democratic dictatorship of the workers and peasants'). Trotsky thought that only a workers' state (with the support of the poor peasantry) could realize the bourgeois democratic tasks of the revolution.

15. In his testament addressed to Trotsky just before his suicide, Yoffe, a leading member of the party and a Soviet diplomat, stated categorically that Lenin told him that Trotsky had been right on the question of 'permanent revolution' since 1906.

16. See the Theses of the Second Comintern Congress on the conditions under which councils should be formed, in Jane Degras, *The Communist International 1919–1943, Documents*, London 1960, vol. 1; also Karl Korsch, *Schriften zur Sozialisierung*, Frankfurt/M 1969.

17. Similar ideas were also developed by the American socialist, Daniel De Leon, although not in such a systematic way.

18. See Geras, 'Political Participation in the Revolutionary Thought of Leon Trotsky'.

19. See George Haupt, *Correspondence entre Lénine et Camille Huysmans*, Paris 1963, p. 130.

20. The increase in labour struggles in Russia after 1912 was without doubt helped by the continuing presence and activity of the Bolsheviks.

21. On the resistance of the 'old Bolsheviks' to Lenin's Theses, see Marcel Liebmann, *Le Léninisme sous Lénine*, Paris 1973, vol. 1, p. 1.

22. Trotsky, *History of the Russian Revolution* (Sphere Books edition in 3 volumes, 1967), vol. 1, p. 167.

23. 'The person who *now* speaks of a "revolutionary dictatorship of the proletariat and peasantry" is behind the times ... that person should be consigned to the archive of "Bolshevik" pre-revolutionary antiques (it may be called the archive of "old Bolsheviks"' (Lenin, 'Letters on Tactics', in *Collected Works*, vol. 24, p. 45).

24. See Roy Medvedev, *Let History Judge*, Oxford 1989, pp. 43ff.

25. Quoted by Trotsky in his *The Stalin School of Falsification*, New York 1971, p. 105.

26. Evidence of this is not only to be found in the results of the free election to the Second and Third Congresses of Soviets but also in the elections to the Constituent Assembly, in which more than 60 per cent of the vote in the towns went to the parties that favoured soviet power.

27. See N. Sukhanov, *The Russian Revolution 1917*, New York 1962, vol. 2, p. 529.

28. Trotsky, *History of the Russian Revolution*, vol. 1, pp. 15–16.

29. See Victor Serge, *Year One of the Revolution*, London 1972; and Alfred Rosmer, *Moscow under Lenin*, London 1971.

30. Alexander Solzhenitsyn, *The Gulag Archipelago*, London 1974, p. 305.

31. On the Workers' Opposition, see Alexandra Kollontai, *The Workers' Opposition*, London 1962; also *Selected Writings*, London 1977 (chapter 5, 'The Workers' Opposition').

32. *The Revolution Betrayed*, pp. 104–5.

33. 'Speech to the Second Comintern Congress', in *The First Five Years of the Communist International*, New York 1945 and 1972, p. 99.

34. Quoted from Deutscher, *The Prophet Armed*, pp. 508–9.

35. Ibid.

36. Isaac Deutscher gives a number of examples of Trotsky's 'substitutionism' in 1920–21 in chapter 14 of *The Prophet Armed*.

37. Christian Rakovsky, a leading member of the Central Committee and Trotsky's closest friend and collaborator in the Left Opposition, has given an unsurpassed account of this process in his article, 'The Professional Dangers of Power' (written in 1928), in Christian Rakovsky, *Selected Writings on Opposition in the USSR 1923–1930*, London 1980, pp. 124ff.

38. In *Marx Engels Selected Works*, London 1968, p. 46.

39. These theses are given clear political expression in 'The Transitional Programme' (1933), in *Documents of the Fourth International. The Formative Years 1933–1940*, New York 1973.

40. These theses are developed concretely in Trotsky's writings on Germany, France and Spain. See *The Struggle against Fascism in Germany*, New York 1971; *The Spanish Revolution 1931–1939*, New York 1973; and *Leon Trotsky on France*, New York 1973. His writings on Britain and on the General Strike of 1926 are in *Trotsky's Writings on Britain*, vol. 2, London 1974.

41. The Fourth International systematized and codified these theses in the programmatic document adopted at its Twelfth Congress, 'Socialist Democracy and the Dictatorship of the Proletariat'.

42. Quoted in Irving Howe, *Trotsky*, London 1978, p. 110.

6

Trotsky and the Liberation
Movement in the Third World

I

Trotsky was convinced that the Russian Revolution of 1905 would
have an effect on other countries even more backward than Russia.
The revolutions that broke out before the First World War, in Persia,
China and Turkey, confirmed him in this view. The shattering effects
of the First World War and the effects of the Russian Revolution,
which far overshadowed those of 1905, gave to the national liberation
movements in the colonies and semi-colonies a completely new
significance for the international labour movement. From then on it
was a fundamental component of the international revolution. For the
communist world movement, this was given programmatic expression
in the 'Theses on the National and Colonial Question' passed at the
Second Congress of the Communist International.[1] Social Democracy
as well responded in a limited way to this new aspect of world politics.
At the Brussels Congress of 1926, partly organized by the Social
Democrats, there were a number of prominent representatives of
national liberation movements (among them Nehru) who, in later
years, were to become founders of states and leading world statesmen.

In a number of these countries, particularly in India, China and some
countries of Latin America, the First World War stimulated a process
of industrialization.[2] This led to the emergence of a national bourgeoisie quite distinct from the classical comprador bourgeoisie who were
the direct agents of foreign capital. The national bourgeoisie was also
tied to foreign capital but it had a higher degree of financial
independence and had quite different immediate interests.

The comprador bourgeoisie and the landowners who depended on
export defended, as did foreign capital, a policy of free trade. This
policy, however, threatened to destroy any possibility of industrialization because of the effects of competition from cheap imported goods.

The national bourgeoisie therefore supported a policy of protective tariffs against foreign manufactured goods, in order to secure for themselves a certain space in the domestic market for their own industrial products. These different economic interests led to different political conceptions and tactics. The slogan of political self-administration and, somewhat later, national independence was an expression of the need to find the appropriate means to defend these specific interests.

With a developing industrialization there emerged also a modern proletariat that was stronger than the national bourgeoisie because it worked, at the same time, for both foreign and domestic industrial capital. Right from the beginning, a fear of the class movement of this proletariat meant that the participation of the national bourgeoisie in the mass movement for national independence contained a core of reluctance and uncertainty.

The main problem with which the national liberation movement in the colonies and semi-colonies confronted the international labour movement was the question of what political position it should take on the increasingly sharp conflicts (including armed conflicts) between imperialism and these national movements. On this question it came to inevitable conflicts between those parties that were prepared to accept government responsibility (or join coalitions or support governments) within the framework of a bourgeois-democratic but imperialist state and those parties that rejected this form of social partnership.

The first party that was forced to take the step from government responsibility, within the framework of an imperialist state, to a maintenance of the colonies was the British Labour Party. Already in 1924, Trotsky pointed out that MacDonald's first Labour Government, following the logic of the British imperialist state, joined in the oppression of the colonies. In his *Where is Britain Going?*, published in Britain in 1926, he wrote:

> They had first, in the quality of a responsible opposition, and then, in the capacity of a government, to answer either 'yes' or 'no' to the most severe questions of state existence ... in other words, it had either to draw revolutionary conclusions from its opposition to the imperialist state, or openly to enter its service. It goes without saying that the latter is what happened. The pacifist MacDonald began to build cruisers, to cast Indians and Egyptians into prison ...[3]

But it was MacDonald's second Labour Government especially that came into conflict with the rapidly growing movement for self-government in India, led by the Congress Party under Gandhi and

Nehru. It tried to resolve this problem by means of the Round Table Conference of 1931, but without success.

Following the Seventh Comintern Congress, which made the turn to a popular front policy, the Stalinized communist parties were confronted with the same dilemma.[4] After the Stalin–Laval Pact the French Communist Party voted for war credits. In Spain, the refusal of the popular front government, supported by the Spanish Communist Party, to grant immediate independence to Spanish Morocco was to have tragic consequences for the course of the civil war.[5]

Trotsky, in his struggle to defend the programme and the continuity of the Marxist tradition, saw it as a question of principle to give unconditional support to the colonies and semi-colonies in their liberation struggle against the imperialist states. For him this was an absolutely fundamental question:

> The movement of the coloured races against their imperialist oppressors is one of the most important and powerful movements against the existing order and demands therefore the full, unconditional and unlimited support of the proletariat of the white race.... For a communist, the war of a colonial nation against an imperialist nation is a bourgeois revolutionary war.[6]

This approach was valid for Trotsky independently of the class nature of the colonial or semi-colonial state, or of the governing regime of that state, that was at war with imperialism. The state of Emperor Haile Selassie was a despotic feudal state. But it was Trotsky's view that its transformation into a colony of Italian imperialism after Mussolini's aggression of 1935 would be a backward step, quite independently of the fascist nature of the Italian state. He took a similar position not just in military but also in economic conflicts, for instance, on the question of Mexico's nationalization of foreign oil companies.

This policy was founded on an assessment of the historically retrogressive nature of imperialism in the twentieth century, something we have already discussed in chapter 1. Trotsky defended this standpoint in the historically important conflicts in Asia in the 1930s: the war between China and Japan and the explosive conflict between Great Britain and India. His supporters consistently followed the same policy during the Second World War.

In both cases, it was not so easy to stick to these fundamental principles. In the case of China, the war was fought under the leadership of the reactionary Chiang Kai-Shek regime. Chiang Kai-Shek was the bloody executioner of hundreds of thousands of workers and peasants. But in spite of this, it was clear for Trotsky that the transformation of China into a colony of Japanese imperialism would bring nothing but misfortune and historical regression for this massive country. A defeat for Japan would be, in any case, the lesser evil.

The same applied for Trotsky to the conflict between Britain and India. In spite of the alleged world-political 'priority' which led both the British Labour Party and the British and Indian Communist Parties to defer the question of Indian independence until after the defeat of Germany and Japan, this postponement was a gruesome policy.[7] It was to have terrible consequences for the lives of millions of Indians (for instance, the famine in Bengal in 1942 caused by British imperialism, which led to millions of deaths). This policy actually facilitated the political and military actions of Japanese imperialism. And it set back the development of an independent socialist/communist mass movement in India. It made it possible for the Indian bourgeoisie under Nehru to keep their total political hegemony over the Indian masses for decades. Through its capitulation to British imperialism, the Indian Communist Party did not strengthen the anti-Hitler coalition, but rather strengthened British and Japanese imperialism and the Indian bourgeoisie.

In the period of the tempestuous rise of the national liberation movements after the Second World War, the terrible consequences of the failure, on the part of the Social Democracy as well as the communist parties of Britain, France and Holland, to live up to these principles reached catastrophic proportions. Governments in which these parties participated were engaged in wars and mass repression in Algeria, Indonesia, Indochina, Madagascar, Malaysia and Kenya, wars which cost the lives of many millions of people. Trotsky's principled position with respect to the reactionary character of every form of imperialist aggression against national liberation movements, every imperialist war against countries of the Third World, is still relevant today.

II

Trotsky hesitated a long time before he applied his theory and strategy of permanent revolution, developed in 1906, to the more developed colonies and semi-colonies. He didn't hesitate simply to prevent Stalin and Bukharin from using this as an excuse to turn the internal party struggle into a 'struggle against Trotskyism'. Some of his closest comrades, Karl Radek, Preobrazhensky and Smilga, and later his allies in the United Opposition, Zinoviev and Kamenev, were also opposed to Trotsky's theory. His hesitation was also a result of his assessment of the level of consciousness and the social nature of the mass movements in some of the most important Third World countries, especially China, India, Indonesia, Indochina and, later, Mexico.

One of Trotsky's political friends, the Dutch communist Hendrik Sneevliet (pseudonym: Maring), was, as representative of the Comintern, involved in the setting up of the Indonesian and Chinese Communist Parties. He had spent many years in Indonesia as a trade union leader.[8] While in Indonesia he had become aware of the massive influence of the Islamic movement, Sarekat Islam, on the Indonesian masses. He therefore advised the young Indonesian Communist Party to work as a faction inside Sarekat Islam (whether as an open or secret faction is not clear from the documents). His assessment of the Indonesian mass movement was that it was overwhelmingly a non-proletarian movement in which the proletarian element was very weak. So one of the central preconditions of the theory and strategy of permanent revolution was not fulfilled.[9]

Trotsky neither rejected nor accepted this argument. His attitude was to wait until historical developments would settle the issue one way or another. Although he had great reservations about this tactic of Sneevliet, he didn't initially oppose its extension to China when Sneevliet proposed and the Comintern accepted that the Chinese Communist Party should enter the Kuomintang.

There was one other important difference between Russia of 1905 and those other Third World countries in the 1920s and 1930s. The theory of permanent revolution said that the *totality* of the historical goals of the national-democratic bourgeois revolution in Russia could only be achieved through an overthrow of the state by the workers allied with the poor peasants. Applied to the most important of the Third World countries, the theory, in this general form, does not answer the question whether the achievement of each one of these historical goals of the national-democratic revolution required a similar precondition. One such goal is the winning of national independence.[10]

It is one thing for the bourgeoisie or the urban petty bourgeoisie to carry on a consistent struggle for national independence; it is something quite different for them to fight consistently for radical agrarian reform, in other words, for a real revolution in property relations in the countryside. Such an agrarian revolution would collide with the political/social interests of the bourgeoisie and, to an increasing extent, also with its immediate economic interests. However, national independence would correspond completely to the economic and political interests of the national bourgeoisie. It was therefore not to be excluded that this national bourgeoisie would fight for and win national independence. On this issue also it was necessary to await actual developments.

The real test came with the Chinese Revolution of 1926–27. What the Chinese Revolution demonstrated was the fundamental weakness of the political position of all those other communists who had refused to extend the theory and strategy of permanent revolution to the major Third World countries. The national bourgeoisie was prepared to fight for national independence. It was even prepared to mobilize the broad masses to this end, as long as it had the control of this movement in its own hands. But this meant divorcing the spontaneously developing agrarian revolution, as well as the spontaneously developing workers' struggles, from the struggle for national liberation. The bourgeoisie could neither control nor tolerate these struggles in the long term. But it was illusory to believe that the peasants, once they had gone over to the stage of mass action, would be prepared to ignore their own socio-economic interests. Equally illusory was the belief that the urban workers, once awoken to mass struggle by the development of the revolution, would not fight for their own interests. The Chinese Revolution confirmed this completely.

As the independent mass actions of the workers and peasants grew in strength, so also did the temptation of the bourgeoisie, led by Chiang Kai-Shek, to turn the revolution into a counter-revolution, with massive repression of the workers and peasants. Trotsky and the United Opposition continued to warn the Chinese Communist Party and the Comintern about this danger.[11] But the more the Stalin–Bukharin faction tried to reduce the Chinese Revolution to the anti-imperialist struggle, to the struggle for national independence, the more they were inclined to give way to the bourgeois demand that decisive issues of worker and peasant emancipation be divorced from the national struggle.

Chiang Kai-Shek's march to the North, especially to Shanghai, to deal with the generals who had allied themselves with imperialism, was completely identified with the revolution.[12] Everything was now subordinated to the success of this campaign, which was materially supported by the Soviet Union. Then, on 11 April 1927, came the Chiang Kai-Shek putsch and the slaughter of tens of thousands of communists and workers. On the eve of the catastrophe, Stalin had praised him as a great friend and hero.

The leadership of the Chinese Communist Party under Ch'en

Tu-hsiu, which had followed this course unwillingly and for reasons of discipline, was now made the scapegoat for this disaster. The Chinese communists and the Comintern were now completely confused about the right strategy or tactics to follow.[13] Eventually the group around Mao Zedong began to apply its own tactics. The Stalinist bureaucracy were at first unhappy with Mao's policies. They tolerated them for a time but eventually were strongly opposed.[14]

From 1926, communists and socialists and revolutionary national-ists in Third World countries, like the Russian socialists in 1905, were confronted with the choice: *either revolution in two stages or perma-nent revolution*. This was the essential lesson that Trotsky drew from the Chinese Revolution. His conclusions were formulated in his book, *The Permanent Revolution*, written in 1928, which he had to defend not only against his factional opponents but also against some of his collaborators, for instance, Radek. Historical events since then have demonstrated that this was one of the most important theoretical and practical struggles in Trotsky's life.[15]

Rejection of a stages theory does not mean a devaluation of the struggle for national independence and an agrarian revolution in the Third World. On the revolution in Indochina, he wrote in 1930:

> Unless the regime of colonial enslavement is overthrown, the expropriation of the large and medium-sized landowners is impossible. The two ques-tions, the national question and the land question, must be linked in the closest possible way in the consciousness of the workers and peasants.... National independence ... is a necessary element in the Indochinese revolution.... The nationalism of the mass of the people is the elementary form taken by their just and progressive hatred of their oppressors, that is, the foreign imperialists. The proletariat does not have the right to turn its back on *this kind* of nationalism. On the contrary, it must demonstrate in practice that it is the most consistent and devoted fighter for the national liberation of Indochina.[16]

Some five years later, he expressed the same view on the importance of the national liberation struggle in South Africa:

> No social upheaval (in the first instance, an agrarian revolution) is thinkable with the retention of British imperialism in the South African dominion. The overthrow of British imperialism in South Africa is just as indispensable for the triumph of socialism in South Africa as it is for Great Britain itself.[17]

In his Introduction to Harald Isaacs's book, *The Tragedy of the*

Chinese Revolution, Trotsky wrote that 'the struggle for the democratization of social relations and for the creation of a national state develops seamlessly into an open rebellion against foreign rule'.[18] His most intelligent critic inside the Left Opposition, Preobrazhensky, accused Trotsky of concentrating on the question of leadership in the revolutionary process and giving only secondary importance to the question of specific tasks. The quotations above demonstrate that this was not the case. On the question of the revolutionary processes in Third World countries, Trotsky developed, as he did in the case of the Russian Revolution, a dialectical analysis based on the law of uneven and combined development. He analysed the concrete social relations in the colonies and semi-colonies and the historical tasks that flowed from these. From this analysis he drew conclusions about the concrete positions that the different social and political forces would take in the revolution and counter-revolution. Far from underestimating the tasks of the agrarian revolution and the conquest of national independence, Trotsky came to the conclusion that these tasks could only be fully achieved under the leadership of the working class in alliance with the rural poor through a dictatorship of the proletariat.

This analysis was based on a concrete and by no means schematic understanding of the actual combination of production and property relations in the countryside. In the more developed Third World countries after the First World War, this could not be reduced to the simplistic formula, 'either feudalism or capitalism'. This was how Trotsky summarized his position in 1929:

> Large and middle-scale landed estates (such as obtain in China) are most clearly interlinked with city capital, including foreign capital. There is no caste of feudal landlords in China in opposition to the bourgeoisie. The most widespread, common and hated exploiter in the village is the kulak-usurer, the agent of finance capital in the cities. The agrarian revolution is therefore just as much anti-feudal as it is anti-bourgeois in character.... The agrarian revolution in China signifies from the outset, as it will signify subsequently, an uprising not only against a few genuine feudal landlords and the bureaucracy, but also against the kulaks and the usurers. If in our country the poor peasant committees appeared on the scene only during the second stage of the October Revolution, in the middle of 1918, in China, on the contrary, they will, in one form or another, appear on the scene as soon as the agrarian movement revives. The drive on the rich peasants will be the first and not the second step of the Chinese October.[19]

History has completely confirmed Trotsky's prediction.[20] The extension of the theory of permanent revolution to the more developed countries of the Third World became part of the first programme of the International Left Opposition.[21]

III

The application of the strategy of permanent revolution to Third World countries means first of all support for and defence of the independent organization of the workers and peasants, regardless of the demands and conditions placed by the bourgeoisie and its political representatives.[22] This presupposes the political and organizational independence of the workers' party (socialists, communists).

With respect to China in the 1920s, Stalin and Bukharin defended the opposite view. They regarded the Kuomintang not as a bourgeois party but as a 'bloc of four classes' (peasants, workers, national bourgeoisie and urban petty bourgeoisie). History has dealt a fatal blow to this un-Marxist definition. The arguments of Trotsky and the United Opposition against this approach have retained their validity.[23]

In a speech to the Communist Academy on 18 March 1927, Radek criticized Stalin's and Bukharin's policy on China with respect to Chiang Kai-Shek and the Kuomintang. He declared that in a very short time Chiang Kai-Shek would turn against the Chinese communists and would betray the revolution. On 6 April 1927 Stalin ridiculed Radek's prediction in a speech to the Moscow party. According to Stalin then: 'Chiang Kai-Shek may have little sympathy for the revolution, but he controls the army and has no other choice but to lead this army against the imperialists.'[24] Just a few days later, on 12 April 1927, Chiang Kai-Shek's army began its notorious slaughter of the Shanghai proletariat and the Chinese Communist Party.

The leadership of the Chinese Communist Party under Ch'en Tu-hsiu reluctantly accepted the Comintern order to subordinate themselves to the Kuomintang. As events unfolded they questioned it more and more. With Wang Fang-si, we can say that both Trotsky and Ch'en Tu-hsiu, at almost the same time but independently of each other, decided to extend the theory and strategy of permanent revolution to China. This led Ch'en Tu-hsiu to join the International Left Opposition. At the same time, and quite independently of Ch'en, a large number of Chinese students in Moscow joined the ranks of the Left Opposition, a step that cost many of them their lives.[25]

The emphasis on the political independence of the working class in the liberation movements of the more developed Third World countries does not, of course, provide an answer to the question of alliances.[26] Is an anti-imperialist united front against the colonial power incompatible with working-class independence? Like Lenin before him, Trotsky was inclined to deny any such incompatibility. He applied the same rule to the anti-imperialist united front as had previously been applied to the proletarian united front: march separately, strike together.

Marching separately means not only total defence of the freedom of action of the workers' party in the defence of the interests of the workers and poor peasants and a refusal to subordinate these interests to the demands of the alliance. It also means making sure that the popular masses are conscious that the alliance depends on the willingness of the bourgeois ally really to fight against the imperialists; that this will only be the case in a limited way and for only a certain period of time; that the masses have to prepare themselves for the day when the national bourgeoisie will break from the alliance and join the camp of counter-revolution.[27]

On the other hand, striking together means that the workers' parties give not just lip-service but really do fight for the common goal of national liberation by means of mass agitation, mass mobilization and mass action, that they make it absolutely clear to their own members and to the masses that this goal of national independence corresponds to the interests of the working people. There is a great similarity here to the workers' united front, for instance in the struggle against fascism. In this sense, the anti-imperialist united front is only a tactical variant of the general strategy for the conquest by the working class of the leadership of the national liberation movement.

After the defeat of the workers in Shanghai and Canton, Trotsky on a number of occasions expressed his doubt that the next Chinese revolution could succeed on the basis of guerrilla war. We have to distinguish two phases of the peasant war. The period from 1930 to 1937 had primarily a defensive character, symbolized by the 'Long March' to Yenan. In this phase there was no question of a revolutionary wave in the whole of China.

With the outbreak of the predatory war of Japanese imperialism against China in 1937, the situation changed fundamentally. It now became possible for a mass mobilization to develop against this aggression. And although, at the beginning, this war was led by Chiang Kai-Shek, an independent armed mass movement against the war was able to develop, which competed with the Kuomintang for hegemony in the national liberation movement. Objectively, a successful development of the third Chinese revolution was once again on the agenda. The national liberation struggle grew into a social revolution.

Trotsky had seen this possibility. Two quotes will suffice:

The immediate task of the Chinese proletariat is to struggle so that the war against Japan will be fought by means of the mobilization and arming of the broad masses of working people so that the defeat and the outbreak of revolution in Japan will be accompanied by a victory of the Chinese proletariat over the Kuomintang traitors and lackeys of imperialism . . .[28]

A people that today, with weapon in hand, knows how to deal with one robber, will tomorrow know how to deal with the other one. A revolutionary party that understands this and consciously and willingly places itself at the head of a people defending its independence – only such a party, both during and after the war, will be able to mobilize to snatch power from the national bourgeoisie.[29]

And here we reach another decisive point in the application of the theory and strategy of permanent revolution to the Third World, in this case to China: the nature of the state power established by national liberation and the agrarian revolution. For Trotsky, the extension of the theory and strategy of permanent revolution to China and the more developed countries of the Third World meant a struggle not only for the political hegemony of the proletariat and of the proletarian parties within the national liberation movement and the agrarian revolution but also a struggle to seize state power, to overthrow the existing state and establish a dictatorship of the proletariat. This entails a judgement on the class character of the state established by the national bourgeoisie and the class nature of the state that can and should replace it.

On this central question, Stalin and Bukharin, and later the Stalinist communist parties in the two periods of popular frontism (1935–39 and 1941–47), defended what was fundamentally a right-Menshevik position. In the semi-colonies the dictatorship of the proletariat is not on the agenda. The goals of the national democratic revolution can be realized in coalition with the bourgeoisie and in the framework of a bourgeois state.

Mao Zedong defended, on paper, an intermediate position. He did not deny that the Kuomintang was capable of leading the national liberation struggle and even the agrarian revolution to victory. But in his book, *The New Democracy*, he defended the thesis that it was possible to have a state and an army with a dual character, half bourgeois democracy and half proletarian democracy. The Maoists initially claimed that the proclamation of the People's Republic of China on 1 October 1949 was the proclamation of such a state. They later revised this position and admitted that the state established by this proclamation was a dictatorship of the proletariat.[30] They thereby implicitly admitted that, in the major historical debate about the conditions for a victorious Chinese revolution which lasted from 1926 to 1940 (1949), Trotsky had been right.

The practice of the Chinese Communist Party was completely different from its theory. Although Mao rejected the path of proletarian dictatorship, and even accepted on paper the subordination of the army to Chiang Kai-Shek, in practice he maintained the independence of the People's Liberation Army, strengthened and steeled it in the battle not only against Japan but also against Chiang Kai-Shek, and thereby created the political-organizational preconditions for the peasant uprising that spread through north and central China after 1946.[31] Mao destroyed the bourgeois army and the bourgeois state and replaced them with an army and state with a different class nature.

Does this mean that the mistaken theory of 'new democracy' was historically unimportant? Unfortunately, no. For the strongest communist party in the capitalist world, the Indonesian Communist Party under the leadership of the unfortunate Aidit, followed, with Mao's full backing, not Mao's practice but his theory. Unfortunately, the Indonesian army did not have a 'dual character'. It was a counter-revolutionary instrument of the Indonesian bourgeoisie. In 1965 it destroyed the Indonesian Communist Party and murdered almost a million communists, trade unionists, peasants and youth. It was the worst catastrophe to hit the international working-class movement since Hitler's coming to power.[32]

The Chinese Trotskyists also made the mistake of not distinguishing between the Chinese Communist Party's theory and its practice. They saw that the same formulas were being used from 1937 to 1946 as had been used in the period 1925–27. What they did not see was the fundamental difference in practice: in the earlier period the communists had really been under the command of the Kuomintang; now an independent popular liberation army was being created independently of the Kuomintang and, at least in the countryside, a practice was developing that was not subordinate to the bourgeoisie.[33] Because of the imprecise information he was receiving at the time, Trotsky came to the wrong conclusion about the conceptions and perspectives of the Chinese Communist Party when, in May 1940, he wrote the Manifesto, 'The Imperialist War and the Proletarian Revolution'.[34]

He also feared that the peasant army, when it occupied the industrial cities, might turn against the workers and consolidate capitalism. For a short time after 1949, this fear did seem to have a real basis. But it very soon became clear that the People's Liberation Army and the state apparatus of the People's Republic were instruments not for the consolidation but for the elimination of capitalist rule. Its class nature was not determined by the social origins of the majority of the soldiers (the majority of the soldiers in the Red Army were also peasants) but rather by the social origins and political convictions of the middle and higher ranks, in other words, of the apparatus of the Chinese Communist Party. And this apparatus was in no sense either peasant or capitalist.

In the light of what happened, however, we must admit that there was a kernel of truth in Trotsky's wrong assessment of the Chinese Communist Party. The victory of the third Chinese Revolution was the victory of a party which, even before the seizure of power, was completely bureaucratized and prey to the illusions of substitutionism. Its refusal, particularly after the conquest of the cities, to base itself on the free self-organization of the Chinese proletariat, in other words, on workers' councils, made the People's Republic of China, from the beginning, the prisoner of a hardened party, military and state bureaucracy. Mao partially recognized this at the end of the 1950s. He tried to fight against it, partly by the use of severe repressive measures, in the Cultural Revolution but was forced to admit, on the eve of his death, that his attempt had been a failure. Deng Xiaoping tried to break the power of the bureaucracy by means of economic liberalization, which also failed and ended in the repression of Tienanmen Square.

Trotsky's policy was not followed in China. In order to overthrow the Chiang Kai-Shek state, the peasant army linked itself not with an independent proletariat and a power based on councils, but with a narrow-minded, all-powerful and arbitrary bureaucracy. For these failures, the Chinese communists, the Chinese workers and the Chinese people have paid a heavy price.

Notes

1. See the minutes and the resolutions of the Second Comintern Congress on the national and colonial question in *The Second Congress of the Communist International*, vol. 1, London 1977, pp. 109–83.
2. Trotsky had foreseen this in his pamphlet, *The War and the International*, published in 1915. Extracts from this pamphlet are in *Lenin's Struggle for a Revolutionary International. Documents 1907–1916*, ed. John Riddell, New York 1984, pp. 150–56.
3. *Where is Britain Going?*, London 1926, p. 161. See also his 'Speech to the Students of Moscow Communist University for the Working People of the East' (1924),

in *The Age of Permanent Revolution. A Trotsky Anthology*, ed. George Novak, New York 1964, pp. 236–7.

4. See the Resolutions of the Seventh Comintern Congress in Jane Degras, ed., *The Communist International 1914–1923. Documents*, vol. 3 (1965), pp. 346ff.

5. 'Franco's main base of operations was Morocco, a colony subjugated by Spain only after many years of brutal desert warfare. Even from the standpoint of bourgeois democracy the republic could have proclaimed the independence of this oppressed colonial people. Strategically, in the fight against Franco there was every reason to do so in order to win the Moroccan people as allies in the fight against fascism. But Stalin and Azaña were afraid of alarming the British and French governments, which held vast colonial empires in Africa. And so the republic defended Spain's imperialist claims to rule Morocco' (Trotsky, *The Spanish Revolution (1931–1939)*, New York 1973, pp. 43–4).

6. *The Third International after Lenin*, New York 1970, p. 171.

7. 'Open Letter to the Workers of India', in *The Age of Permanent Revolution*, pp. 246ff.

8. On Sneevliet, see Fritjof Tichelman, *Henk Sneevliet*, Paris 1988.

9. Sneevliet was secretary of the Commission for the National and Colonial Question of the Second Comintern Congress and played an important role in developing Lenin's Theses on this question. In his speech to the plenum of the Congress he defended the participation of the Indonesian communists in the Sarekat Islam, without meeting any opposition. See his speech in *The Second Congress of the Communist International*, vol. 1, pp. 150–56.

10. After the Second World War, the national bourgeoisie of India, Egypt, Kenya, Ghana, Nigeria, etc. won political independence but were unable to break out of their subordination to the imperialist world system.

11. These warnings can be read in Trotsky, *Problems of the Chinese Revolution*, Michigan 1967; and in *Leon Trotsky on China*, New York 1976.

12. See the resolution on the Chinese situation adopted at the Seventh Plenum of the ECCI (November/December 1926) in Jane Degras, *The Communist International 1919–1943. Documents*, vol. 2 (1960), pp. 336ff. On the question of the Kuomintang the resolution says: 'The Communist Party of China should seek to make the Kuomintang a genuinely national party, a firm revolutionary bloc of the proletariat, peasantry, the urban petty bourgeoisie and other oppressed strata who are waging an energetic struggle against imperialism and its agents' (p. 345).

13. After the right-opportunist course of 1926–27 there followed the ultra-left turn, with the proclamation of the Canton Soviet Republic which, in view of the defeat of the Shanghai proletariat and the decline in the peasant movement, had no chance of success.

14. Mao succeeded in winning support inside the Chinese Communist Party against the Stalin faction and enjoyed a certain amount of support from the Kremlin between 1934 and 1941. Kremlin resistance hardened, however, and the conflict with Stalin came to a head over Mao's refusal to dissolve the People's Liberation Army into the forces of Chiang Kai-Shek. From 1946 Mao's course was set on the seizure of state power.

15. We have to remember that not only Stalin and his supporters but also Bukharin, Zinoviev, Kamenev, Radek, Preobrazhensky and others forgot that Lenin himself, in unambiguous terms, had formulated the central political class lesson of the October Revolution as follows:

> We know from our experience – the revolutions all over the world confirm it if we take the modern epoch of, say, a hundred and fifty years – that the result has always been the same everywhere: the petty bourgeoisie in general, and the peasants in particular, have failed in all their attempts to realize their strength, and to direct economics and politics their own way. They have to follow the leadership either of the proletariat, or the capitalists – there is no middle way open to them.
>
> ('Speech Delivered at the All-Russian Congress of Transport Workers', 27 March 1921, in *Collected Works*, vol. 33, pp. 277–8.)

16. 'On the Declaration of the Indochinese Opposition' (18 September 1930), in *Wirtings of Leon Trotsky 1930–31*, New York 1973, pp. 29–31.

17. 'On the South African Theses' (20 April 1935), in *Writings of Leon Trotsky 1934–35*, New York 1977, p. 249.

18. In *Leon Trotsky on China*.

19. *The Third International After Lenin*, New York 1970, pp. 182–3.

20. See, for instance, Jack Belden, *China Shakes the World*, New York 1970.

21. 'The International Left Opposition, its Tasks and its Methods' (1932), in *Documents of the Fourth International*, New York 1973, pp. 19ff.

22. This was emphasized in Lenin's Theses on the national and colonial question adopted by the Second Comintern Congress. Key elements of the strategy of permanent revolution were contained in these Theses but were not developed.

23. See Trotsky's critique of the Comintern programme in *The Third International after Lenin*.

24. Quoted from Pierre Broué, *Trotsky*, Paris 1988, pp. 509–10. It appeared in the *China Press*, 14 April 1927.

25. 'Li Fu-yen: Revolutionary Teacher of the Colonial Peoples', in *Fourth International*, August 1944.

26. Trotsky stated explicitly that this applied only to the more developed Third World countries.

27. Lenin clearly emphasized this need in his Theses on the national and colonial question.

28. This quote is translated from a German collection of Trotsky's writings on China: *Trotzkis Schriften über China 1928–1940*, Hamburg 1990, p. 46.

29. Ibid, p. 885.

30. For instance, in the polemic with Liu Shao-shi during the Cultural Revolution.

31. This turn occurred under a dual pressure: on the one side, the anti-communist military offensive of Chiang Kai-Shek and, on the other side, the spontaneously developing uprising of the peasants in northern China.

32. See, for instance, Taylor, ed., *Repression and Exploitation in Indonesia*, Nottingham 1974.

33. Trotsky had explicitly warned the Chinese Trotskyists not to limit themselves to general formulas in their assessment of the peasant army. Unfortunately they didn't follow his advice. Some however had second thoughts, especially Ch'en Tu-hsiu.

34. 'At the beginning of the Sino-Japanese war, the Kremlin again placed the Communist Party in bondage to Chiang Kai-Shek, crushing in the bud the initiative of the Chinese proletariat' (*Writings of Leon Trotsky 1939–40*, New York 1969 and 1973, p. 202).

Trotsky's Struggle against Fascism

The history of fascism is, at the same time, the history of the theory of fascism. An adequate theory of fascism was and remains a precondition for an effective anti-fascist practice. For no other newly emergent social phenomenon of the modern age is the simultaneity of emergence and explanatory effort so striking as in the case of fascism.

The reasons for this simultaneity are obvious. Fascism arose suddenly and immediately; it threatened and shattered first the living conditions, then the very lives of millions of people. Historical and individual destiny suddenly coalesced for innumerable people. It is understandable that those affected by this tried to comprehend the fate that had befallen them. The first arson attack by the fascist bands in Italy immediately raised the question: 'What is this fascism?' For seventy years the leading thinkers of the working-class movement, the bourgeois intellectuals and the historians have been fascinated by this question.

Fascism, the victory of the political counter-revolution in the imperialist countries, was as difficult to conceptualize as Stalinism for contemporary social, including Marxist, thought. Once again it was Trotsky who, in his explanation of this phenomenon, was head and shoulders above his contemporaries. No other thinker grasped so clearly the nature of fascism, the threat it represented for the working-class movement and for human civilization. He alone warned the working class in time about this danger, insisting that it was necessary to defeat it and mapping out the kind of resistance that was necessary. It would not be an exaggeration to say that, with the exception of Marx's *Class Struggles in France 1848 to 1850* (1850) and his *Eighteenth Brumaire of Louis Bonaparte* (1852), there is no other Marxist analysis of contemporary political and social issues comparable in depth and clarity with Trotsky's writings on Germany from 1929 to 1933.[1]

Trotsky's passionate commitment, his Cassandra-like calls about the horrendous danger that threatened the German and the European working-class movement and indeed whole nations, were based from the beginning on a clear though theoretically complex understanding of this novel historical phenomenon. We seldom find such an immediate and direct coincidence of theoretical insight, concrete political analysis and guidance to political practice, as we do in Trotsky's work on fascism in the decade from 1930 to 1940.

What is Specific about Fascism?

Fascism is a product of a severe systemic crisis of monopoly capitalism (imperialism), in which the normal valorization of capital under conditions of bourgeois parliamentary democracy is being increasingly undermined. Parallel to this crisis in the economy and in the political institutions, there is a radicalizing discontent among *déclassé* social layers, primarily among the petty bourgeoisie, and their growing organization in new forms of mass organizations.[2] These operate initially in an autonomous way, but are then used to an increasing extent by big business in its attempt to destroy the organized labour movement and to atomize the working class. This, very briefly, was the core of Trotsky's theory of fascism.

In his approach to the phenomenon of fascism, Trotsky was again powerfully assisted by his thorough grasp of the law of uneven and combined development: that synthesis of materialist dialectics applied to class society. Like a few other Marxist thinkers (e.g. Ernst Bloch and Kurt Tucholsky), he understood the partial non-synchronism of socio-economic and ideological forms; in other words, the fact that ideas, feelings and irrational images of pre-capitalist epochs continue to exist in large sections of capitalist society (especially in the middle classes threatened with impoverishment, but also, to some extent, in the ranks of the bourgeoisie, the *déclassé* intellectuals and even in certain layers of the working class). From this Trotsky drew the following social and political conclusions: Under conditions of growing pressure from the increasingly insurmountable socio-economic class conflicts, significant sections of the middle class and the other social layers mentioned above – what Trotsky so aptly described as human quicksand – fuse to form a powerful mass movement which, hypnotized by a charismatic leader and armed by sections of the bourgeoisie and their state apparatus, serve as a kind of battering-ram to crush the working-class movement through intimidation and bloody terror, and to atomize the working class.

This application of the theory of uneven and combined development to fascism made it possible for Trotsky to avoid two errors, two one-sided views of fascism: either as a relapse into pre-capitalist reaction and obscurantism, or as a late, 'catching up' form of modernization.[3] In reality, fascist ideology and fascist rule contain both 'logically' contradictory elements. But the historical dialectic does not follow the laws of formal logic. Not to have understood this was the misfortune of numerous opponents of fascism.[4] It is also a weakness of many later interpretations.

This analysis of fascism unites and combines several analytical elements, each with a relative autonomy that corresponds to particular aspects of the social and political reality of the imperialist states in a time of deep socio-economic crisis. Their combination – as opposed to their simple juxtaposition – provides an instrument for comprehending the totality of this phenomenon, the rise of fascism.

Fascism and the Petty Bourgeoisie

Fascist ideology and fascist political groupings began to develop, independently of the *immediate* needs of the capitalist class, from that point in time where the middle classes, ground between the power of monopoly capitalism and the power of the trade unions, fell prey to exasperation and hopelessness. (The relative independence of their ideology is another matter. Racism is deeply rooted in the typical ideology of the colonial imperialist epoch, although it is mixed with remnants of pre-bourgeois prejudices.)

During the initial phase there are many such groupings, with fierce competition breaking out between rival 'Führer' candidates.[5] It is only after a complex selection process that a leader emerges out of this underworld cock-fight. It is not only charismatic personality that is needed, but also a high level of unscrupulousness and the ability to sacrifice even one's closest confederates.

When the petty bourgeoisie is so hard hit by the structural crisis of late capitalism that it becomes increasingly desperate and without hope (inflation, bankruptcy of small businesses, mass unemployment among academics, technicians and higher civil servants, etc.), then at least a section of this social class, motivated by a mixture of ideological reminiscences and psychological resentments, will gradually adopt somewhat rabid views and engage in violent actions. Fascism is, in the first instance, a mass movement of the petty bourgeoisie gone wild. In this mass movement we find a combination of extreme nationalism and at least a verbal anti-capitalist demagogy[6] with an even greater hostility towards the organized labour movement ('against Marxism', 'against Bolshevism', 'against the trade union bosses'). When this developing mass movement begins to use physical violence against the workers, the workers' actions and their mass organizations, then we have the beginning of a fascist party.

Trotsky summarized magnificently the social-ideological background to the autonomous emergence of these petty bourgeoisie gone wild:

> The rapid growth of German capitalism prior to the First World War by no means signified a simple destruction of the middle classes. Although it ruined some layers of the petty bourgeoisie it created others anew: around the factories, artisans and shopkeepers; within the factories, technicians and executives. But while preserving themselves and even growing numerically – the old and the new petty bourgeoisie compose a little less than one half of the German nation[7] – the middle classes have lost the last shadow of independence. They live on the periphery of large-scale industry and the banking system, and they live off the crumbs from the table of the monopolies and cartels, and off the spiritual alms of their professional theorists and politicians ...
>
> The post-war chaos hit the artisans, the peddlers and the civil employees no less cruelly than the workers. The economic crisis in agriculture was ruining the peasantry. The decay of the middle strata did not mean that they were made into proletarians, inasmuch as the proletariat itself was casting out a gigantic army of chronically unemployed. The pauperization of the petty bourgeoisie, barely covered by ties and socks of artificial silk, eroded all official creeds and first of all the doctrine of democratic parliamentarism.
>
> The multiplicity of parties, the icy fever of elections, the interminable changes of ministries aggravated the social crisis by creating a kaleidoscope of barren political combinations. In the atmosphere brought to white heat by war, defeat, reparations, inflation, occupation of the Ruhr, crisis, need and despair, the petty bourgeoisie rose up against all the old parties that had bamboozled it.[8] The sharp grievances of small proprietors never out of bankruptcy, of their university sons without posts and clients, of their daughters without dowries and suitors, demanded order and an iron hand.
>
> The banner of National Socialism was raised by upstarts from the middle and lower commanding ranks of the old army. Decorated with medals for distinguished service, commissioned and non-commissioned officers would not believe that their heroism and suffering for the fatherland had not only come to naught, but also gave them no special claims to gratitude. Hence their hatred of the revolution and the proletariat. At the same time, they did not want to reconcile themselves to being sent by the bankers, industrialists and ministers back to the modest posts of bookkeepers, engineers, postal

clerks and schoolteachers. Hence their 'socialism'. At the Yser and under Verdun they had learned to risk themselves and others, and to speak the language of command, which powerfully overawed the petty bourgeoisie behind the lines. Thus these people became leaders ...

The petty bourgeois is hostile to the idea of development, for development goes immutably against him; progress has brought him nothing but irredeemable debts. National Socialism rejects not only Marxism but Darwinism.[9] The Nazis curse materialism because the victories of technology over nature have signified the triumph of large capital over small. The leaders of the movement are liquidating 'intellectualism' because they themselves possess second- and third-rate intellects, and above all because their historic role does not permit them to pursue a single thought to its conclusion. The petty bourgeois needs a higher authority, which stands above matter and above history, and which is safeguarded from competition, inflation, crisis and the auction block. To evolution, materialist thought and rationalism – of the twentieth, nineteenth and eighteenth centuries – is counterposed in his mind national idealism as the source of heroic inspiration. Hitler's nation is the mythological shadow of the petty bourgeoisie itself, a pathetic delirium of a thousand-year Reich.

In order to raise it above history, the nation is given the support of the race. History is viewed as the emanation of the race. The qualities of the race are construed without relation to changing social conditions. Rejecting 'economic thought' as base, National Socialism descends a stage lower: from economic materialism it appeals to zoologic materialism ...

On the plane of politics, racism is a bombastic and vapid form of chauvinism in alliance with phrenology. As the ruined nobility sought solace in the gentility of its blood, so the pauperized petty bourgeoisie befuddles itself with fairy tales concerning the special superiorities of its race ...

Personality and class – liberalism and Marxism – are evil. The nation – is good. But at the threshold of private property this philosophy is turned inside out. Salvation lies only in personal private property. The idea of national property is the spawn of Bolshevism. Deifying the nation, the petty bourgeois doesn't want to give it anything. On the contrary, he expects the nation to endow him with property and to safeguard him from the worker and the bailiff ...

Fascism has opened up the depths of society for politics. Today, not only in peasant homes but also in city skyscrapers, there lives alongside the twentieth century the tenth or the thirteenth. A hundred million people use electricity and still believe in the magic power of signs and exorcisms. The pope of Rome broadcasts over the radio about the miraculous transformation of water into wine.[10] Movie stars go to mediums. Aviators who pilot miraculous mechanisms created by man's genius wear amulets on their sweaters. What inexhaustible reserves they possess of darkness, ignorance and savagery! Despair has raised them to their feet, fascism has given them a banner. Everything that should have been eliminated from the national organism in the form of cultural excrement in the course of the normal development of society has now come gushing out from the throat; capitalist society is puking up the undigested barbarism. Such is the physiology of National Socialism.[11]

Fascism, the Petty Bourgeoisie and Big Business

The autonomy of the fascist–petty-bourgeois mass movement, however, runs up against insurmountable barriers that correspond to the actual social relation of forces in late monopoly capitalism. A large mass movement with a lot of paid officials and an even larger number of paid thugs needs a lot of money.[12] The only source of such a continuous flow of money is big business. But only a very specific combination of circumstances can convince capital to finance fascist parties with something more than small subsidies.[13] These conditions are met when the economic crisis deepens, when big business has an urgent need to dispense with essential elements of bourgeois democracy, when there is an objective need for a greater concentration of political power in order to achieve a number of pressing economic goals and when there is sufficient public support for at least one of the dictators in waiting.

From the point of view of the long-term interests of the capitalist class and the relative stability of bourgeois society, the bourgeois parliamentary regime is preferable to any form of dictatorship, not to speak of fascist dictatorship. The rule of the bourgeois class rests on a specific combination of repressive and integrative mechanisms. Where the repressive element dominates, there is a greater long-term risk of social instability. Fascism and other extreme forms of bourgeois dictatorship are an ongoing state of siege, a form of permanent civil war (a special form of civil war, however, since one camp is disarmed and at the mercy of the other camp).[14] These governmental forms are much more dangerous for bourgeois society since they tend to raise social tensions and, in times of crisis, push matters to an explosive point, in a situation where there are no mechanisms for class conciliation.

It is a historical fact that all successful socialist revolutions took place in countries that had, over a long period of time, one form or another of dictatorial regime (Czarism; a monarchical and then a fascist dictatorship in occupied Yugoslavia; the Chiang Kai-Shek dictatorship in China; the Batista dictatorship in Cuba; Bao Dai, Diem and Thiu in South Vietnam; the Samoza dictatorship in Nicaragua, and so on).

The objective contradiction, from the standpoint of bourgeois class interests, lies in the fact that although the long-term social and political price of repressive dictatorships is high and very dangerous, the short- and medium-term economic price for bourgeois democracy may become intolerable *in certain conditions*.

In the industrially developed countries, bourgeois democracy includes a developed labour movement (mass trade unions), which in turn implies that the commodity labour-power is sold not individually but collectively. Under such conditions, the price of labour power will be higher than under conditions in which the workers are atomized. On top of this higher price come such additional costs for capital as social security and other social expenditure, all of which lower the proportion of surplus-value in the net product. When the total value product stagnates or begins to fall as a result of unfavourable changes in inter-imperialist competition following a lost war, a severe economic crisis or a combination of these factors, then the material ability to continue paying this price begins to disappear. The bourgeoisie has no choice but to try to get rid of bourgeois democracy.

It is therefore wrong to see fascism, exclusively or even predominantly, as a terrorist attack on the more radical sections of the working-class movement – as mainly an anti-communist dictatorship. It is something quite different. Fascism is the attempt to destroy the entire organized labour movement, including its moderate sections, even including its 'yellow' trade unions. It is an attempt to atomize the class as such. To achieve its goal of preventing any form of collective sale of the commodity labour-power, it has to prohibit, attack and destroy even the most elementary forms of class organization.[15]

Although the fascist leaders, by means of some 'good examples' of anti-proletarian terror, may be able to attract generous contributions from some individual capitalists, this is still not enough to open up the road to power. For that they have to make decisive ideological and political concessions.

With his sense of tactic and his unlimited cynicism, Hitler, like Mussolini before him and Franco after him, found the right words at the right time: 'I will apply the Führer principle to the factories.' In the factories the entrepreneurs are the only leaders. Their rule in the factories is unlimited. We will put an end to the interference of trade unions, local governments, parties and parliament. This was music to the ears of the big factory owners. At the same time, this wiped out almost every claim of 'German socialism' and almost the entire economic space of the petty bourgeoisie. If, outraged by this 'new betrayal', the petty-bourgeois 'old fighters' are tempted to undertake a 'second revolution', then they are mercilessly eliminated, as actually happened in the Third Reich on 30 June 1934. Big business cheered them on – in spite of the fact that every form of 'constitutional state' was being cynically eliminated in full public view and the pure arbitrary will of the 'Führer' was now becoming the only 'law'.

But this is still not the end of the road to Calvary for the petty bourgeoisie, who have been betrayed by their fascist leaders. Their mass movement is bureaucratized and incorporated into the state apparatus. When the valorization conditions of capital have decisively improved, then the destructive domestic dynamic of fascism becomes transformed into an equally destructive international dynamic.[16]

The share in the world market now has to be decisively increased. This drive is given added impetus by the threat of state bankruptcy. The adventurist policy of fascism is carried from the social into the financial sphere, clearing the way for a military build-up. This stokes up inflation and leaves, in the final analysis, no way out other than foreign military adventures. This whole development, both politically and economically, does not strengthen but weakens the position of the petty bourgeoisie, except for the small number that are nourished by sinecures in the inflated state apparatus. There follows an accelerated concentration and centralization of capital.

Now, the petty bourgeoisie are proletarianized on a mass scale; later, they are pauperized as a consequence of the war. Here we see clearly the *class character of the fascist dictatorship which does not at all correspond to the class character of the fascist mass movement. The fascist dictatorship represents the historic interests not of the petty bourgeoisie but of monopoly capital.*

We must add here that the disastrous underestimation of the difference between bourgeois-parliamentary democracy and fascism, which led to the catastrophic 'social-fascism' theory of 1930–33, was already present in official Comintern theory at the time of Mussolini's seizure of power, nurtured by Bordiga, Fischer, Maslov and partly also by Zinoviev, in other words, by the so-called 'Left' of the time, who were to a not insignificant extent actually ultra-left.[17] The fact that the Bordiga Group inside the Italian Communist Party supported Trotsky against the Stalin faction did not prevent Trotsky from persisting in his theoretical critique of this ultra-left deviation.[18]

Big Business and Fascism

The project of handing over government power to fascist parties always unleashes discord and doubt among the bourgeoisie. It is never a smooth operation. This differentiation corresponds to economic, political and ideological stratification in the bourgeois class. We could formulate a thesis in the following way: Those sectors that produce directly for mass consumption are more reluctant openly to support and finance a fascist seizure of power, while big and heavy industry, those sectors involved in the production of armaments and means of production, are more inclined to consider such a step.

To the last group belonged, in Germany, the big chemical industries, especially IG-Farben, the steel and mining companies, most of the big banks and especially the Deutsche Bank. But sections of the electro-industry, textiles and clothing belonged to the first group.[19] Although this thesis is often applied too mechanically, there is strong empirical support for it. Different political goals are partly determined by differences in material interest. The key role played by the Herrenklub in Hitler's nomination to Reich Chancellor is well known. The *Osthilfe* scandal was an important factor.[20]

But more important than the conjunctural-sectoral aspect was a difference in political judgement about the possibility of really control-ling the obviously nihilistic adventurer Hitler, in the interests of big business. Some were sceptical, others not. The conservatives around Papen and Hugenberg, and later even the catholic Centre party believed that, under certain conditions, this would indeed be possible. From a purely political point of view, they obviously erred.

We should not forget that the whole history of the bourgeois class has been characterized by this historical difference between liberals and conservatives, a difference that dates from the French Revolution, if not earlier. In this process of differentiation, sometimes one, sometimes the other current has the upper hand, for reasons which have to be analysed concretely in every case. In the last decades of the nineteenth century in Germany the liberals were the dominant current, in France the conservatives. But there was a change at the beginning of the twentieth century. In France it was the Dreyfussards that were victorious, while in Wilhelmine Germany it was the national-militarist conservatism that came increasingly to the fore. Hitler's coming to power is part of the continuity of this conservatism, which was reinforced by the First World War, the defeat and the revanchism after Versailles. It was anticipated in the Harzburg Front.[21] It was not, however, an unbroken continuity, but rather one filled with doubt and self-doubt. It led not just to 30 January 1933 but also to 20 July 1944.[22]

What, however, unites all these layers and groupings within the bourgeoisie is their common class interest in the defence of property, the freedom of capital accumulation and the guarantee of valorization of capital. And on this level the balance sheet of fascism is unequivocal. The fundamental features of the capitalist mode of production were not only kept and consolidated. They were able to freely develop as never before.

Economically, the Third Reich was the unconstrained rule of monopoly capital. What appeared as state 'interference' in the economy turned out, in nine cases out of ten, to be measures aimed at strengthening the self-management of monopoly capital, including support for big business in its disciplining of weaker firms (forced cartelization) in the run-up to the predatory imperialist war.[23] There was no economic disempowerment of big business by the Nazis. There is an element of mystification in the endless discussion about the 'primacy of politics' versus the 'primacy of economics' in the Third Reich.[24] Consciously or unconsciously, the historically irredeemable guilt of the so-called elite for the crimes of Nazism is either played down or denied. We are not concerned here with the small fellow travellers, with the 'silent majority' that at best closed its eyes or at worst knew and collaborated. We are dealing here with the crucial responsibility of the bankers, factory owners, big traders, army leaders, top civil servants, judges, barristers, university professors, doctors, engineers, who in their majority not only 'tolerated' or 'went along with' Nazism, but planned, introduced, guided, led and gave ideological cover to this whole course with absolutely concrete class-specific interests and goals.

On only one occasion did Hitler try to impose his will against the interests of the bourgeoisie: in the final phase of the war when he wanted to destroy their factories. He didn't succeed.[25] The totalitarianism thesis, in its most logical form, does not stand up to the historical evidence. The totalitarian dictatorship never succeeded in controlling, much less eliminating, the independent economic interests of capital.

Trotsky's theory of fascism leads to the following synthesis of these contradictory elements of fascist dictatorship as exemplified in the Third Reich: a temporary political expropriation (disempowerment) of monopoly capital with the goal of consolidating its economic power and guaranteeing the valorization of capital. This is history's answer to the mechanical counter-position: primacy of politics versus primacy of economics.

Fascism and the Working Class

We said just now that the bourgeoisie could *try* to eliminate bourgeois democracy with the help of fascist bands. But the establishment of a fascist regime does not depend only on what happens inside the petty bourgeoisie and the capitalist class. It depends also on what happens inside the working class, in other words, on the reaction of the organized labour movement.

In contrast to the 'human quicksand' that Führer candidates might be able to attract to themselves in large numbers, the modern working class in all the industrially advanced countries has in its hands the potential of an enormous social, economic and political power. All the creative and productive functions of society are concentrated in this class or in social layers closely linked to it. In most of these countries the cultural and political mass organizations of the working class were very active, in some cases up to the end of the 1920s or the beginning of the 1930s. They brought together hundreds of thousands, if not millions, of workers who were capable of fighting for their common class interest with commitment and enthusiasm. And in all these countries there were big and powerful trade unions that were in a position to cripple the capitalist economy and that had the potential power to paralyse the capitalist state itself.

To take on such a strong opponent, the class-conscious representatives of the top bourgeoisie layers must not only, for the reasons outlined above, see themselves as having no other way out, but they must also be convinced that they at least have a chance of coming out of this without losing life and limb – in the massive test of strength without which the destruction of bourgeois democracy would seem impossible. Any mistake in these calculations, any wrong assessment of the social relation of forces, would have disastrous consequences for the bourgeois class. From an individual as well as from a social point of view it could be suicide. Barcelona, Madrid, Valencia and Malaga in June 1936 were an important object-lesson.[26]

In a period of increasing fascist danger, but before the fascist seizure of power, the most important leaders of monopoly capitalism pay a great deal of attention to everything that is happening inside the working class and inside the organized labour movement in response to this fascist threat. In fact, their analysis of the changing relation of forces has similarities with the analysis of revolutionary Marxists, although from different angles.

Every sign of united and strong resistance that becomes visible in the working class, every indication that there is a move towards mass armed self-defence, every sign of a growing willingness to fight with a firm determination to defend themselves against the fascist beast, increases the hesitation and doubt of monopoly capital about the wisdom of a test of strength.

Similarly, any sign of division, passivity or resignation in the working class, every tactical success on the part of the fascists that doesn't meet with resistance or a counter-attack, every sign that the leaders of the mass organizations, in spite of their phraseology, will capitulate to fascism in the end, every sign that the masses are not able to mount a spontaneous counter-offensive to the fascist threat, will convince monopoly capital that the price to be paid for a change of regime is less than it had feared. Such signs of weakness accelerate the process of seizing power by the fascists because they show that the civil war will be a one-sided affair and that the defeat of the working class will be both crushing and long-lived.[27]

Hence the vital need to oppose the rise of fascism from its inception by a resolute, united and energetic response, by a struggle to defend the free organizations of the working class, the right to strike and all other basic democratic freedoms, without which the working class would be crucially weakened for a whole historical period.

Such a united, resolute and energetic response sets off a chain reaction that alters the whole political climate in the country. It makes the petty bourgeoisie more doubtful about whether the fascists will actually win, thus weakening their mass base and improving the chances of neutralizing a significant section of the middle classes, if not actually winning them for the cause of the workers and for socialism. To achieve this, however, the workers need a programme which takes the interests of these social sectors into account. The petty bourgeoisie must have the feeling that the working class is serious in its resolve to create an alternative to the fascist solution of the problem of political power.

The capitalists themselves will also learn through sad experience that the capital invested in the fascist bands is bringing no returns and promises only heavy losses. Their support for the fascist solution will move into the background and cease to be a major element in their political perspective. As for the working class, every tactical success in the fight against fascism will consolidate the unity in its ranks, strengthen its militancy and determination. Their belief in their own destiny and in a socialist alternative solution to the social crisis that is shaking the country will continue to grow. In this way, the ground is prepared for a powerful social and political counter-offensive which can bring the socialist revolution onto the agenda very quickly.

All these chances and opportunities depend on the unity and political independence of the working class. If the class is politically divided, if the Social Democrats and communists (Stalinists) fight each other instead of uniting their ranks to fight the fascists, if the communists (Stalinists) believe that they have to defeat the Social Democrats first before they can deal with the fascists, if the Social Democrats think that it would be impossible to 'neutralize' the fascists as long as there is a 'communist danger', in other words, if the united intervention of the class in this historic struggle is prevented in the name of abstract and sectarian 'principles' – then there will be less and less chance of a timely, resolute and successful response to the growing fascist terror (aided and abetted by the bourgeois state apparatus and increasingly financed by big business). Instead, a chain reaction of hesitation, disorientation and demoralization will set in, leading finally to defeat. This is what happened in Germany, despite Trotsky's numerous warnings, which found an echo beyond Trotskyist circles in other oppositional communist circles, such as the KPO (Communist Party Opposition) under Brandler and Thalheimer and the SAP (Socialist Workers Party), a left split from the SPD.

Fascism and Bonapartism

The most important Marxist contribution to an understanding of fascism, which led to similar political-tactical conclusions as Trotsky's, was the theory of August Thalheimer. It can be very briefly summarized as follows: fascism is the final stage of the counter-revolution which began with the defeat of the German Revolution of 1918/19 and which was characterized by an increasing autonomy of the state apparatus (the executive). This autonomy he defined as 'Bonapartism', a direct reference to Marx's analysis in *The Eighteenth Brumaire of Louis Bonaparte*.[28]

This analysis of Thalheimer contains a germ of truth. The state apparatus, completely cut off from parliament, parties and trade unions, was a constitutive element of political rule in the Third Reich, much more so than had been the case in the Weimar Republic. But in Thalheimer's theory, not enough attention is paid to the role of the fascist groups and the later fascist apparatus (the party, the SS, etc.). But this is how fascism makes its first appearance. It is the *differentia specifica* of fascism, as distinct from Bonapartism. This difference is neither accidental nor of secondary importance. It is essential to the goal of fascism: the total destruction of every form of working-class organization. A Bonapartist state alone cannot achieve this. It needs an instrument of institutionalized mass terror and mass control, and neither the police nor the army can provide this. This is the task of the fascist mass party. Trotsky recognized this from the beginning. Hence his rejection of the Bonapartist interpretation,[29] although he clearly saw that both Bonapartism and fascism had certain features in common.

Under the Bonapartism of the latter period of government under Brüning, Papen and Schleicher, the labour movement became increasingly weaker and subject to repression. But it was still capable of resisting. The Hitler government between 30 January 1933 and the burning of the Reichstag could be described as a 'late Bonapartist', semi-fascist regime. It was only after the total defeat of all legal labour organizations that we can describe the regime as a fascist and no longer a Bonapartist dictatorship.

This is not an abstract theoretical debate. It has an extremely practical dimension, namely the possibility of massive popular resistance to fascism. Such a possibility exists under a Bonapartist regime, but under fascism it disappears rapidly.[30]

This analytical and political debate is also relevant today. The theory of 'creeping fascism', defended by many left-wing circles today, is attempting, with inadequate concepts, to throw light on a very real process, namely, the development of a 'strong state', the growing autonomy of the state executive, which has been a feature of bourgeois parliamentary democracies since the Second World War. What we are witnessing is a growing symbiosis between parts of the state apparatus, top military leaders, the secret services, the judiciary and right-wing extremist groups, including openly terrorist and putschist-oriented groups.[31] Certain sections of society are becoming increasingly indifferent to this weakening if not elimination of parliamentary control and are, in many cases, even hostile to the 'parliamentary talk-shop'. This general development can be conceptualized as a 'creeping Bonapartism'. We can confidently predict that, until there is a radical deterioration of the economic and social crisis, the main threat to democratic freedoms comes from this 'creeping Bonapartism' and not from the relatively weak open fascist currents. These fascist groups are being used by sections of the state apparatus, but they themselves are not pulling the strings.

The conclusion of this analysis is that what we are witnessing today is not creeping fascism. Fascism means more than increasing autonomy of the state apparatus. When fascist thugs begin to attack strikes and union headquarters physically, and intimidate and defeat striking workers, then we are dealing with 'fascism'. Fascism never creeps, it is always open and brutal.

Trotsky's Struggle for the Workers' United Front

Trotsky's painstaking analytical work on the German problem in the period 1930–33 had an immediate practical goal: to warn the German and international labour movement about the terrible threat that was imminent, to propose tactics and goals to overcome this threat in time. His message can be summarized in the words of his solemn warning of 8 December 1931:

> Worker-Communists, you are hundreds of thousands, millions; you cannot leave for any place; there are not enough passports for you. Should fascism come to power, it will roll over your skulls and spines like a terrific tank. Your salvation lies in merciless struggle. And only a fighting union with the Social Democratic workers can bring victory. Make haste, worker-Communists, you have very little time left![32]

Concretely, the right tactic for the workers' united front had to include the following:

- A rejection of defeatism. The victory of fascism is not inevitable as long as it is practically possible to mobilize the mass of the workers.
- A rejection of ultimatums. A break by the Social Democratic workers with their party and its leaders cannot be a precondition for the united front. Systematic proposals for a united front should be made to the leaders. The united front should be from above and from below.[33]
- A rejection of parliamentary cretinism. The fascist seizure of power will not be decided by the ballot box but on the streets, in extra-parliamentary mass struggles.
- A concentration on direct anti-fascist actions, aimed at mobilizing the broad masses, supported by the mass organizations of the workers, the final goal of which is the armed general strike.

Subsequently, those who shared in the responsibility for the catastrophe of 1933 have claimed that, in the period from 1932 to March 1933, the workers, ground down by unemployment, divided and demoralized, were not prepared to undertake mass action against the fascists. Today, however, there is a large amount of evidence to show that Trotsky's view was more realistic than this apologetic for their own passivity, confusion and failure.[34] The willingness of millions of German workers to take up mass action was even greater than Trotsky had assumed.[35] This is admitted today in some social-democratic circles.[36]

One of the central social-democratic illusions that, like the sectarianism of the Stalinist ultra-left, played a decisive role in the German labour movement's capitulation without a fight to the fascists in 1933 was that of the need to 'neutralize' the bourgeois state apparatus in order to prevent a fascist seizure of power. The unfortunate Rudolf Hilferding, later murdered by the Nazis, who before 1920/21 had been a radical socialist and theoretician of the labour movement and later became the main theoretician of the right-wing of Social Democracy, gave the clearest formulation to this illusion when he wrote in 1933 that history would regard Social Democracy's success in preventing co-operation between the state apparatus and the Nazis as its greatest historical achievement.

Unfortunately, Hindenburg had already nominated Hitler as Reichs Chancellor when these lines appeared in print.[37] This illusion arises from a failure to understand the class character of the bourgeois state, especially its military and state apparatus,[38] as well as from an underestimation of the depth of the capitalist crisis which can lead to the elimination of bourgeois parliamentary democracy.

The Workers' United Front and the Popular Front

The German catastrophe, the capitulation without a fight of the world's mightiest working-class mass organization, dealt a crushing blow to the self-confidence and class-consciousness of the German and international working class. The negative results of that defeat stretch far beyond its immediate economic and political consequences. Trotsky correctly predicted this, and from the spring of 1933 onwards he tried to guide his small band of followers in the developing situation.

The first result of this shock was an irresistible pressure for a united front of all working-class organizations against the danger of fascism or other forms of reactionary dictatorship in countries outside Germany. The right-wing offensive in France on 6 February 1934 triggered an actual united front between the Socialist Party and the Communist Party, which completely reversed the relationship of forces and the dynamic of French society for at least three years. Working-class strength grew by leaps and bounds. Finally, the June 1936 general strike with factory occupations brought France to the threshold of a socialist revolution.[39]

Similarly in Spain, the reactionary offensive of 1934, which led to a right-wing regime with one wing resting on clerical, semi-fascist formations, triggered a powerful united working-class response, first expressing itself in the abortive insurrection of October 1934, then in the uninterrupted rise of mass struggles in the first half of 1936, and finally in the incipient socialist revolution which broke out in nearly all the big cities and important parts of the countryside in answer to the military-fascist coup of July 1936. But in both cases, France and Spain, the tremendous potential of this unitary thrust of the working class was deflected into channels perfectly compatible with the survival of private property and the bourgeois state. In fact, this was a conscious policy of class collaboration on the part of the social-democratic, Stalinist and trade union bureaucrats (and, in Spain, the main leaders of the mass anarchist movement).[40]

Starting in 1935, the Communist International under Stalin's leadership took over lock, stock and barrel the old social-democratic/ Menshevik 'lesser evil' strategy of a bloc with the 'liberal' bourgeoisie against 'reaction'. This Popular Front policy, coinciding with a deep structural crisis of the capitalist economy and bourgeois democracy as a whole, that was in no way alleviated by sundry reforms, not only meant the loss of another historical opportunity for the workers to conquer power, this time mainly through the fault of Stalinism, as it had been the fault of the Social Democrats in the 1918–23 period. (The same experience occurred for a third time in the 1944–48 period in France, Italy and Greece.) It also meant that the collapse of the labour movement under the onslaught of reaction and fascism was merely postponed, not avoided.

In Spain, the fascists eventually won the civil war after the Stalinists and the reformists had crushed the social revolution in the Republican camp. In France the tremendous build-up of working-class strength crumbled through the capitulation of successive Popular Front governments and the ensuing disenchantment and demoralization of the working class. Little more than two years after the glorious general strike of June 1936 came the defeated general strike of September 1938, then the whittling away of working-class liberties, the illegalization of the Communist Party, the paralysis of the trade unions and the ignominious self-immolation of the Third Republic when the senile Bonapartist regime of Marshal Pétain took over in 1940 without any reaction from the workers.

It is no accident that Trotsky's sharp criticism of the divisive policies of German Social Democracy and Stalinism before Hitler's conquest of power wins approval and admiration in very wide circles today;[41] whereas his no less convincing demonstration of the disastrous consequences of popular frontism meets with a great deal of mis-understanding and even rejection from historians and critics, both hostile and friendly.[42] For fascism represents a physical threat to the very survival not only of revolutionary organizations but even of the most moderate social-democratic ones; it is seen as a barbaric menace not only by the vanguard of the working class but by a large part of the petty-bourgeois intelligentsia and by the labour bureaucracy in its entirety. This is precisely the material basis for a united front policy at the top as well as at the bottom.

Popular frontism, however, is nothing but a variant of the classical policies of class conciliation and class collaboration practised by reformist labour leaders and labour bureaucracies ever since the beginning of the century, and generally greeted with approval by the majority of intellectuals. To approve Trotsky's criticism of popular frontism would mean for them not only to reject their own past and tradition, but in many cases to go directly against the defence of their own immediate material interests.

Nevertheless, for Marxists and advanced workers today, it is crucial to understand the logical nexus between Trotsky's fight for a united front in Germany in 1929–33 and his fight against the Popular Front in France and Spain in 1935–38. The rise of fascism as an immediate threat to the organized labour movement coincides with a deep structural crisis of bourgeois parliamentary democracy, itself bound up with a deep structural crisis of the capitalist economy and bourgeois society as a whole. Under such circumstances, to tie resistance against the fascist danger to the defence at all costs of bourgeois parliamentary democracy is to wager everything on the survival of institutions already in their death throes. While it is correct to defend against reaction every single one of the conquests of the working class in the political as well as the economic field, including universal franchise, it is suicidal to limit the scope of such defence to the narrow and decaying framework of bourgeois-democratic state institutions.

If the strength gathered through successfully defending working-class organizations and freedoms is not used as a launching-pad for a revolutionary socialist solution to the crisis of bourgeois democracy and bourgeois society, then that strength will rapidly fade and crumble away. After a temporary retreat, fascist or semi-fascist reaction will once again take the offensive against a working class demoralized by a lack of positive results from its tremendous militant efforts. There is no future for bourgeois democracy under conditions of extreme crisis of capitalism. Either it is replaced by proletarian democracy or it collapses into right-wing dictatorship. Refusal to draw that lesson led in Spain (and later in Chile) to defeats no less tragic, costly and lasting than those caused by disunity in Italy and Germany.

Some sectarians have attempted to reduce the difference between the popular front and the workers' united front to the question of participation of bourgeois or petty-bourgeois politicians or parties in coalitions. This abstract, schematic approach is actually quite similar to that of popular front supporters. The latter see the alliance with liberal-bourgeois parties as a necessary precondition for the alliance with the middle classes. The sectarians see the participation of bourgeois politicians in the alliance as the inevitable prelude to class betrayal.

What both overlook is the really decisive issue, namely, the free development of anti-capitalist mass action. If the participation of bourgeois politicians or parties results in – or is used as an excuse for – this mass action being reduced or prevented, then what we have is a popular front, that is, the surrender of the class political independence of the proletariat. The workers' parties then become the prisoner of the bourgeoisie. But if the participation of bourgeois politicians or groups in the alliance does not put a brake on the developing offensive against the bourgeois state, then these bourgeois politicians are objectively the prisoners of the working class.

Notes

1. Trotsky's writings on German fascism are in the collection *The Struggle against Fascism in Germany*, with an introduction by Ernest Mandel, New York 1971. There is also a German collection, in two volumes, *Schriften über Deutschland*, Stuttgart 1971.

2. The concept of *déclassé* (*Deklassierung*) used by Marx in *The Eighteenth Brumaire of Louis Bonaparte*, sometimes identified with the term *lumpenproletariat*, is in need of a more thorough Marxist analysis.

3. This was the view of Max Horkheimer.

4. The best example here is Rudolf Hilferding, who at the end of his life rejected the capitalist nature of fascist dictatorship.

5. The conflict between Hitler and the Strasser brothers remained tense right up to the time of the fascist seizure of power.

6. The fixation on a 'Jewish world conspiracy' was nurtured by the fact that some of the big bankers and socialist/communist leaders were Jewish. The myth was none the less an irrational and paranoid one: in both groups the Jews were a small minority.

7. The concept of petty bourgeois here is too wide, including as it does large strata of wage-earning white-collar employees and civil servants. In the text, however, the petty bourgeoisie are actually identified with the class of small proprietors.

8. Later research has shown that the majority of Hitler's electoral support came

from the traditional base of the conservative parties and not from the base of the SPD or Communist Party.

9. Hitler's concept of history could actually be described as a degenerate form of primitive Social Darwinism. In the bitter 'struggle of nations' it is the racially strongest that win.

10. The present pope has stated not only that the devil exists but that he met him on two occasions, once in the form of a goat, once in the form of a woman.

11. 'What is National Socialism?' (10 June 1933), in *The Struggle against Fascism in Germany*, pp. 399–407.

12. See Jochen von Lang, *Die Partei*, Hamburg 1991.

13. On financial support for Hitler, including foreign financial support (for instance, Henry Ford), see James and Suzanne Pool, *Who Financed Hitler?*, New York 1978.

14. Nicos Poulantzas (*Fascism and Dictatorship*, London 1974, pp. 61–2) raises two criticisms of Trotsky's theory of fascism. First, by characterizing fascism as a state of 'civil war', Trotsky is supposed to have shared the Comintern's mistaken view of fascism as a response to the 'insurrectional' working class on the offensive. This is obviously a misrepresentation of Trotsky's position. He saw fascism as a 'one-sided civil war', in other words, a bourgeois offensive to crush a working class evidently on the defensive. Poulantzas, in his eagerness to combat 'economism', does not understand the economic compulsion which, under specific circumstances, leads towards such one-sided civil war. Secondly, Trotsky is supposed to have 'mechanistically' contrasted the way in which a declining bourgeoisie leans on fascism and the support given by a stable bourgeoisie to social democracy. But in reality, Trotsky made no such sweeping statements about a whole epoch. He stressed time and again the specific conjunctural circumstances under which big business turned to fascism.

15. The German Labour Front (*Deutsche Arbeitsfront*), established by Hitler in May 1933 after having liquidated the unions, cannot be regarded as a union, not even as a 'yellow' union. It was simply a subordinate part of the Nazi state apparatus.

16. The proportion of income from capital in the national income rose from 17.4 per cent in 1932 to 26.6 per cent in 1938. The total capital of all German corporations rose from 20.6 billion Reichsmark in 1932 to more than 29 billion Reichsmark in 1942.

17. In his speech to the Fourth Congress of the Comintern, Zinoviev completely underestimated fascism and spoke of a 'comedy' which 'after a few months or years' would end 'in the working class's favour'. He saw the fight against reformism as 'the main task'. See documents from the Fourth Congress, in Jane Degras, *The Communist International 1919–1943. Documents*, vol. 1.

18. Trotsky's writings on Italy have been published in *Scritti sull' Italia*, Rome 1990.

19. See Daniel Guérin, *Fascism and Big Business*, New York 1973; Franz Neumann, *Behemoth*, Toronto 1942.

20. *Osthilfe* was the agrarian aid programme launched in 1927 to rescue insolvent, mainly small East Prussian farmers. In practice, nearly all the vast sums involved were lavished on the Junkers, the biggest landowners of them all. Hindenburg's son Oskar had been prominent in these shady dealings, and this was to prove a useful lever in securing his collaboration with the Nazis in persuading his father to appoint Hitler Chancellor.

21. The Harzburg Front was a bloc between the Nazis, the conservative party of Hugenberg and the equally conservative *Stahlhelm* (the Steel Helmets, a right-wing para-military veterans organization formed in 1918 under the leadership of Franz Seldte, who later became a minister for a short time under Hitler).

22. 20 June 1944 was the date of the attempt to assassinate Hitler organized by Count von Stauffenberg, one of his earlier supporters.

23. See Eberhard Czichon, *Wer half Hitler zur Macht?*, Cologne 1967.

24. See the discussion between Tim Mason and Eberhard Czichon in *Das Argument*, December 1966 and June 1968.

25. Albert Speer, minister for arms production in Hitler's government, was a direct representative of German big business and was probably influential in persuading Hitler in this case.

26. This is dealt with in great detail in Guérin, *Fascism and Big Business*.

27. It is interesting to note that the *Reichswehr* waited to see the Communist Party reaction to the provocative SA demonstration of January 1933 in front of the Berlin Communist Party headquarters, before it finally gave the green light to Hitler's nomination as Reich Chancellor. Similarly, according to a well-known interview given after his successful coup, General Pinochet reached the conclusion that there was no serious risk in overthrowing the Allende government only after he had studied the passive attitude of the working-class mass organizations to the failed *tankatazo* early in 1973 (the abortive coup of a Santiago armoured car regiment). The Spanish bourgeoisie gravely miscalculated the situation in 1936, thinking that the fascist-military coup would be a walk-over. As a result, it nearly lost power in the major part of the country. Half the generals lost their lives.

28. August Thalheimer, *Über den Faschismus*, Hamburg 1989.

29. In the 1930s Trotsky wrote quite a few articles on the issue of Bonapartism and fascism. The most important is 'Bonapartism and Fascism' (15 July 1934), in *Writings of Leon Trotsky 1934–1935*, New York 1977, pp. 51–7.

30. After the catastrophic error of 'social fascism', the German Communist Party in 1933/34, after the defeat of the organized labour movement, began to agitate for mass action.

31. The Gladio scandal in Italy is a good example. We have also learned, in the meantime, that the apparently absurd putsch attempt by the Spanish Lieutenant Tejero in 1981 was actually supported by a significant section of the army leadership.

32. *The Struggle against Fascism in Germany*, p. 141.

33. Detailed evidence about the disastrous consequences of the ultra-left theory of 'social fascism' is to be found in Theo Pirker, *Komintern und Faschismus 1920–1940*, Stuttgart 1961; also in Herman Weber's introduction to Ossip K. Flechtheim, *Die KPD in der Weimarer Republik*, Frankfurt 1969.

34. See Otto Braun, *Von Weimar zu Hitler*, New York 1940.

35. There is now a large amount of documentary evidence for the willingness of the social-democratic workers to resist and to unite with the communists.

36. For instance, in the memoirs of the later Bavarian prime minister, Hoegner.

37. Rudolf Hilferding, in *Die Gesellschaft*, No. 1, 1933.

38. Trotsky dealt at length with the sympathy of the officer corps for right-wing conservatism and fascism in his 'The Lessons of Spain' (30 July 1936), in *The Spanish Revolution 1931–1939*, pp. 234ff.

39. Trotsky analysed developments in France between 1934 and 1936 in his pamphlet *Whither France*, published by Pathfinder Press, New York 1968.

40. See *The Spanish Revolution 1931–1939*.

41. For an assessment of Trotsky's role in the fight against fascism, see, among other sources, Baruch Knei-Paz, *The Social and Political Thought of Leon Trotsky*, Oxford 1978, pp. 354–5.

42. For instance, Isaac Deutscher, *The Prophet Outcast*, Oxford 1970; Monty Johnstone, 'Trotsky and the World Revolution', *Cogito*, 1976, pp. 10–14; I. Howe, *Trotsky*, London 1978.

8

Trotsky as Military Leader

Old and New Myths

The attitude to Trotsky in the Soviet media and in the media of the
official communist parties has reflected in a striking way the political
development of the Soviet Union and, to a lesser extent, Eastern
Europe and the so-called World Communist Movement.

Before Lenin's death Trotsky was seen as the organizer of the
October uprising, the founder and leader of the Red Army and the
second man in the party and state alongside Lenin. In numerous books,
pamphlets, journals and newspapers reference was to 'the regime
(country, government, etc.) of Lenin and Trotsky'.[1] Between 1924 and
1929 Trotsky's image gradually changed to that of the main political
opponent of Lenin and Bolshevism. After 1929 he was described as a
Menshevik counter-revolutionary and after 1935 as public enemy
number one, spy, agent of Nazi imperialism, Hitlerite (the French
communists coined the phrase 'Hitlero-Trotskyist'), supporter of
capitalist restoration in the Soviet Union and organizer of terrorist
attacks.

After the beginning of de-Stalinization under Khrushchev and
particularly in the first phase of Glasnost, there was a significant shift:
Trotsky was now described as the real inspiration behind Stalin; Stalin
implemented his programme; had he won the struggle for power, he
would have been a 'second Stalin'. To support this view new historical
myths were created and old ones resurrected from the second half of
the 1920s. For instance, in the late 1980s General Volkogonov, in his
biography of Stalin, claimed that Lenin did not propose a bloc with
Trotsky against Stalin on the Georgia question, although the documentary evidence on this is absolutely unequivocal. Volkogonov also
claimed that Lenin did not regard Trotsky as his successor, although
the documents that have been now published show that this was

indeed the case. Volkogonov's claim that Trotsky wanted to use the army against Stalin has no basis whatever in empirical evidence.[2]

More recently, however, General Volkogonov, having done a more thorough study of the archive material, wrote a book about Trotsky's role in the Russian Revolution and revised practically all the negative judgements previously contained in his Stalin biography.[3] He still maintained, however, that Trotsky's practice in the civil war contributed to the aspect of terror in the dictatorship of the proletariat.

The myths and the accusations have finally undergone a 180 degree shift. In the 'liberal' (in reality, liberal-conservative) and social-democratic circles of the old CPSU and other communist parties, Trotsky is said to have been the inspiration behind, not Stalin, but Lenin. It was Trotsky who was responsible for drawing Lenin away from the bourgeois-democratic path along the road of the socialist revolution and the dictatorship of the proletariat. It was he who was mainly responsible for the 'utopian' and 'violent' October Revolution. He was responsible for Stalin to the extent that Stalinism was the inevitable result of the October Revolution. At the same time, he is cleared of all criminal slanders and his contribution to the construction of the Soviet Union is recognized.

This to and fro in the assessment of Trotsky's role reflects by and large the to and fro in attitudes to the revolution and in the revolution itself. The ambivalent attitude to Trotsky in Russia today is influenced by the still limited involvement and political confusion of the masses and by the ideological regression of the intelligentsia. This is no accident. For together with Lenin and Rosa Luxemburg, Trotsky incorporated the two main trends of the proletarian revolution – self-activity of the proletariat and internationalism. And it is typical of Trotsky's consistent and principled behaviour that we should find these main trends once again in his activity as military leader.

The Creator of the Red Army

No one contests that Trotsky was the creator of the Red Army. We know today that the famous decree of 21 February 1918, 'The Fatherland in Danger', mistakenly included in Lenin's *Collected Works* (vol. 27, pp. 30–33), was actually written by Trotsky. Leonard Shapiro has said that 'the creation of the Red Army must be credited to Trotsky more than to anyone else.'[4] This was also Lenin's view, which he expressed in his well-known conversations with Gorky.[5] Numerous contemporaries, including Lunacharsky, have said the same thing. One of the most important American specialists on Russian history, W. Bruce Lincoln, refers to 'Trotsky's Red Army'. He writes:

> With his brilliance at organization and his genius for leading men, Trotsky understood that Russia's embryonic Red Army could not develop without a large corps of officers trained in the methods of modern warfare.[6]

It was an impressive organizational achievement. From almost nothing he created an army of 5.5 million men, most of them peasants. He succeeded in uniting and disciplining this army in such a way that it was able to maintain its cohesion and morale without any large measure of repression, certainly less than is normal in bourgeois armies in time of war. Even more impressive was his success in recruiting and using tens of thousands of ex-Czarist officers, among them one thousand generals, who made up a significant proportion of Red Army commanders. Lenin supported this, but it was Trotsky's idea. It was necessary as a way of bridging the time until an adequate number of trained and experienced 'red commanders' were available. He had to create an operative centralized army to counter the counter-revolutionary White Armies and to prevent them from annihilating the young Soviet state. A number of Bolshevik leaders, including Stalin, wanted to fight the Whites mainly by means of a decentralized partisan war. In the international relation of forces at the time, this would have led to a rapid Soviet defeat.

Trotsky's organizational success is expressed in the fact that the overwhelming majority of the ex-Czarist officers remained loyal to the Red Army, as did the vast majority of the peasant soldiers, although neither group was politically close to Bolshevism. This organizational achievement was closely linked to Trotsky's political practice in building the army. Discipline was achieved mainly by agitational and moral means. Deserters were treated generously, the aim being their reintegration. In nine times out of ten this worked.

In *My Life* Trotsky describes his encounter with thousands of deserters in the region of Ryazan and quotes from his speech of 24 February 1919 to the young Red Army commanders gathered in the Hall of Columns in Moscow:

> Give me three thousand deserters, call them a regiment; I will give them a fighting commander, a good commissary, fit officers for battalions, companies and platoons – and these three thousand deserters in the course of four weeks in our revolutionary country will produce a splendid regiment.[7]

Civil War as Class War

His impressive achievement in building the Red Army was matched by his role as overall commander during the civil war and in the victory against the counter-revolutionary White Armies and foreign intervention. The Swiss expert, Commander E. Léderrey, has written: 'It is no exaggeration to say that it was Trotsky who was mainly responsible for the victory in the civil war.'[8] Trotsky's strategy in the civil war was based on a particular political-moral concept of civil war under proletarian leadership and on an understanding of what specifically was needed in the actually existing situation of the young Soviet power encircled by hostile forces.

Trotsky had a unique and bold concept of the special character of a proletarian-led civil war. It can be summarized in the following formula: destroy the hostile army by appealing systematically to the elementary class interests of its soldiers. The first decrees of the young Soviet power – the decree on peace and the decree on the immediate distribution of land to the peasants in the villages – had precisely such an effect. The soldiers deserted the Czarist army in masses in order to be able to take part in the distribution of land.[9] Later, the promise to return to the peasants in the White-occupied territories the land taken by the landowners played a similar role. The systematic emphasis on the proletarian and international character of the Red Army,[10] on its defence of the workers' power and of the gains of the October Revolution, played a similar role in relation to the urban workers.

Trotsky saw every civil war as a class war. He saw the parallels between the Russian civil war and the war of the Vendée, supported by foreign intervention, against the French Revolution. He often referred to the White armies as the Russian Vendée. He also saw striking parallels with the American civil war. The decisive turn in this civil war came when Lincoln proclaimed the emancipation of the slaves and permitted the formation of black regiments. Trotsky later systematized his concept of class war in his analysis of the civil war in Spain.[11]

The special geopolitical position of the Soviet Union in this civil war also had its own military logic, which Trotsky soon recognized in spite of his limited military experience. The White armies, with their professionalism and mobility, had a great advantage over the Red Army. They also had the support of foreign regiments and had access to money, weapons and munitions. Their weakness, however, apart from their narrow social base, was that they never succeeded in effectively uniting their forces. They were fighting on geographically discrete fronts. This lack of unity among the White generals was linked to the different economic and political interests of the imperialist powers that were leading the war of intervention against Soviet Russia: Germany (allied with Finland), France (allied with Poland), Japan, Britain and the USA.[12]

To exploit these weaknesses, the Red Army availed itself of all the advantages of its 'inner circle' and, supported by a central reserve, it struck now in the east, now in the north, the south, or the west, in such a way that the enemy was only able to muster a fraction of its forces against them. Trotsky's famous train played an important role in this.[13] The main problem in the execution of this strategy was the poor condition of the transport system in the Soviet-controlled areas. Hence the importance which Trotsky attributed to the restoration of the transport system. A successful application of this strategic principle also required a centralization of the forces of the young Red Army. This was opposed by the supporters of decentralized guerrilla tactics. But Trotsky had his way, fully supported by Lenin.[14]

Trotsky rejected any notion of a special 'proletarian' military science.[15] This was identified by quite a few communists with the 'principle of the offensive'. There was an intense debate over this with a group of communist military specialists around Michael Frunze (supported by Tukhachevsky). In the period 1923–24, this group supported the troika of Stalin, Zinoviev and Kamenev against the Left Opposition, contributing in no small way to the victory of the Stalin faction.[16]

Trotsky rejected the concept of 'proletarian military science' just as energetically as he did the notion of 'proletarian culture'. He was also critical of bourgeois military leaders such as Marshal Foch of France, who paraded a few platitudes as 'fundamental principles' of military science. What Trotsky emphasized above all else was the historically and sociopolitically relative character of a successful military strategy, which, in every case, corresponded to particular interests and particular situations. What was decisive for him was the ability to manoeuvre. His rule was to act in accordance with the specific situation and on the basis of a realistic assessment of the relation of forces, operating offensively or defensively as the situation required. The main thing was at no cost to lose one's most important positions while aiming to take the main positions of the enemy. The defence of Petrograd against Yudenich was crucial for him because Petrograd was the bastion of the Russian Revolution and therefore the bastion of Soviet Russia. Trotsky literally rescued red proletarian Petrograd, as Bruce Lincoln described in his history of the civil war:

Trotsky sent men and women to Petrograd's defence with their hearts seared by his revolutionary passion and comforted by his abiding belief in the new world the Bolsheviks were building. As Yudenich's forces at Pulkovo prepared their final assault, this legion of workers transformed Petrograd into the labyrinthine fortress Trotsky had envisioned during his lonely night journey from Moscow.

Red Victory: A History of the Russian Civil War, p. 298

He approved the offensive to drive the Polish army out of Ukraine but, in the next phase, he was deeply worried about the Red Army offensive against Warsaw. For the same reason, he tended to reject altogether the concept of 'military science', preferring to describe it as a military art linked with good military skills.[17]

Certain authors make insinuations about allegedly disastrous mistakes made by Trotsky as military commander during the civil war. He certainly made mistakes, as does everyone. But what concretely these were and what precisely the grave consequences were remains a mystery. Roy Medvedev also makes similar hints, without presenting anything concrete.[18] Walter Laqueur, although a critic of Trotsky, makes a very positive assessment of him as military leader,[19] as does the Leningrad historian, Vladimir Billik.

The Myth of the 'Militarization of Labour'

At the end of the civil war Russia was faced with the problem of the demobilization of the massive Red Army. To prevent mass unemployment, which would weaken the position of the working class in Soviet society, Trotsky proposed that a significant number of the armed forces should be transformed into a 'labour army'. This army should be used mainly to restore the shattered rail and road transport system. This proposal, described in the later polemic as 'militarization of labour', was unanimously agreed by the Ninth Congress of the party and was supported by the later members of the Workers' Opposition around Shlyapnikov and Kollontai, as well as by Lenin.[20]

Trotsky went a step further. Not only should the red soldiers become red workers, but the hungry and unemployed workers should be taken into the factory to stimulate and normalize industrial production. Because of the extensive lumpenization (*Deklassierung*) of the working class, strong discipline in the workplace would be essential. The same methods that led to victory in the civil war could now lead to victory on the production front. This was the origin of Trotsky's formula, 'militarization of labour'. Lenin completely supported this proposal, although it met with opposition in certain party circles.[21]

Trotsky was accused, in the later controversy, of wanting to introduce a policy that was hostile to the workers and the trade unions. His mistakes in the trade union controversy certainly contributed to the construction of this myth.[22] Today, however, 'liberal' circles in Russia claim that Trotsky's proposals on the 'militarization of labour' paved the way for the repressive and authoritarian policy of the Stalin faction and the bureaucracy against the workers. Stalin only put into practice in a more energetic and brutal manner what Trotsky had proposed.

But this in no way corresponds to the historically ascertainable facts. There are no examples of repressive actions against the workers in the factories during the period of the so-called labour armies. Not only the new myth-builders but also friendly critics such as Isaac Deutscher and Tony Cliff overlook the fact that one of the motives for Trotsky's attitude in the trade union debate was his concern about the growing gulf between the ordinary workers and the administrative apparatus and his desire to prepare the workers to take the key positions in factory management. Trotsky's proposals, in spite of appearances and in spite of the fact that this wasn't understood by them at the time, were actually closer than Lenin's to the position of the Workers' Opposition. This was why Bukharin, who at this time was acutely aware of the dangers of bureaucratization, supported Trotsky in the trade union debate.

Trotsky's psychological and political mistakes in the debate about 'militarization of labour' and in the trade union debate undoubtedly weakened him in the decisive conflicts within the party in 1922 and 1923. They also had a negative effect on Lenin's attitude. He replaced the first party secretariat around Preobrazhensky and Krestinsky, which was close to Trotsky, with a new general secretary, Stalin, with the disastrous consequences that Lenin himself only became aware of in 1922–23. They also, at the beginning, placed a question mark, in the eyes of the party and of the workers outside the party, over the credibility of the proposals made by Trotsky and the Left Opposition. In this sense, they were a secondary link in the fateful chain of causes that led to the victory of the Stalin faction and the Soviet bureaucracy.

All these discussions in 1921 and 1922 took place in the context of a wider economic problem: should the party preserve War Communism or is the partial return to market relations in agriculture and trade, the end of requisitioning in the countryside, a precondition for stimulating productive forces in the countryside and in the cities? Deutscher was quite right in pointing to the importance of this overall context. And as has already been pointed out on many occasions, Trotsky, in proposing that War Communism should be replaced by NEP, was at least a good year ahead of the rest of the party leadership, including Lenin.

The Militia and Election of Officers

The myth of the authoritarian Trotsky as precursor to the repressive Stalin is also contradicted by another historical fact. After 1922/23, Trotsky wanted the Red Army to be reorganized on the basis of a territorial militia system. As J. M. Mackintosh has correctly emphasized, this was because Trotsky wanted 'to increase the weight of the urban proletariat in the army by stationing and recruiting territorial troop formations in the industrial centres'.[23]

This proposal brought him into conflict with the military specialists of Czarist origin, whose spokesman at the time was General Svechin, author of a standard work on strategy and professor at the Military Academy.[24] But now the fronts in this debate had completely changed. During the civil war it was Trotsky who had argued for a centralized army commanded by ex-Czarist officers. Now he was the main defender of a proletarian militia. Another important element of the debate concerned the principle of election. In the Red Army the commanding staffs were appointed, not elected; but now Trotsky proposed a return to the elective principle for the militia. In 1924 Trotsky wrote:

> We must always have before our eyes two circumstances: If the very possibility of going over to the militia system was first created by the establishment of a Soviet structure, still the tempo of the change is determined by the general conditions of the culture of the country – technique, means of communication, literacy, etc.[25]

In *The Revolution Betrayed* he added: 'The correlation between regular troops and militia can serve as a fair indication of the actual movement towards socialism.'[26] According to Peter Gosztony, in 1925 the Red Army consisted of 36 territorial divisions and 26 regular divisions. In 1930, 58 per cent of the infantry divisions were territorial and in 1934 as much as 74 per cent.[27] In 1935 the situation was radically reversed. In that year only 35 per cent of the infantry divisions were territorial, in the following year the figure sank even further to 23 per cent. Trotsky described the events in the army in 1935 as a kind of 'state revolution'.[28]

Of course, this reversal of policy was partly dictated by the growing threat of war and by the objective need for motorization and the construction of a professional tank division.[29] Trotsky commented:

> Nevertheless, the slide from 74 per cent to 23 per cent seems excessive. It was not brought to pass, we may assume, without a 'friendly' pressure from the French general staff.[30] It is still more likely that the bureaucracy seized on a favourable pretext for this step, which was dictated to a considerable degree by political considerations.
>
> The divisions of a militia through their very character come into direct dependence upon the population. This is the chief advantage of the system from a socialist point of view. But this is also its danger from the point of view of the Kremlin . . .
>
> The army is a copy of society and suffers from all its diseases, usually at a higher temperature. The trade of war is too austere to get along with fictions and imitations. The army needs the fresh air of criticism. The commanding staff needs democratic control. The organizers of the Red Army were aware of this from the beginning, and considered it necessary to prepare for such a measure as the election of the commanding staff.[31]

But the Soviet bureaucracy didn't introduce the election principle in 1935. Instead, at the same time as dismantling the territorial divisions, it reintroduced the old officer caste, with its 'classical' hierarchy, stripes, medals and growing material privileges. This was the expression of the victory of the Soviet Thermidor in the Red Army. Trotsky's struggle for the militia and for the election of commanders was part of his general struggle against the Soviet Thermidor. It is of some interest that in 1990 a Soviet army commander and deputy to the Congress of People's Deputies, Podziruk, openly argued for a democratization of the army and for a return to its original structures, the same structures that Trotsky had argued for.[32]

Notes

1. I will limit myself to just three of numerous possible examples. Rosa Luxemburg, in *The Russian Revolution* (1918), in *Rosa Luxemburg Speaks*, New York 1970, refers constantly to the Bolshevik leadership and government 'of Lenin and Trotsky'. The same is true of John Reed's book, so highly praised by Lenin, *Ten Days That Shook the World*, London 1961. Likewise, numerous messages sent to the Second Comintern Congress were addressed to Lenin and Trotsky.

2. Dmitri Volkogonov, *Stalin*, Düsseldorf 1989, p. 145.

3. Dmitri Volkogonov, *Trotsky, the Janus Face of the Revolution*, 1992.

4. Quoted in B. H. Liddel Hart, *The Red Army*, New York 1956, p. 27.

5. In the first edition of Gorky's pamphlet, *V. I. Lenin*, published in Moscow in 1924, we find the following: 'Banging his fist on the table, Lenin said: "Show me another

man able to organize almost a model army within a single year and win the respect of military experts. We have such a man"' (p. 37).

6. W. Bruce Lincoln, *Red Victory. A History of the Russian Civil War*, New York 1989, p. 173.

7. Trotsky, *My Life*, New York 1960, p. 413.

8. Quoted in Liddell Hart, *The Red Army*, p. 43.

9. Trotsky, *Comment la révolution s'est armée*, Paris 1967, pp. 45–6; *The Russian Provisional Government 1917. Documents*, ed. by R. P. Browder and Alexander Kerensky, Stanford 1961, vol. 3, pp. 1614ff.

10. The soldiers of the Red Army swore an oath to the world revolution. The two cruisers in the Red Fleet were renamed 'Proletarian Revolution' and 'Paris Commune'.

11. See 'The Lessons of Spain. The Last Warning', in *The Spanish Revolution (1931–1939)*, New York 1973, pp. 320–22.

12. A good contemporary analysis of these conflicts was provided by M. Philip Price, the then correspondent of the *Manchester Guardian*. See his *The Russian Revolution*, London 1921.

13. Larissa Reissner, *Sviask* (*Cahiers Leon Trotsky*, no. 12).

14. 'On one occasion Lenin emphasized his confidence in Trotsky by giving him a blank piece of paper with the letterhead of the chairman of the Council of People's Commissars. On it he had written in longhand at the bottom of the page: ' "Comrades: Knowing the strict character of Comrade Trotsky's orders, I am so convinced, so absolutely convinced, of the correctness, expediency and necessity for the success of the cause of the order given by Comrade Trotsky, that I unreservedly endorse this order. V. Ulyanov/Lenin." Naturally, Trotsky kept this document for the rest of his life' (Roy Medvedev, *Let History Judge*, Oxford 1989, p. 105).

15. Quote from Liddell Hart, *The Red Army*, p. 30.

16. Trotsky, *L'Art de la guerre et le marxisme*, Paris 1975, pp. 88ff.

17. 'War bases itself on many sciences but war itself is no science – it is a practical art, a skill ... a savage and bloody art ...' (quoted in Isaac Deutscher, *The Prophet Armed*, Oxford 1970, p. 482).

18. Medvedev, *Let History Judge*, pp. 103–8.

19. Walter Laqueur, *Stalin*, Munich 1990, p. 73.

20. Deutscher, *The Prophet Armed*, pp. 494, 496.

21. Ibid., pp. 491–3.

22. See chapter 3.

23. In Liddell Hart, *The Red Army*, p. 53.

24. Ibid., pp. 53ff; see also *The Revolution Betrayed*, pp. 220–25; Deutscher, *The Prophet Armed*, pp. 477ff.

25. *The Revolution Betrayed*, p. 217.

26. Ibid., p. 219.

27. Peter Gosztony, *Die Rote Armee*, Vienna 1980, p. 124.

28. *The Revolution Betrayed*, p. 215.

29. Tukhachevsky was one of the most brilliant military strategists in Europe in the 1930s. He understood the importance of mobile independent tank divisions much better than did Liddell Hart, Manstein, Guderian, de Gaulle, etc. He began to reorganize the Red Army along those lines. Stalin put an end to this and disbanded the tank divisions – with disastrous consequences after June 1941. This was the background to the murder of so many Red Army commanders in 1937, including Tukhachevsky himself.

30. In 1935 there was an alliance between France and the Soviet Union known as the Laval Pact, involving co-operation of the general staffs of both countries.

31. *The Revolution Betrayed*, pp. 220, 222.

32. In an interview in the Mexican daily, *Excelsior*, 20 August 1990.

9

Trotsky and the National Question

Trotsky was born in the biggest multi-ethnic state in Europe, in Czarist Russia. He lived for many years in the second biggest multi-ethnic state, the Austro-Hungarian Empire. As correspondent for a liberal Russian newspaper, he experienced the wars in the Balkans, that area of Europe in which many ethnic groups live alongside each other without clear territorial boundaries, creating extremely complex political problems which are still with us today. Under such conditions, it was inevitable that he would take an interest in the national question. In fact it was to occupy his attention for thirty-five years.

We cannot deal here with all the specific national questions on which Trotsky took a position, nor do we want to approach this chronologically. We shall instead look at those statements of his on the national question which express most clearly his principled attitude to this question.

The National Question at the Twelfth Party Congress of the Russian Communist Party

As is generally well known, Lenin, in what he wrote on the so-called Georgian question in his Testament, was preparing a bombshell against Stalin. What is probably less well known are the theoretical, political and constitutional controversies that accompanied the debate over Georgia and that concerned the problem of the relations among the nationalities in the multinational Soviet Union.

This was a problem inherited from Czarist Russia, a specific type of colonial power, the distinctive features of which were its incorporation of conquered territories into the Russian motherland and its partial colonization by non-autochthonous groups. This led to complex social relations between the Czarist rulers, their agents (officials, military), local rulers, peasants, local intelligentsia and, later, workers. These relations were themselves affected by national conflicts.

To resolve this complex problem the Bolsheviks had to have a correct understanding of the kind of federal state structure that they needed to develop and a correct attitude to surviving or newly emergent forms of nationalism. In the first case, what was required was a real and not merely formal equality of rights of all nationalities of the Soviet Union, including their right to separate. Stalin's original draft constitution for the Soviet Union, which proposed a simple adhesion of the Caucasian republics to Soviet Russia, the RSFSR (which would give them less autonomy than they already had), was an example of Great Russian over-centralization and contradicted the most elementary requirements of national equality.[1] It was severely criticized by both Lenin and Trotsky, who supported the efforts of the Georgian communists around Budu Mdivani.[2] Stalin gave way formally but did not relinquish his Great Russian chauvinist views. Lenin's proposal, for instance, to have a rotating presidency (Russian, Ukrainian, Caucasian) was not followed; the Great Russian, Kalinin, remained president.

Worse still was Stalin's attitude to nationalism. Although, in his speech to the Twelfth Party Congress, he was critical of Great Russian chauvinism, he equated it with the nationalism of the minority nations, both of which the Bolsheviks should fight against.[3] Stalin's policy was wrong in principle and could only lead to disastrous political consequences. Although, as internationalists, communists are opposed to all forms of nationalism, they do not equate the nationalism of the oppressor nation with the nationalism of the oppressed. For such an approach to be politically effective, one has to demonstrate understanding and tact with respect to the nationalism of an oppressed people. To do otherwise would be grist to the mill of radical nationalists in the different republics. On the eve of the Twelfth Party Congress, Stalin had even proposed a tripartite division of the nations of the Soviet Union depending on their degree of economic development, a proposal that contradicted the most basic principles of equality among nations and ethnic groups. As a result of pressure from Lenin and others in the party, the proposal had to be withdrawn.

Albeit unsuccessfully, it was Rakovsky and Bukharin who defended a principled position on this at the Twelfth Congress.[4] It is not true that Trotsky rejected the bloc proposed by Lenin on the Georgian and national question. He defended their common viewpoint in the Central Committee, the Politburo and in the press.[5] He didn't speak out on the issue at the Twelfth Congress, for reasons that are still unclear.[6]

The Independence of Soviet Ukraine

What surprised his contemporaries the most, friends and foes alike, was Trotsky's defence of Ukrainian independence in 1939.[7] His article, 'The Ukrainian Question' (22 April 1939), has to be seen against the political background at the time. Hitler and the *Wehrmacht* had established links with Ukrainian nationalists. The Ukrainian question was meant to provide the explosion that would facilitate the planned invasion of the Soviet Union. Following the dissolution of Czechoslovakia and the separation of Carpatho-Ukraine, the Nazis had secured a territory under their control with a Ukrainian-speaking population.

At the same time, there was nowhere in the Soviet Union where the hatred of the Stalinist dictatorship was so great as in Ukraine. It had been nurtured by the deportation of the peasants, the ensuing famine and the intensification of national oppression.[8] There was a real danger that the Ukrainian nationalists, who were collaborating with the Nazis, would find sympathy among the rural population.[9] Under such circumstances, it was politically necessary to hinder or disrupt this manoeuvre. The slogan of an independent Soviet Ukraine served precisely this function.

But, over and above this, it also reflected a more general approach to the Ukrainian question. According to Trotsky's analysis, the national question was an important factor in politically reactivating the people of the Soviet Union. This would enable the proletarian vanguard once again to win the leadership of the peasant masses. His bold defence of an independent Ukrainian workers' state was meant to be an impulse to the political revolution and the renewal of the Soviet Union as a whole.[10]

Certainly, the separation of Soviet Ukraine from the Soviet Union would represent a step backwards economically. But it would be a step backwards that actually corresponded to the consciousness of the peasant masses, similar to the division of the big estates in 1917 and 1918. Without such a compromise it would be impossible to re-establish the alliance of workers and peasants. Trotsky then came to the important conclusion which is still so relevant today:

> Naturally an independent workers' and peasants' Ukraine might subsequently join the Soviet federation; but voluntarily, on conditions that it itself considers acceptable, which in turn presupposes a revolutionary regeneration of the USSR.[11]

This led Trotsky to a more general conclusion: the state created by the October Revolution had not succeeded in resolving the national question.[12] Trotsky attributed this mainly to objective circumstances. In his writings on Ukraine he only deals in a peripheral manner with the subjective mistakes of the Bolsheviks on the national question. This aspect of the problem was very important with respect to the nationality problems in the Caucasus and in Central Asia.[13] Trotsky dealt with this in his last book, the biography of Stalin, although not in a systematic way.[14] The Georgian communists persecuted by Stalin and Ordzhoni-kidze and so energetically defended by Lenin were close political friends of Trotsky. Although he was closely linked to the Georgian question, he didn't devote as much space to it in his writings as he did to Ukraine.

Self-determination for the Black People of the USA

The American Communist Party grappled for a long time with the problem of their attitude to the black population of the USA. In the so-called Third Period they argued for the right of self-determination of the black people and their right to set up their own independent state in the south which would have the same rights as the other states in the Union.

The American Trotskyists were divided on this question. In general they preferred to agitate for the social, economic and political equality of the blacks. In other words, they didn't regard the blacks as a 'national minority' or 'ally of the proletariat', but rather as an overexploited and oppressed section of the American proletariat.[15]

Trotsky didn't agree with this. For him the right of self-determination was an inseparable part of elementary democratic rights in general. In view of the undeniable racism of the white working class, it would be unacceptable for them to prescribe to the blacks certain limitations on their self-determination. One had to demand that blacks have the right to choose whatever form of political organization they wanted: autonomy, state rights, separation. The unrestricted right of self-determination for the black population of America was a concrete element of the strategy of permanent revolution in that country.[16]

For Trotsky there was a big difference, however, between the unrestricted right of self-determination and the demand for the formation of a black state in the south. There should be no restriction of the right of blacks to make their own choice in this matter. For the white majority to impose a separate state on them, which could be a ghetto, would be just as tactless as the attempt to deny them this choice. If the majority of blacks wanted to emigrate to the northern states, they had the full right to do so.[17]

Self-determination of the Black Population of South Africa

Trotsky spoke out clearly for the right of the black population of South Africa to self-determination, including the right to a 'black republic'. In a response to a programmatic document of the South African Left Opposition he wrote in 1935:

> From the point of view of the black majority, South Africa is a slave colony.... Under these conditions, the South African Republic will emerge first of all as a 'black' republic; this does not exclude, of course, either full equality for the whites or brotherly relations between the two races – depending mainly on the behaviour of the whites. But it is entirely obvious that the predominant majority of the population, liberated from slavish dependence, will put a certain imprint on the state.
>
> Insofar as a victorious revolution will radically change the relation not only between the classes but also between the races and will assure to the blacks that place in the state corresponding to their numbers, thus far will the *social* revolution in South Africa also have a *national* character.
>
> We have not the slightest reason to close our eyes to this side of the question or to diminish its significance. On the contrary, the proletarian party should in words and in deeds openly and boldly take the solution of the national (racial) problem in its hands ...
>
> When the theses say that the slogan of a 'black republic' is *equally* harmful for the revolutionary cause as is the slogan of a 'South Africa for the whites', then we cannot agree with the form of the statement. Whereas in the latter there is the case of supporting complete oppression, in the former there is the case of taking the first steps towards liberation.
>
> We must accept decisively and without any reservations the complete and unconditional right of the blacks to independence. Only on the basis of a mutual struggle against the domination of the white exploiters can the solidarity of black and white toilers be cultivated and strengthened ...
>
> In any case, the worst crime on the part of the revolutionaries would be to give the smallest concessions to the privileges and prejudices of the whites. Whoever gives his little finger to the devil of chauvinism is lost.
>
> The revolutionary party must put before every white worker the following alternative: either with British imperialism and with the white bourgeoisie of South Africa or with the black workers and peasants against the white feudalists and slave owners and heir agents in the ranks of the working class.[18]

This warning is as relevant today as it was then.

The Right of Self-determination of the Catalan Nation

Trotsky concerned himself for many years with the problems of the Spanish revolution and he expressed his views a number of times on the national question in Spain. On the eve of the revolution in 1931 he wrote that the communists should defend the right of self-determination of the Catalan people, including their right to separate from the Spanish state. This was a matter for the democratic decision of the Catalan people. This did not mean, however, that the communists should raise the slogan of the secession of Catalonia. In view of the popular revolution in the whole of Spain which was being led by the proletariat, it would perhaps be advisable for the Catalan working class to aim their propaganda towards Catalonia remaining in some form of Spanish (or Iberian) federation. Trotsky's own political judgement suggested such a solution.[19]

Some months later, after the outbreak of the revolution, he expressed a similar view for both Catalonia and the Basque nation. The proletarian vanguard, argued Trotsky, should fully and completely defend the *right* of the Catalans and Basques to organize their state life independently in the event that the majority of these nationalities express themselves for complete separation, but he thought that extensive autonomy of national districts within a Spanish federation would represent great advantages for the workers and peasants.[20] This position of Trotsky's was all the more important in that the major part of the Spanish communist movement, the Catalan Federation led by Joaquin Maurin, threatened to become separated from the rest of the Spanish vanguard through its excessive emphasis on the national question.[21] This was to have very bad consequences when the majority of the Spanish Left Opposition fused with Maurin's organization to form the POUM and thereby lost any chance of influencing broad left-oriented sections of the working class outside Catalonia.

For a Balkan Federation

During his stay in the Balkans in 1912/13 Trotsky had first-hand experience of the explosive nationality problems in this area. In 1909 he had argued for a transformation of the Balkans into a democratic federation of all the dispersed nationalities.[22] He condemned the big power chauvinism of the Young Turks for their rejection of such a solution.

In the years that followed he often returned to the central importance of this slogan.[23] After the peace of Bucharest, which led to the partition of Macedonia, he again argued intensely, for economic as well as national reasons, for a Balkan Federation.[24] In its early years, the Comintern adopted this demand for a Balkan Federation which had been the traditional position of socialists in the region before the First World War. Under pressure from Stalin, this demand was later dropped, with well-known disastrous consequences as the different factions of the bureaucratic apparatus in these countries inflamed nationalist sentiments with their territorial demands against each other, which promoted the rise of pre-war reactionary nationalist currents.

The Nationality Problem in the Austro-Hungarian Monarchy

Trotsky did not make any special study of the nationality problem in the Austro-Hungarian monarchy. In his *History of the Russian Revolution*, however, in a chapter dealing with the national question, he devoted a section to the nationality problem in the old Austria-Hungary. Unlike his writings on the national problem in other countries, this is more of a systematic and theoretical analysis and deserves to be looked at for that reason. Trotsky remarks, first of all, that the belated arrival of the bourgeois revolution in nationally heterogeneous states such as Turkey, Russia and Austria-Hungary unleashed powerful centrifugal forces because it used national unity as a fundamental industrial reserve.[25] He then continues:

> Bolshevism based itself on the assumption of an outbreak of national revolutions continuing for decades to come, and instructed the advanced workers in this spirit. The Austrian social democracy, on the contrary, submissively accommodated itself to the policy of the ruling classes; it defended the compulsory citizenship of ten nations in the Austro-Hungarian monarchy, and at the same time, being absolutely incapable of achieving a revolutionary union of the workers of these different nationalities, fenced them off in the party and in the trade unions with vertical partitions. Karl Renner, an educated Habsburg functionary, was never tired of probing the inkwells of Austro-Marxism in search of some means of rejuvenating the rule of the Habsburgs – until one day he found himself the bereaved theoretician of the Austro-Hungarian monarchy. When the Central Empires were crushed, the Habsburg dynasty again tried to raise the banner of a federation of autonomous nations under its sceptre ...
>
> And Otto Bauer, representing the 'left' wing of the Austrian social

democracy, considered this a suitable moment to bring forward the formula of national self-determination. That programme which during the preceding decades should have inspired the struggle of the proletariat against the Habsburgs and the ruling bourgeoisie, was now brought in as an instrument of self-preservation for the nation which had dominated yesterday, but today was in danger from the side of the liberated Slavic peoples ...

On 3 October 1918, when the matter no longer depended on them in the slightest degree, the social-democratic deputies of the Reichsrat magnanimously 'recognized' the right of the peoples of the former empire to self-determination. On 4 October the bourgeois parties also adopted the programme of self-determination. Having thus outstripped the Austro-German imperialists by one day, the social democrats immediately resumed their waiting policy. Only on 13 October, when the conclusive collapse of the army and the monarchy had created, in the words of Otto Bauer, 'the revolutionary situation for which our programme was designed', did the Austro-Marxists raise the question of self-determination in a practical form. In very truth they now had nothing to lose ...

Thus the new programme was put in circulation not because it was needful to the oppressed, but because it had ceased to be dangerous to the oppressors. The possessing classes, driven into a tight place historically, had found themselves obliged to recognize the national revolution juridically, and Austro-Marxism found this an appropriate moment to legitimize it theoretically. This was a mature revolution, they said, timely, historically prepared – it is all over anyway. The spirit of the social democracy is here before us as though in the palm of our hand.[26]

The way in which Austrian Social Democracy accepted the dual monarchy had disastrous consequences not only for its policy on the self-determination of nations. Up to and even into the First World War, they approved of annexations. When, under pressure from Otto Bauer, they shifted their line on self-determination in 1918, this effectively meant a shift in the direction of unity with the German Empire and provided an added justification for their failure to promote a socialist transformation in the pre-revolutionary period 1918–19.[27]

Notes

1. See Lenin's letter to the Politburo of 26 and 27 September 1922, also the final part of his Testament, in *Collected Works*, vol. 36. There is a good general account of this controversy in Ditte Gerns, *Nationalitätenpolitik der Bolsheviki*, Düsseldorf 1988, pp. 380ff.

2. See Trotsky's *Stalin*, London 1969, vol. 2, pp. 170ff; also *My Life*, New York 1960, pp. 482–6.

3. Gerns, *Nationalitätenpolitik der Bolsheviki*, pp. 429ff.

4. Rakovsky's speech to the Twelfth Congress in *Christian Rakovsky. Selected Writings on Opposition in the USSR 1923–1930*, London 1980. See also Pierre Broué, *Trotsky*, Paris 1988, pp. 326ff.

5. See especially Moshe Lewin, *Lenin's Last Struggle*, London 1975.

6. We have already dealt with this in chapter 3.

7. 'The Ukrainian Question', in *Writings of Leon Trotsky 1938–1939*, pp. 301ff.

8. The Secretary of the Ukrainian Communist Party, Skrypnik, was accused of petty-bourgeois nationalism and committed suicide in protest in 1933.

9. In the summer of 1941 during the early phase of the Nazi invasion, and before they were aware of the full extent of Nazi crimes, many of the Ukrainian peasants, unlike the workers, were sympathetic to the occupying forces.

10. The mass movements in the Baltic republics after the beginning of Glasnost confirmed Trotsky's views on this.

11. 'The Ukrainian Question', pp. 305–6.

12. 'Independence of Ukraine and Sectarian Muddleheads' (30 July 1939), in *Writings of Leon Trotsky 1939–1940*, p. 47.

13. A fascinating and still not adequately clarified part of this history concerns the leading Asian Bolshevik, Sultan Galiev, who defended an organizational autonomy of the communists in the Central Asian Soviet territories. He was later expelled from the party. The Stalinists referred to him as the 'Asian Trotsky' (Alexandre Bennigsen and Chantal Lemercier Quelquejay, *Sultan Galiev*, Paris 1986.) We are not aware of Trotsky's attitude to Sultan Galiev.

14. *Stalin*, pp. 170ff.

15. Trotsky, *On Black Nationalism and Self-Determination*, New York 1978.

16. Ibid., pp. 25–6.

17. Ibid., pp. 45–8.

18. *Writings of Leon Trotsky 1934–1935*, New York 1977, pp. 248–55.

19. Trotsky, *The Spanish Revolution*, New York 1973, pp. 60–61.

20. Ibid., pp. 77–8.

21. Ibid., p. 107.

22. Trotsky, *The Balkan Wars*, New York 1980, p. 12.

23. Ibid., p. 41.

24. Ibid., pp. 366–7.

25. *History of the Russian Revolution*, London 1967, vol. 3, pp. 53ff.

26. Ibid., pp. 59–60.

27. Peter Kulemann, *Am Beispiel des Austromarxismus*, Hamburg 1979.

Trotsky and the Jewish Question

The Marxists of the Second International were convinced that the consolidation of the capitalist system of production and bourgeois society would lead inevitably to Jewish emancipation. It would also lead unavoidably to their assimilation. The Jews would be absorbed into the bourgeoisie and middle classes. There would no longer be a Jewish question. It would simply be absorbed into the more general problematic of the bourgeois class.[1]

The extent to which the emancipated Jews would still regard themselves as Jews would depend exclusively on what remained of anti-Semitism.[2] To the extent that the assimilated Jews were not accepted by certain sections of society as equal members with equal rights, they would retain their Jewish identity. But this anti-Semitism was rooted mainly in the nobility, the Church and the officer corps (which also came from the nobility) and it had a pre-bourgeois, semi-feudal character. With the advance of bourgeois society, it too would disappear.

The view that the Jews would be assimilated and that anti-Semitism, as a pre-bourgeois phenomenon, was destined to disappear, had undoubtedly a rational core.[3] The fact that, in the sixty-five years between the revolution of 1848 and the First World War, semi-feudal Czarist Russia was the only major European state to have an openly anti-Semitic ideology and practice seemed to confirm this view. There were significant differences, however, between the Jewish emancipation process in those countries which had bourgeois-democratic revolutions backed by mass popular movements (the Netherlands, Britain, France, USA), and countries like Germany and Austria, where the revolutions came 'from above' and where Jewish emancipation was introduced from the top, only to be revoked later.[4]

But the attitude of Marxists at that time to the Jewish question was marked by a strong element of mechanistic economic evolutionism, largely resulting from the influence of Karl Kautsky. It was also based on a rather simplified image of the social composition of the Jewish population. In this respect, it was more a semi-Marxist than a Marxist attitude.[5]

In Czarist Russia and in the Austro-Hungarian Empire (in Galicia, Slovakia) there was a large population of impoverished Jewish petty bourgeoisie and lumpen proletariat. There was a large Jewish proletariat in Czarist Russia (especially its Polish part), Salonika, Amsterdam, London and New York. In all these places it played an important role in the creation of the modern labour movement.[6] Kautsky and his followers were largely unaware of this dimension of the Jewish question. Bernstein, Bebel, Lenin, Rosa Luxemburg and Gramsci had a more flexible but still limited approach.

This inadequate theory led to a defective practice. When French society was literally torn in two by the Dreyfus affair, French Marxists around Guesde maintained a strict neutrality. For them this was simply a conflict between different factions of the bourgeoisie.[7] There were even anti-Semitic overtones in the propaganda of the Austrian Social Democrats (SPÖ).[8] The Austrian Social Democracy was, to a certain extent, responsible for the fact that anti-Semitism was more prevalent in the Austrian working class than it was among the German workers, with tragic consequences at the time of the *Anschluss*.

When the young Soviet Republic came to deal with the status of its Jewish population, it opted, under pressure from Jewish communists, the *Jewsektia*, for a half-way solution between assimilation and recognition of the Jews as a nation.[9] In Russia it was only the Jews that were declared a nationality without having their own territory.[10] Although they were numerically larger, territorially more concentrated and characterized by a higher level of cultural homogeneity than many of the other nationalities that were given an autonomous territory or autonomous republic, the Jews were not granted the right to their own state. Nevertheless their passports and identity cards described their nationality as Jewish. Both aspects of this half-way solution made it objectively easier for the Nazis later to organize their campaign of extermination.

It was only the older Friedrich Engels and Rosa Luxemburg who managed to free themselves from the Kautskian straitjacket on the Jewish question. In the last two decades of the nineteenth century, Engels became familiar with the growing anti-Semitic mass movements around the court chaplain, Adolf Stöcker, in Germany and the mayor of Vienna, Karl Lueger, in Austria. He recognized that this anti-Semitism resulted from an ideological fusion of pre-capitalist and capitalist motivations and interests, and that these were to be found not only in the nobility, the church and the officer corps, but also in the impoverished middle classes and in the free professions exposed to Jewish competition.

Engels was not satisfied simply to condemn anti-Semitism as 'the socialism of blockheads'.[11] He understood that there was a significant Jewish proletariat in the West whose struggles had to be supported (he didn't say anything about the Jews in Eastern Europe). He was probably influenced here by Marx's daughter Eleanor, who once said: 'My happiest hours are when I'm in the East End with the Jewish workers.'[12] Engels also recognized that the Jewish workers in London's East End were among the most exploited of the English proletariat. Jewish tailors, bakers and cobblers went on strike three times to demand that their 14–16-hour day be reduced to 12 hours.

Influenced by what happened in the Dreyfus Affair, Rosa Luxemburg went one step further. She recognized that the restriction of Jewish political rights, or any form of discrimination against the Jews, including the Jewish bourgeoisie, was an attack on democratic rights in general.[13] Therefore, these anti-Semitic tendencies should be seen not just as an expression of pre-capitalist petty-bourgeois mentality, but as the ideology of present-day militarism and chauvinism and as such should be energetically opposed.[14]

In 1914, Lenin edited for the Bolshevik Duma faction a draft law for the elimination of all restrictions on Jewish rights. In his commentary to this draft, he wrote:

> The Black Hundreds [armed bands of the ultra-right] are carrying on a hate-filled agitation against the Jews. The followers of Purishkevich [an extreme right-wing leader in the Duma] are trying to make the Jewish nation a scapegoat for their own misdeeds. Therefore the Russian Social Democratic Labour faction gives such prominence, in its draft law, to the arbitrary persecution of which the Jews are victims.[15]

Among all the prominent Marxists of the Second and Third International, it was Trotsky alone who developed the positive aspects of Rosa Luxemburg's and Engels's ideas into a less simplistic and less mechanical approach to the Jewish question. The background to this was his experience with Black Hundred anti-Semitism as a young man, the pogroms against the 1905 revolution and the famous Beilis trial of 1913.[16] At that time he still did not reject the Kautskian thesis that the Jews did not constitute a nation. But he had been from his early childhood extremely sensitive to injustice and was temperamentally inclined to protest against every form of oppression. We find in his early writings on the Jewish question a much greater feeling of solidarity with the victims of anti-Semitism than was the case with Kautsky, Viktor Adler, Otto Bauer or even Lenin and Rosa Luxemburg.

At the same time, he was deeply outraged by the barbarism he witnessed under Czarism. In the pogroms, the lies, the brutality of the Black Hundreds and the injustice of the Beilis trial, he saw the expression of this barbarism. Revolt against the persecutor, identification with the persecuted: this was the impulse to a new approach to the Jewish question, which went beyond what had been achieved by Engels and Luxemburg.

In the Russian Revolution of 1917 and in the civil war that followed the internal contradictions in Trotsky's approach became clearer.[17] He made no personal intervention in the debate on the status of the Jews. The Jewish problem was not part of his agitation in the period before the October Revolution. He did not intervene in the party's internal debate about the *Jewsektia* proposal to regard the Jews as a nationality without a territory. But, unlike the other leading Russian revolutionaries of Jewish descent, he became increasingly aware of his own Jewish origins and of the political reaction to this in significant sections of the Russian population.

Trotsky was unquestionably the second man in the state and party. He was the unchallenged leader of the Red Army. The hatred of the counter-revolution concentrated itself on Trotsky because of his Jewish origin, much more so than in the case of Felix Dzerzhinsky, leader of the Cheka. The most reactionary currents of the counter-revolution used Trotsky's Jewish origins to stir up real or latent anti-Semitic tendencies in the petty bourgeoisie and in the more backward sections of the proletariat against the revolution. It was because of this that Trotsky refused to take on certain positions in the state.[18] At the meeting of the Central Committee on 26 October 1922, Lenin proposed that Trotsky should become first deputy chairman of the Council of Peoples' Commissars, tantamount to being Lenin's designated successor as head of government, but Trotsky declined, giving his Jewish origins as a reason.[19]

Trotsky was more aware than the other revolutionary leaders, including Lenin, of the potential horrors of active anti-Semitism.[20] The pogroms of Petlyura in Ukraine, with more than a hundred thousand innocent victims, most of them women, children and older people (the biggest number of Jewish victims before the Nazi murders), were a traumatic shock for Trotsky. He was firm in his resolve to deal with the perpetrators of these atrocities and he didn't allow his Jewish origins, or the fact that the reactionaries might use this against him, to hold him back in his bitter struggle against the counter-revolution.

Like the other Bolshevik leaders, Trotsky hoped that the new social relations in the Soviet Union, public education and the dominant ideology would lead to a gradual decrease in anti-Semitic prejudice and behaviour. The first examples of what was an initially covert but later increasingly systematic use of anti-Semitism by the Stalin faction in its fight against the opposition were a heavy blow for Trotsky.[21] This was followed by an increase in both official and traditional anti-Semitism in the USSR during the period of the mass purges.[22] The worst manifestations of this anti-Semitism were during the period of the Hitler–Laval Pact and then again in 1950 to 1952, the time of the 'doctors' plot'. (The doctors, many of whom were of Jewish origin, were accused of murdering Andrei Zhdanov and of conspiring to kill top government officials.) During this period, Stalin destroyed Jewish culture in the Soviet Union and, under the pretext of a struggle against Zionism, there was a widespread distribution of anti-Semitic literature. The long-term disastrous consequences of this break with Bolshevik tradition are still evident today.[23]

The anti-Semitism that was increasing in the Soviet Union was insignificant, however, compared with the tragedy now beginning to unfold in Europe. After the First World War, there developed in many countries of Europe an increasing number of anti-Semitic organizations, products, in the final analysis, of the systemic crisis of capitalism. But this development reached a qualitatively new stage when the NSDAP, the Nazi Party in Germany, won a mass base and an electorate which made it an effective instrument of power, using terror as a means to achieve the national and international goals of German big business, of the German ruling elite. Hitler now had at his disposal the political and technical means to implement his own special ideology, a form of Social Darwinism based on biological racism.[24] From 1939 at the latest, the goal was genocide. With the invasion of the Soviet Union on 22 June 1941, Hitler was now ready to implement this policy systematically.[25]

Trotsky was well aware of the link between the structural crisis of capitalism, the murderous dynamic of the Nazis' Third Reich and the fate of the European Jews. Just as the emancipation of the Jews had symbolized the historic development of civil rights in the period of capitalism's ascent, now the restriction and elimination of Jewish civil rights gave expression in a rather concentrated form to the reactionary historical development since 1914. The final chapter of Trotsky's autobiography, My Life, has the title 'A Planet Without a Visa', a phrase he also used to describe the situation of the European Jews in his Manifesto on the war written in May 1940.[26] The Evian Conference of world governments in 1939, treated with contempt by the Nazis, offered to the many millions of threatened European Jews only a few hundred travel visas.[27] What was required, of course, was a mass evacuation of the European Jews.

Trotsky knew that the intense imperialist struggle for world domination that would result from the emergence of fascist and semi-fascist regimes in Europe would also mean the physical destruction of the European Jews. In his 'Appeal to American Jews' of 1938, he wrote:

> It isn't difficult to imagine what will happen to the Jews in the case of an outbreak of world war. But even without war, the developing worldwide reaction will lead with certainty to the physical extermination of the Jews.[28]

This certainty provided the final stimulus for Trotsky to change his position on one decisive aspect of the Jewish question. From 1937 he recognized the right of the Jewish nationality to its own state at least in those territories in which it constituted a self-contained population with its own language. He had already written in 1934:

> A workers' government must create for the Jews, as for all other nations, the best conditions for their cultural development. This means, for those Jews who want it, their own schools, their own press, their own theatre, as well as their own territory to be administered by them. This is how the proletariat will behave when it is master of the whole planet. There will be no restrictions with respect to the national question. On the contrary: there will have to be material assistance for all the cultural needs of all nationalities and all ethnic groups. If one or other national group is destined to disappear (in the national sense), then this can only be the result of a natural process and not the consequence of any territorial, economic, or administrative difficulties.[29]

Three years later he expressed a similar view:

> On the Jewish question, first of all, I can say that it cannot be resolved within the framework of the capitalist system, nor can it be resolved by Zionism. At one time I thought that the Jews would assimilate into the peoples and cultures they lived among. This was the case in Germany and even in America, and for this reason it was possible to make such a prediction. But now it is impossible to say this . . .
>   The territorial question is pertinent because it is easier for people to carry out an economic and cultural plan when it lives in a compact mass . . .

[This] is necessary for cultural development.... If the Jews desire this, socialism will have no right to deny it to them.[30]

Although Trotsky changed his position on the question of territory, this did not alter his complete rejection of Zionism.[31] At most, one could conclude from this analysis that he would not have rejected the right to a limited state-political autonomy for the Hebrew-speaking minority in Palestine.[32]

Trotsky's formulation places the emphasis, quite rightly, on the freedom of choice of the relevant national/ethnic group. In the concrete situation in Soviet Russia between 1918 and 1923, the Yiddish-speaking population of Ukraine, Byelorussia and the Crimea would probably have opted for a Jewish state, while the Russian-speaking Jews of Moscow, Petrograd, possibly Kiev, Odessa and Kharkiv would have rejected this.[33] But the latter would then have been free to live where they chose and would not have been forced to carry the description 'Jewish' in their passports. This would have been a positive solution to the antinomy: 'preservation of nationality or assimilation'.

Trotsky's analysis of contemporary anti-Semitism and his recognition of the right of self-contained Jewish populations to a territorially and politically secure national existence constitute a coherent unity and a decisive step forwards in the Marxist attitude to the Jewish question.[34] We do not claim that this was the last word of historical materialism on the Jewish question. On this, as on any other historical debate, there is probably no last word. There were still weaknesses in Trotsky's position of the 1930s, among them his underestimation of the cultural and religious element in the persistence of anti-Semitism and indeed in the survival of Jewish identity.[35] The French Marxists Maxine Rodinson and Vidal Naquet have been right in pointing these out, as have other historians. This weakness in Trotsky's analysis is all the more surprising in that this cultural and religious element is another example of the non-simultaneity of ideological and socio-economic phenomena which played so important a role in his dealing with the question of fascism and with the national question, as we have already pointed out in a previous chapter.

But, all in all, Trotsky's analysis of the Jewish question represented a qualitative advance in relation to what other Marxists had achieved, including Marx and Engels themselves. It comes therefore as no surprise that the most important Marxist contributions on the Jewish question since Trotsky's death have come from authors whom we could describe as pupils of Trotsky: Abraham Leon's *Interprétation matérialiste de la question juive*; Isaac Deutscher's *The Non-Jewish*

Jew in History; Nathan Weinstock's *Le Pain de la misère*; and, at least to some extent, Enzo Traverso's *Le Marxisme et la question juive*.

The period since the Second World War has witnessed a new development which paradoxically appeared to confirm the original analysis of the Second International. As a combined result of Nazi genocide and the long expansive postwar boom, there has been a general de-proletarianization of the major Jewish population groups (USA, USSR, Britain, France), with the exception of the state of Israel itself. The big majority of the Jewish population was assimilated into the middle-ranking bourgeoisie and the intelligentsia. Even in Israel itself, the Jewish working class became, to some extent, a labour aristocracy with respect to the Arab wage-earners.

The traumatic psychological and political consequences of the Nazi genocide, and the resultant feeling of guilt on the part of the non-Jewish population, had the effect of marginalizing anti-Semitism in Europe and North America for decades. The structural dependence of the Zionist state on US imperialism also had an effect on the ideological and political development of the Jews: there was a general move to the right within the Jewish population. They were no longer the traditional recruiting ground for radical left politics.

But since the 1980s this development has come to a halt. With the general growth in poverty and uncertainty in Western Europe and North America and with the horrific social consequences of the Stalinist collapse in Eastern Europe, there has been a renewed growth of anti-Semitism. Many Jewish groups are experiencing the end of upward social mobility in the economic depression. How strong this trend will be is difficult to say. And the state of Israel offers no solution for either of those problems.

For the first time since 1941, revolutionary socialists who fight consistently for human rights, against every form of anti-Semitism and discrimination, rejecting both Stalinism and capitalism, may find a sympathetic hearing from the Jewish people who are once again threatened by this society.

Notes

1. Marx's early article, 'On the Jewish Question', is in *Marx. Early Writings*, Harmondsworth 1975.

2. A Jewish solicitor in Antwerp, assimilated and married to a Catholic woman, said in an interview that he would think of himself as a Jew if there was only one Jew somewhere in the world who was persecuted or oppressed (*Zeit-Magazin*, 23 November 1990).

3. There is a variety of examples from the nineteenth and twentieth centuries in

which Jews living in a hospitable milieu gradually lost their special identity over three generations through mixed marriages.

4. Walter Grab, *Der deutsche Weg der Judenemanzipation 1789–1938*, Munich 1991.

5. In his whole political development, Kautsky never completely cut the umbilical cord between Darwinism (mechanical evolutionism) and historical materialism.

6. See Nathan Weinstock, 'Geschichte der jüdischen Arbeiterbewegung', in his *Le Pain de la misère*, Paris 1984.

7. This attitude was also to be found in the Marxist journal, *Neue Zeit*, which in one of its leading articles equated anti-Semitism and philo-Semitism and proclaimed a strict neutrality with respect to both. This was the position of Viktor Adler, leader of the Austrian Social Democracy. With his passionate defence of Dreyfus, Jean Jaurès rescued the honour of the French socialists.

8. Leopold Spira, *Der Jud ist Schuld*, Vienna 1978. In the history of the socialist movement, there have been some very bad examples of anti-Semitism. Bakunin was a vicious anti-Semite, as was Makhno, the Ukrainian peasant leader.

9. The *Jewsektia* was the Jewish section of the Russian Communist Party. In January 1918 a Commissariat for Jewish Affairs was established as a department of the Commissariat for National Affairs led by Stalin. 'When the *Jewsektia* had done its job of silencing all opposition in the Jewish milieu, it was dissolved in 1930' (John Bunzl, *Klassenkampf in der Diaspora*, Vienna 1975).

10. Kalinin, formally head of state in the USSR, admitted in 1934 that the Jewish nationality was the only one in the USSR without its own territory. He was attempting to justify the establishment of the Jewish Autonomous Region in the Far East in 1934. Its capital was Birobidzhan. This was an area not inhabited by Jews, and it was a way of avoiding giving them their own state in the west of the USSR where they actually lived. Trotsky called Birobidzhan a 'bureaucratic farce'.

11. The phrase 'socialism of the blockheads' came originally from Bebel. In a letter to Bernstein in 1881, Engels wrote that he had never read anything as stupid and childish as anti-Semitic literature (*MEW*, vol. 35, p. 214). Ten years later, in a letter to the Vienna *Arbeiterzeitung* (9 May 1890), he severely condemned anti-Semitism (*MEW*, vol. 22, p. 49) and, a year later, expressed in a letter to Bebel his pleasure over the fact that many Jews were joining the Social Democracy under the pressure of anti-Semitism (*MEW*, vol. 38, p. 228).

12. Chushichi Tsuzuki, *The Life of Eleanor Marx, 1855–1898*, Oxford 1967.

13. Marx's article, 'On the Jewish Question', had a dual aspect missed by most critics. He not only says that the emancipation of society from capitalism would be the emancipation of society from the Jews as a component part of big business, but he also starts off from the assumption that the emancipation of the Jews would be an essential element of the general emancipatory movement. Political emancipation, in other words, equal rights for all citizens, including Jews, was progressive.

14. In her article, 'The Socialist Crisis in France', written in 1900, this is what Rosa Luxemburg had to say about the French socialists' struggle against reaction in the Dreyfus Affair:

> Jaurès was right. The Dreyfus Affair aroused all the latent forces of reaction in France. The old enemy of the working class, militarism, was exposed, and all weapons had to be directed against it. For the first time, the working class was called upon to wage a major political battle. Jaurès and his friends led them in this battle and thereby inaugurated a new epoch in the history of French socialism.
>
> *Gesammelte Werke*, vol. 1/2, pp. 27–8

August Bebel expressed similar sentiments. He opposed anti-Semitism and, in a letter to Engels, expressed his opposition to 'all emergency laws, all forms of political and social oppression' (August Bebel, *Briefwechsel mit Friedrich Engels*, The Hague 1965, p. 101).

He had the illusion, however, that there was a socially progressive element among the anti-Semitic electoral base which would, in the end, find its way to the Social Democracy. Viktor Adler and even, for a time, the KPD shared this illusion. It was a tragic mistake.

15. *Collected Works*, vol. 20.

16. Beilis, a young Jew, was accused in 1913 of murdering a child to obtain blood for a secret ritual. Although found innocent in both trial and re-trial, the Czarist administration made a rigorous effort to prove that Jews used Christian blood in certain rituals. When the war started the following year, the police and military went into immediate action against the Jews. Trotsky's article on the Beilis case appeared in *Die Neue Zeit*, no. 9, 1913. See Joseph Nevada, *Trotsky and the Jews*, Philadelphia 1971; also Robert Segal, *The Tragedy of Leon Trotsky*, Harmondsworth 1983, which contains a critique of the Nevada book.

17. This becomes very clear in the chapter devoted to the national question in his *History of the Russian Revolution*. Initially, he doesn't mention the Jews in his list of oppressed nationalities, although they were numerically stronger that the Lithuanians, Estonians and Latvians. But then he writes: 'This formal equality gave most of all to the Jews, for the laws limiting their rights had reached the number of 650' (vol. 3, p. 42). So they were obviously an oppressed minority. Trotsky also focused exclusively on the Jewish bourgeoisie and intelligentsia, completely ignoring the existence of the Jewish proletariat and semi-proletariat.

18. See *My Life*, New York 1960, p. 340.

19. Victor Danilov, in *History Workshop Journal*, Oxford 1990.

20. Between 1918 and 1920, as leader of the Red Army, Trotsky, more than all the other revolutionary leaders, had travelled all over the country on his legendary train and was personally better acquainted with the moods of the population, especially the small and middle peasants.

21. He expressed this in a letter to Bukharin on 4 March 1926: 'Is it true, is it possible, that *in our party, in Moscow, in workers' cells*, anti-Semitic agitation should be carried on with impunity?!' (quoted from Isaac Deutscher, *The Prophet Unarmed*, Oxford 1970, p. 258).

22. Trotsky, 'Thermidor and anti-Semitism'. This article is dated 22 February 1937 and first appeared in the American magazine, *The New International*, 22 February 1937. Jean-Jaques Marie indicates that in 1926 Soviet Jews, mostly urban-dwellers, already made up 25 per cent of Soviet functionaries (bureaucracy). In 1939, 40 per cent of the heads of Jewish families were functionaries, against only 17.2 per cent of the average Soviet heads of families. These facts made Soviet Jews, in Stalin's eyes, an easy scapegoat for the masses' hatred of the bureaucracy (*Les derniers complots de Staline*, Brussels 1993, p. 212).

23. On anti-Semitism in present-day Russian, see Ernest Mandel, *Beyond Perestroika*, London 1989, pp. 18–20.

24. Social Darwinism should not be confused with extreme nationalism or chauvinism.

25. In absolute figures, the number of victims of imperialist repression in India and of the imperialist mass terror in China during the Second World War are equal to if not greater than the number of Jewish victims of Nazi genocide. The difference is that neither Britain nor Japan set out with the goal to murder all the Indians or all the Chinese. This was Hitler's goal – to murder every Jewish man, woman and child. The Sinti and Roma (gypsies) were also threatened with extinction.

26. 'The Imperialist War and the Proletarian Revolution', in *Writings of Leon Trotsky 1939–1940*, New York 1973.

27. The Zionist leader Ben Gurion, and Naum Goldmann, also anticipated the holocaust. See David Ben Gurion, *Israel, A Personal History*, Tel Aviv 1972, p. 50.

28. Trotsky's 'Appeal to American Jews' is in *Leon Trotsky on the Jewish Question*, New York 1970.

29. Ibid.

30. 'Interview with the Jewish Daily, *Forward*', in *Writings of Leon Trotsky 1936–1937*, New York 1970 and 1978, pp. 102ff.

31. See Trotsky, 'A Trip to Palestine' (14 February 1939), in *Writings of Leon Trotsky. Supplement 1934–1940*, pp. 827–8.

32. Trotskyists in Israel call for a transformation of the Zionist state into a bi-national Palestine.

33. See also Nora Levin, *The Jews in the Soviet Union since 1917*, New York 1988.

34. For Marxists, federalism is the best – the only possible – solution for nationalities that live in mixed populations over a wider area.

35. Religion and cultural traditions are by no means identical. For instance, the different cultural and linguistic traditions of the Jews in India prevented them from uniting in a single nation in spite of their common religion.

11

Trotsky as Literary Critic

Trotsky, from an early age, was a passionate devourer of literature. The numerous reviews of classical and contemporary authors published before his return to Russia in 1917 are evidence of this. Jean Van Heyenoort reports that, during his exile in Turkey, France and Norway, Trotsky always took two hours off after lunch to rest and read novels.[1] But the dialectic of the general and the particular, the abstract and the concrete, the theoretical and the practical, which dominated Trotsky's thinking, led his passion for literature inevitably beyond judgements about particular authors and works to more general theoretical considerations.

Trotsky had a very keen sense for the social effects of popular literature and he was one of the first to recognize the enormous popular influence of the film.[2] Books and films, with their ability to reach and influence millions, would be an absolutely essential instrument in the education of the masses, in the development of class-consciousness and later in the construction of a classless society. But this generalization did not in itself answer a further question: Under what conditions can it fulfil this function, under what conditions can it promote the self-understanding, self-activity and self-realization of the enormous mass of wage-earners?

To approach a solution to this question, Trotsky looked at it from both ends: the writer as artist and the reader as consumer of art.[3] In his writings on literature and art he demonstrated a profound understanding for the specificity of art and of the work of art, and these writings are an impressive example of a unity of theory and practice, of practice and sensitivity.[4]

In art, according to Trotsky, man expresses his need for harmony and for the full utilization of all the possibilities that life has to offer; something that he cannot find in class society. Therefore, every authentic work of literature is, at the same time, a protest against a humanly inadequate social reality. He therefore makes a fundamental distinction between writers such as Marcel Proust, who contemplate only their own navel, and those writers whose works portray a social reality and social problems which a reading public can recognize as its own.

More generally, Trotsky adopted a rather positive view of the intelligentsia's social qualities that made it unlike the commercial and industrial petty bourgeoisie and peasantry:

> its occupational ties with the cultural branch of society, its capacity for theoretical generalization, the flexibility and mobility of its thinking, in short, its intellectuality. Confronted with the inescapable fact of the transfer of the entire apparatus of society into new hands, the intelligentsia of Europe will be able to convince itself that the conditions thus established not only will not cast them into the abyss but, on the contrary, will open before them unlimited possibilities for the application of technical, organizational and scientific forces.[5]

At least under the specific conditions of civil war and decline of productive forces in Soviet Russia, this prediction proved too optimistic. It became, however, increasingly true after 1921.

But the creative writer writes his novels and poems not like an alchemist who uses the instruments and tools of his laboratory in the search for gold or the secret of youth. His own individuality, his own emotional experiences act as a mediating element between the inadequate social reality in general and the individual work of art. Art is always the junction between human history and individual destiny. What Trotsky valued most in writers therefore was honesty about themselves and others, characteristics he described as spontaneity and authenticity.[6] Hypocrisy came ultimately from self-deception, and self-deception led inevitably to the deception of others.

Alongside spontaneity, what Trotsky considered important in the evaluation of a literary work was the will of the writer, a will generally reflected in the characters of the novel. Trotsky felt a strong dislike for passive people, people without a will of their own, who reconciled themselves to an inhuman destiny. Hence his negative reaction not only to Proust and Giraudoux but also to Dostoyevsky.[7] Rebellion, rejection, resistance to everything that was inhuman and anti-human was, for Trotsky, an elementary human duty. Only such an instinctive rejection could lead ultimately to an understanding of the need for socialism, for a classless society, to an understanding of the need for revolution. Hence his great admiration for Balzac and Tolstoy, regardless of their ideological limitations. These writers brought living, active people on to the stage, people who attempted, with or without success, to determine and to alter their own destiny.

Spontaneity, authenticity, honesty and a strong will – these were the essential preconditions of creativity and these demanded absolute independence. Just as Marx, the authentic scientist, had the greatest contempt for the scholar who falsified the results of his research or adapted to the requirements of the moment, so also did Trotsky, as an authentic writer, despise the novelist who subordinated his pen to the requirements of paymasters, ruling classes, states, or party leaders. *Without independence, in other words, without moral integrity, there is no true art.*

This does not, of course, mean that Trotsky suffered from the illusion that the thinking and work of the individual artist or writer could be free of all social influence. There are no writers who can stand outside their own time and their own society, who can write without expressing, consciously or unconsciously, the influence of social movements and social interests. But partisanship (conscious, semi-conscious or unconscious) is one thing, objectivity and honesty are something else. A writer can be passionately in favour of the existing order, can defend its interests and can be a convinced conservative reactionary. But he can only be a great writer if he mediates this message in a way that does not distort reality; in other words, if he does not deceive himself and others. Therefore, Goethe and Balzac were brilliant and great writers in spite of their conservative ideology. So also was the conservative anarchist Tolstoy.

What is valid for writers with a reactionary ideology is also valid, if not even more so, for writers who regard themselves as progressive or socialist. The writer can condemn class society, praise the revolution, admire the proletarian class struggle – but without embellishment, without portraying reality in a dishonest way, without painting a picture of conditions that do not exist, without pretence. As Lenin said: only the truth is revolutionary. In Trotsky's eyes, Emile Zola, Anatole France, Ignacio Silone, Marcel Martinet and especially Jack London were great writers; Aragon, Simonov and Barbusse (except for *The Fire*) were not.

The requirement that the writer should have absolute independence meant that the workers' state should refrain from any form of prescription or interference. In his *Literature and Revolution*, written in 1924,[8] Trotsky insisted absolutely on this. A resolution of the Central Committee of 1925, which Trotsky influenced, said:

> The communist critic must be free from any form of pretentious, semi-literate and self-satisfied communist superiority.... The Party favours the free competition of literary schools and currents.... Any other solution

would be formal and bureaucratic.... The Party will not grant any group a monopoly in literary production. The Party can give no group a monopoly position, even a group that is completely proletarian in its ideas. This would be tantamount to a destruction of proletarian literature itself. The Party believes it is necessary to root out every kind of high-handed and incompetent administrative interference in literary matters.[9]

This is the alternative to Zhdanov's 'cultural policy', to Mao's Machiavellian slogan, 'Let a Hundred Schools Bloom', which was only a trap for 'right-wing deviationists' who were subjected to repression when they did bloom. The demand for complete independence of the writer is directed not only at the despotic bureaucracy of the Soviet Union. It is also directed at the bourgeois state and at the capitalists who put political as well as monetary pressure on the artist. Sometimes they both worked in unison: during the Second World War, the Kremlin put pressure on the British authorities to prevent George Orwell from publishing his satire, *Animal Farm*.[10]

But there is another side to the coin: freedom and objectivity do not mean the same thing as non-partisanship or abstinence with respect to defence of workers' interests. In *Literature and Revolution* Trotsky often passes severe judgement on numerous literary currents, for instance, the Symbolists, the Formalists and the Futurists. He was also very critical of the literary 'fellow travellers' of the Revolution, such as the 'Serapion Brothers' and Vsevolod Ivanov. Any other attitude would have been insincere and illogical. One cannot demand that others should have the freedom of criticism and opinion while at the same time denying it to oneself. One cannot demand that a Marxist should not avail himself of Marxist criteria when assessing a literary work.

There is no contradiction, therefore, between both parts of *Literature and Revolution*: the part in which Trotsky demands that the workers' state should not interfere with writers and the part in which he formulates his own severely critical judgements of both Russian and foreign writers.

He had high praise for Mayakovsky and Yesenin and he portrayed their tragic fate as a product of the Soviet Thermidor. In his assessment of Maxim Gorky, he distinguished two periods in the writer's life. The young Gorky developed from a vagrant poet to a writer who, influenced by the revolution of 1905, went over to the side of the proletariat. At the same time, this auto-didact writer became a passionate defender of what was called the 'cultural treasure'. This made him critical of what he saw as the worst excesses generated by the October Revolution. This was the bridge which made it easier for Gorky to pass over to the authoritarian Stalin camp later, in spite of his political attitudes of 1917. Then began the second, the non-creative period of his life. Gorky died, said Trotsky, when he had nothing more to say. But 'the great writer, the great man, left his mark on a period of history. He helped in opening up new historical paths.'[11]

This dual aspect of Trotsky's literary criticism derives from something more fundamental, something he shared with Lenin and partly with Bukharin: a rejection of the myth of 'proletarian culture'. The proletariat is an oppressed class in bourgeois society and in the transitional period between capitalism and socialism it remains a culturally underdeveloped class. Its task, therefore, under the dictatorship is not the creation of a proletarian culture. Its main task is to appropriate for itself the valuable parts of pre-bourgeois and bourgeois culture. This opens the way for the first elements of a future socialist culture to appear. There will be a magnificent socialist culture, but there will be no proletarian culture.[12]

These views were increasingly rejected by the Proletkult movement, which had the support of the authorities in the period from 1932 to 1934. As in the economy and social relations in general, this ultra-left period was merely a transition to the consolidation of the Soviet Thermidor. The main characteristic of Thermidor with respect to literature and art was not an ultra-left Proletkult, but a hackneyed imitation of petty-bourgeois narrow-mindedness. Trotsky had nothing but contempt for 'socialist realism':

> The style of contemporary official Soviet art has the title 'socialist realism'. This name was clearly given to it by some director of some artists' association. Its realism consists of an imitation of the provincial clichés of the nineteenth century. Its 'socialist' character is expressed in its use of falsified photographs to portray events that have never happened.... Officials armed with pens, paint brushes and chisels pay honour, under the supervision of officials armed with mausers, to 'great' and 'brilliant' leaders, who in reality are devoid of greatness or brilliance.[13]

But Trotsky was convinced that this 'Babylonian exile' of Soviet literature and art would not last forever.[14] Developments in Russian and Soviet society in recent years have shown him to be right. He also emphasized the growing importance of art and science for the final victory of socialism:

> Even when the basic problems of food, clothing, housing and elementary education have been resolved, this still won't mean the final victory of the new historical principle, i.e. of socialism. Only the progress of scientific thought and the development of a new art will demonstrate that the historic

seed has not only grown into a plant but has already begun to bloom. In this sense, the development of art is the highest test of the vitality and significance of every historical epoch.[15]

There can be no pure proletarian art or literature. Nevertheless, bourgeois society, and even more the transitional period between bourgeois and socialist society, can contain the initial elements of a socialist culture and literature. These can be found primarily in the material itself. Trotsky asked that writers concern themselves with the actual problems and issues that affect the workers – once again without embellishment.

These beginnings of socialist literature – Trotsky often used the phrase 'revolutionary literature' – should be educational, in the best sense of the word (not formally didactic), in that they serve, in the first instance, to raise the general cultural level of the working class. Trotsky deals here with very elementary problems: know the language and speak it correctly, express yourself clearly, think critically, put events in their wider context, link personal destiny with the destiny of the class, and so on. Trotsky's most important disciple in questions of literature and literary criticism was undoubtedly Victor Serge. He used the term 'proletarian humanism'.[16]

Another problem was how to overcome the gulf between literary production and literary consumption, in other words, how to encourage the workers themselves to write.[17] Neither Trotsky nor Victor Serge had any illusion that this problem could be resolved easily or in a short time.

From the analysis of the problems of literary creation and the literary and cultural policy of the proletarian state we now arrive at another problem: How is literature to influence the broad masses? We are dealing here with the dialectic of content and form: which forms of literary expression will help a large reading public to reach a higher cultural level? The form of presentation has to interest the reader. It must offer an incentive to further reading. Characters and actions have to be comprehensible. They must remind the reader of what he is familiar with, but also lead him beyond this to the unfamiliar. It must be simultaneously entertaining and thought-provoking. It must stimulate the reader's critical faculties. At the end of the book he must have the feeling that he now knows more about people and society than he did before.

The novels that Trotsky highly praised, for instance, Silone's *Fontemara* and Jack London's *The Iron Heel*, had all these features. There are, of course, numerous other examples. Primo Levi's *The*

Wrench (1978, Penguin edition 1987), one of the great literary achievements of the century, would have delighted Trotsky. Its hero is a manual worker in constant conflict with all kinds of institutions bent on commanding and manipulating him, including Soviet bureaucrats. Primo Levi was actually close to Trotsky's ideas. The Old Man would have loved these telling words from *The Wrench*:

> Sure, of course, we lodged a protest: witnesses, another inspection, lawsuit.... Years have passed but the lawsuit is still going on.... How do you think it will end? I already know what happens when things of iron become things of paper. It ends wrong.

This does not mean, of course, that novels and stories that are not accessible to the broad masses because of their specific form are without aesthetic or social value. Trotsky strongly rejected this narrow pseudo-proletarian prejudice against avantgardist or complex forms of expression. He knew that a living creativity cannot move forwards without deviating from official tradition and from the established canon of ideas and emotions, without breaking away from images and linguistic usages that have been covered with the varnish of habit.

Every new direction in literature looks for a more direct and more sincere relation between words and perceptions. The struggle against dissimulation and hypocrisy becomes a struggle against falseness in social relations:

> Every authentic work of art contains a conscious or unconscious, active or passive, optimistic or pessimistic protest against reality. Every new artistic current begins with a rebellion. The power of bourgeois society has been seen in its ability, over a longer period of time, to use a combination of pressure, admonition, boycott and flattery to discipline and assimilate every 'rebellious' artistic current and to give it official 'recognition'. For the current in question this 'recognition' was always the beginning of the end. But later the left or more radical wing of the officially recognized school started a new rebellion, or a new generation of creative bohemians began a new rebellious movement which, in its own time, would also enter the doors of the academy.[18]

Hence Trotsky's spontaneous sympathy for the surrealist movement. This led in 1938, during a trip of André Breton to Mexico, to the manifesto 'For an Independent Revolutionary Art', formally signed by Breton and Diego Rivera, though in reality written commonly (not without controversies) by Breton and Trotsky. Simultaneously, a 'Federation for Independent Revolutionary Art' was created.

It is not enough for the writer to fight mendacity and hypocrisy in form and content. The pessimistic, hopeless fighter of hypocrisy who can neither find nor even point to a way out of this society built on falsehood will, in the end, defend the existing order as the only possible one. The new style of Céline's *Journey to the End of Night* fascinated Trotsky but he instinctively recognized the reactionary element in Céline, something confirmed by later events.[19]

The apparently pessimistic Jack London, however, who in his novel *The Iron Heel* describes with almost prophetic intuition the possibility of a fascist dictatorship, is a truly revolutionary writer. In London's book it is the masses who are the potential source of rebellion, unlike Orwell's *Nineteen Eighty-Four*, in which it is a few individuals.[20] As literary critic Trotsky remains a revolutionary realist. In order to change society and life consciously, one first has to know, recognize, understand and explain. But he is a realist who integrates the dream, the 'principle of hope', into his reality.

Notes

1. See Jean Van Heyenoort, *With Trotsky in Exile*, Cambridge, Mass. 1978.
2. For Trotsky's view on films, see his *Problems of Everyday Life*, New York 1973.
3. Trotsky used the unexpected but appropriate expression: 'Every artist creates with his nerves.'
4. Trotsky was also a 'practitioner' of literature, one of the major stylists of the twentieth century.
5. 'The Intelligentsia and Socialism' (1910), in *The Fourth International*, 1964/65.
6. This quotation is from the French collection, *Littérature et révolution*, Paris 1974, pp. 362–3. This collection contains more material than the English publication, *Literature and Revolution*, Michigan 1968.
7. See Pierre Naville, *Trotsky vivant*, Paris 1962, p. 96.
8. The first English edition was published by International Publishers, New York, in 1925. It was published in German in Vienna in 1924.
9. Quoted from *Victor Serge: Schriftsteller und Proletarier*, Frankfurt/M 1977, pp. 63–4. It remains a mystery to me why Trotsky never made comments on Victor Serge's novels, some of which, like *Naissance de notre force* and *L'affaire Toulayev*, are among the great revolutionary novels of this century.
10. See George Orwell, *The Last Writings*, ed. W. J. West, New York 1988, p. 61.
11. Trotsky, *Portraits – Political and Personal*, New York 1977, pp. 160–61.
12. *Littérature et révolution*, pp. 162–4, 196ff. The American novelist James T. Farrell, who would later join the Trotskyist movement, developed a similar position in his book, *A Note on Literary Criticism*, originally published in 1936; reprinted New York 1962. We don't know whether Farrell had read Trotsky's *Literature and Revolution* at the time.
13. Ibid., p. 358.
14. Ibid., p. 353.
15. Ibid., p. 21.
16. See Serge, ibid., pp. 97ff.
17. *Littérature et révolution*, p. 74.
18. Ibid., p. 354.
19. See the chapter 'Céline and Poincaré: Novelist and Politician', in *Leon Trotsky on Literature and Art*, ed. Paul Siegel, New York 1970, especially pp. 201 and 205.
20. *Littérature et Révolution*, pp. 346–8.

12

Trotsky the Man

Self-confident, unshakeable in the conviction of his historic mission, strict with others and with himself, indifferent to material privileges and to the small joys and sorrows of life: this is the dominant image of Trotsky in the history books and reports (excluding, of course, the Stalinist slanders). This image is not pure invention. It reflects certain aspects of Trotsky's personality, his strengths and his weaknesses. But they are only aspects. What they portray is not Trotsky the whole man, the active participant in world history for forty-five years.

At the highpoints in his life he knew how to communicate directly with the masses, probably more directly than any other socialist leader this century. Jaurès was also a great orator, maybe even greater than Trotsky, but Jaurès never had the opportunity to speak directly to the revolutionary masses. The ability to do this is not just an oratorical gift; it is an eminently political one. These aspects of his character mentioned above don't show us the man who, in moments of political triumph, was able to keep the sympathy and unlimited admiration of large numbers of people, and in times of most bitter defeat was able to win and keep the close friendship of many. They also don't show us the man who, after the greatest personal defeats and bitter disappointments, was still able to express his historical optimism, his belief in the future of humanity, his belief in a non-violent society, his almost child-like devotion to the beauties of nature and art, and his unshakeable affirmation of life.

His Testament, written in February 1940, ended with the words:

> Natasha has just come up to the window from the courtyard and opened it wider so that the air may enter more freely into my room. I can see the bright green strip of grass beneath the wall, and the clear blue sky above the wall, and sunlight everywhere. Life is beautiful. Let the future generations cleanse it of all evil, oppression, and violence and enjoy it to the full.[1]

This belief in a future without violence was by no means obvious at a moment when it appeared that the two mass murderers, Hitler and Stalin, were about to triumph.

This man Trotsky, who, like Karl Marx and Friedrich Engels before him, applied to himself the old Roman saying, 'I am a man, nothing human is alien to me', is not adequately described by the character traits listed at the opening of this chapter. His personality, his thinking, his actions and his emotions are dominated by three characteristics: a spontaneous revolt against every form of injustice and oppression which led, at a very early stage in his life, to a commitment to the working class and its emancipation; an equally spontaneous urge for rationality, for an understanding and explanation of social reality as a precondition for changing it; a constant view of the world and of history as contradictory processes in which progress and regression, evolution and revolution, revolution and counter-revolution, rationality and irrationality, humanity and inhumanity are carrying on a constant struggle, the outcome of which we cannot exactly foretell, in other words, a view that was uniquely and profoundly dialectical.

These three basic features of his character made Trotsky a revolutionary Marxist, a Marxist who was severely critical of the political fatalism of the Second International and who attributed to the subjective factor in history a decisive role in the drama of our century.[2] They also contained a strongly anti-dogmatic element, a certainty that *only the long-term* results of our political actions will allow us to pass judgement on their rationality, effectiveness or historical justification. This was why, throughout his life, he was politically not as self-confident as Lenin. At some decisive moments in his political life he hesitated to fight immediately and ruthlessly for his convictions. One of his closest friends, Adolf Yoffe,[3] wrote this of him in his testament.

He had an unusual intellectual ability and literary talent. In spite of weak health, he remained very energetic and maintained a well above-average workload. He exercised the strictest self-discipline and he expected the same from his closest friends and colleagues. His political hardness, his sharp polemics and his biting irony are reminiscent of Lenin, with one important difference: more so than with Lenin, they contained a personal note which made later reconciliation all the more difficult. Bernard Shaw once said of him, in his typically sarcastic manner, that Trotsky chopped the heads off his opponents to show that there was nothing inside. There were only five instances of such reconciliation in his political life: for a short time with Bukharin in the period 1919–22 and with his brother-in-law, Kamenev, in 1925–27; for many years with his close personal friend, the French revolutionary

Marxist, Alfred Rosmer;[4] with Lenin after the February Revolution of 1917; and in the last days of his life with Raymond Molivier and Pierre Frank. Although he felt himself politically superior to Bukharin, Kamenev and Rosmer, his relation to Lenin after 1917 was that of a talented colleague and student to his teacher. This didn't change during his disagreement with Lenin after 1917, for instance over Brest-Litovsk and in the trade union debate.

His limited ability to seek reconciliation after a polemic meant that Trotsky was less successful than Lenin in grouping around him a team of leaders who were independent and willing to criticize him in spite of his massive authority. His closest colleagues were a more homogeneous, if not monolithic, group compared to the team that worked with Lenin. Of course, there was also a smaller number of people to choose from. There were, however, significant exceptions. The Mezhrayonka group of 1917 included such personalities as Lunacharsky, Manuilsky, Ryazanov, Uritsky, Petrovsky, Yoffe and Volodarsky. Although Lunacharsky later became very critical of Trotsky[5] and Manuilsky became a Stalinist, Uritsky, Volodarsky and Yoffe remained friends for life. His close co-workers in the famous train during the civil war, particularly Sklyansky, Butov, Sermux and his secretary, Glasman, whom Stalin drove to suicide, remained political comrades to the end. The leadership of the Left Opposition between 1923 and 1932 included such prominent personalities as Christian Rakovsky, Beloborodov, Smirnov and Mrachkovsky, who were a functioning leadership team for ten years. Trotsky also worked closely for eight years with such prominent Bolshevik leaders as Preobrazhensky, Pyatakov, Radek and Smilga before they capitulated to Stalin. In the preparation and founding of the Fourth International he worked closely for many years, and in spite of many disagreements, with former Comintern leaders such as Sneevliet, Andres Nin, Ch'en Tu-hsiu, James Cannon and Léon Lesoil.[6]

Although hard in the way he carried out political polemics, he was, by contrast, an exceptionally warm person in the circle of his family and friends. This is something strongly emphasized by most of the people that worked with him. This is how Van Heyenoort described him:

> To visitors and new acquaintances, Trotsky was extremely friendly. He talked, explained, gesticulated, asked questions, and was on occasion really charming.... Of all the people I saw around Trotsky between 1932 and 1939, it was Diego Rivera that Trotsky responded to with the greatest warmth and openness. In his encounters with Rivera he was trusting, natural and relaxed in a way he was with no one else.[7]

Angelica Balabanoff emphasized his modesty:

> Men are usually judged not according to their qualities or defects but rather on the basis of what makes the contact with them pleasant or difficult, and opinions about Trotsky were often one-sided or unjust. Very few, for example, knew of his self-inflicted privations. Had he been willing to avail himself of the privileges to which his position entitled him, he and his family could have lived in much better circumstances.[8]

Max Eastman, although in general quite negative about his meeting with Trotsky in Prinkipo, admitted that 'Trotsky is the most modest of all the famous Marxists that I have known. He never boasts, never talks about himself or his own achievements, never dominates the conversation.'[9]

This apparent contradiction between the hard polemicist and the modest man resolves itself when we recall an important characteristic of Trotsky as a man: his desire to preserve, separate from his political commitments, a free space for his own private life, for his own rich and varied private interests and feelings. This was something he shared with Marx and Engels. Among all the great socialists it was probably Rosa Luxemburg who managed this better than all others, including Trotsky. Bukharin was like Trotsky in this respect, but his interests were not so diverse or profound. Lenin had a similar desire, but he saw it as a temptation. He was the most strongly politicized of all the great socialists, ruled in all his activities by a singleness of purpose. Whether this deliberate constriction of one's private life strengthens one's political judgement or, on occasion, clouds it is, on the basis of concrete historical experience, at least unclear.

In his biography, Isaac Deutscher described Trotsky's diverse interests and activities in Vienna, where he lived with his wife and two children and was the Vienna correspondent of *Kievskaya Mysl*, a widely read radical liberal daily:

> By all accounts the family led a quiet and happy existence. The revolutionary lion was a devoted husband and warm-hearted father. Anxious to help his wife and to enable her to pursue her artistic interests and to follow the political life of the Russian colony, he lent a hand in domestic chores and in the upbringing of the children. Later, when the boys went to school, he regularly helped them in their homework, and found time for this even in the fever of the war years, after the family had moved to Paris. Sedova, for her part, resumed in Vienna her husband's artistic education, which she had begun in Paris without initial success in 1902. The couple spent many a day together amid the rich art collections in the Burgschloss and in Viennese galleries. His interest in the arts was growing appreciably: on his

frequent visits to Paris, Munich or London he would steal away from political conventicles to the Louvre, the Tate Gallery and other collections; and his writings of this period, especially his reviews of the annual Viennese exhibitions, written for *Kievskaya Mysl*, show a slightly more than dilettante appreciation of trends in European art. While politics and journalism claimed only part of his time, he also enlarged his already wide familiarity with the French and the Russian novel and with German poetry; and this too is reflected in his literary essays of the time.[10]

In his portrait of the Austro-Marxists, Trotsky draws attention to two dimensions of the revolutionary, the purely political and the psychological:

I was meeting the flower of the pre-war Austrian Marxists, members of parliament, writers and journalists. At those meetings I learned to understand the extraordinary variety of the elements that can be comprised within the mind of one man, and the great distance which separates the mere passive assimilation of certain parts of a system from its complete psychological re-creation as a whole, from re-educating oneself in the spirit of a system. The psychological type of Marxist can develop only in an epoch of social cataclysms, of a revolutionary break with traditions and habits; whereas an Austrian Marxist too often revealed himself a philistine who had learned certain parts of Marx's theory as one might study law, and had lived on the interest that *Das Kapital* yielded him. In the old, imperial, hierarchic, vain and futile Vienna, the academic Marxists would refer to each other with a sort of sensuous delight as 'Herr Doktor'. Workers often called the academicians 'Genosse Herr Doktor'. During all the seven years that I lived in Vienna, I never had a heart-to-heart talk with any one of this upper group, although I was a member of the Austrian Social Democracy, attended their meetings, took part in their demonstrations, contributed to their publications and sometimes made short speeches in German. I felt that the leaders of the Social Democrats were alien, whereas I found, quite easily, a mutual language with the Social Democratic workers at meetings or at May Day demonstrations.[11]

The versatility of Trotsky's character surprised many observers. Hendrik De Man, the Belgian Social-Democratic leader, admits he found it difficult to believe in Trotsky's leading role in founding the Red Army. He knew Trotsky during his Vienna exile, and from his appearances at the Brussels Buro of the Second International, as the prototype of 'the nervous, coffee-house-literatus without self-discipline'.[12] He saw that this image did not correspond to the Trotsky of 1917–20. With his typical semi-Marxist approach to things, he concluded: a revolution changes a person. What he didn't recognize, of course, was that the core of this new dimension that manifests itself in the life of every historical personality must already have existed previously.

This versatility, with all its weaknesses, should not cloud our overall judgement of his role in history. The certainty of his own historic mission was not the product of an exaggerated sense of his own self-importance. At the following turning-points in world history, Trotsky played a role which, because of the interplay of social and personal development, only he could have played:[13]

1. In the decisive weeks before the October Revolution in the Petrograd Soviet and among the soldiers of the Petrograd garrison, as well as during the decisive days and hours of the October uprising and in the concrete link between the uprising and the democratically elected Second All-Russian Soviet Congress.

2. In the construction of the Red Army and in determining the political and social strategy which would lead to victory in the civil war and to the consolidation of the Soviet power (1918–20).

3. In his early recognition of the extent of the process of bureau-cratization in the party, the state and the trade unions and in his decision to wage an uncompromising struggle against the Stalin faction which supported this process (1923–27).

4. In his recognition of the historical defeat that a victory for Hitler's fascism would represent and in his attempt to prevent this by means of the united front 'from above and below' (1930–33).

5. In his almost hopeless efforts to rescue the historic continuity of revolutionary Marxism in light of the historic defeat of the inter-national labour movement, the 'midnight of the century', which was about to envelop everyone (1936–40).

Trotsky has often been accused of dogmatism, for instance, by the French philosopher, Merleau-Ponty, the American philosopher, John Dewey, and by his Israeli biographer, Baruch Knei-Paz. This accusa-tion rests on an incorrect understanding of science and raises a fundamental question of epistemology. Scientific theories are always tentative; they are working hypotheses which have to be internally coherent and capable of verification or falsification by empirical data. Therefore, both dogmatism (the refusal to submit a hypothesis to this process of verification) and absolute scepticism are unscientific. But the scientific character of a hypothesis cannot be denied if this hypothesis, for instance, the thesis of the immanent systemic character of the capitalist crisis of overproduction, has been verified by historical experience. To deny the scientific character of this hypothesis would be tantamount to a regression to non-scientific superstition. Trotsky's defence of this thesis and of other equally scientific theses central to an understanding of this century are not an indication of dogmatism but of his scientific seriousness.

Another accusation, made for instance by Merleau-Ponty, concerns the problem, allegedly originating from Marx, of objectivism/subjectivism: 'For someone who thinks he knows the future, individual events have no meaning or importance; the future unfolds, come what may.' But this conclusion does not follow; it is a logical fallacy. Let us assume that someone takes for granted that there are empirically verifiable (and empirically verified) regularities in history. Why would such a person be incapable of critically testing the validity of these regularities whenever there is new empirically relevant evidence?

Behind this accusation of the 'subjectivism' of Marxists, sometimes described, in the case of Trotsky, as messianic prophecy, lies a failure to grasp the dual nature of Marxism. Marxism combines a strict scientificity with a categorical imperative, formulated by the young Marx and restated and completely reaffirmed by the old Marx: 'the categorical imperative to overthrow all conditions in which man is a debased, enslaved, neglected, and contemptible being.'[14]

Trotsky expressed this duality of Marxism in a classical and remarkable manner in his article, 'The USSR in War' (25 September 1939):

If however it is conceded that the present war will provoke not revolution but a decline of the proletariat, then there remains another alternative: the further decay of monopoly capitalism, its further fusion with the state and the replacement of democracy wherever it still remained by a totalitarian regime...

The historic alternative, carried to the end, is as follows: either the Stalin regime is an abhorrent relapse in the process of transforming bourgeois society into a new socialist society, or the Stalin regime is the first stage of a new exploiting society. If the second prognosis proves to be correct, then, of course, the bureaucracy will become a new exploiting class. However onerous the second perspective may be, if the world proletariat should actually prove itself incapable of fulfilling the historic mission placed upon it by the course of development, nothing else would remain except only to recognize that the socialist programme, based on the internal contradictions of capitalist society, ended as a utopia. It is self-evident that a new 'minimum' programme would be required – for the defence of the interests of the slaves of the totalitarian bureaucratic society.[15]

The first part of the argument demonstrates the strictly scientific element of Marxism. The second confirms the validity of the categorical imperative, even under extraordinary conditions (which, happily, have not come about).

Jan Meijer, the editor of *The Trotsky Papers*, believes that he has discovered a major contradiction in Trotsky's personality, in the tension between his historical and immediate political role, between the strategist and the tactician.[16] This tension is undoubtedly real. But it is not a characteristic or a weakness that is peculiar to Trotsky. It is a general anthropological characteristic.

Human activity is always (consciously, semi-consciously, unconsciously) goal-oriented, i.e. functional. Its goal is always to bring about certain changes in the existential conditions of the individual (or of humanity or of the community), in his relation to nature or to society. But in the dialectic of initial situation, active subject and end-result, the object as well as the subject are changed. The end-result can never be exactly predicted from the start. The end-result can be completely at odds with what was intended. And our judgement on the result may vary with the time-span. Short-term success can turn out to be long-term failure, and vice versa. In addition, every human action has not just a positive but also a negative alternative. Not to do something, to remain passive, can also affect our own and others' lives. The scholastics quite rightly regarded sins of omission to be just as reprehensible as sins of commission.

The only conclusion that we can draw from these general observations is that a perfect goal-oriented political action – perfect strategy and perfect tactics – is humanly impossible. What remains is to make the optimal choice, based on an optimal awareness, among priorities. Trotsky did this. But optimal is not perfect.

Those who fought by Trotsky's side for the continuity of a living, revolutionary Marxism and for the construction of a revolutionary international, as well as those who continued this work after his death, are generally described as Trotskyists. This term was coined by his opponents.[17] Trotsky himself never used it. The supporters of the Fourth International prefer to describe themselves as revolutionary Marxists because they value, alongside Trotsky, the contributions of the other great socialists of the twentieth century to the body of socialist theory and strategy. But they are not embarrassed by being called Trotskyist and are quite happy to describe themselves as such. Trotsky, for them, is not a new idol that should replace Stalin in the famous pantheon of four. He is certainly no infallible pope of politics. Like Marx, Engels, Luxemburg, Gramsci and others, Trotsky made some analytical and political mistakes. Our task today is to examine these critically and such a critique is part of contemporary revolutionary socialism.

But in the light of the whole historical experience of this century, Trotskyists would claim that among all the thinkers and socialist politicians it was Trotsky who most clearly recognized the decisive problems of our century and proposed the best solutions to these problems. To fight for these solutions today is just as important for the future of humanity as it was in 1906, in 1917–23, or in 1936–40. That's why we are and remain Trotskyists.

Anti-Trotskyist prejudices remain strong in the Western European left. I will give one interesting example. In Germany, Bernt Rabehl and his colleagues have done valuable work in republishing interesting articles by Kurt Mandelbaum from the 1920s on the ideological and social background to reformism. In 1928 Kurt Mandelbaum came to the conclusion that 'the socialist success of the revolution that began in Russia will depend on the victory of the proletariat in the industrially developed countries.'[18] Maybe owing to a lack of information, he did not mention Trotsky's theory of permanent revolution or his struggle against the theory of socialism in one country. Now, thirty-five years later, in their comments on Mandelbaum in the republished work, Rabehl and his colleagues also ignore Trotsky. They list Rosa Luxemburg, Lukács, Korsch and Mandelbaum, but not Trotsky, as sources for the concept (strategy) of socialist revolution based on the self-organization and self-activity of the proletariat. This is, from every point of view, unacceptable.

A few weeks after the fiftieth anniversary of his assassination, Soviet television showed a biographical film on Trotsky with the title (taken from his Testament), 'Life is Beautiful'. He is portrayed in this film as a warm and modest man. On 17 August 1990, *Izvestia* published an article on Trotsky which described him as 'a great and irreproachable revolutionary', the second man in the party and in the state.

On the day after Trotsky was murdered, the German writer, Arnold Zweig, wrote an impressive obituary. It was published in the GDR fifty years later, in 1990:

> The death of Lenin was a great blow to the man that he used to call 'the pen', a man who had in his head the most valuable and best-organized brain that was ever crushed by a hammer. Trotsky came to Lenin from the Mensheviks. He brought with him the whole treasure of his energy, his intellect, and his revolutionary zeal ... L. D. Trotsky, throughout his whole life, fought for all of us who love human civilization, for whom this civilization is our nationality. His murderer, whoever he is, tried, in killing him, to kill this civilization, our fatherland. Our task now is to rescue

Trotsky's life-work from the ever-present threat of decay. For Trotsky, this life-work was world revolution: expressed modestly and in a simple manner, this meant the extension of human culture to the hundreds of millions of the illiterate or, as Lunacharsky expressed it, it meant a different expression in the eyes of all these people.[19]

The South African writer, Ronald Segal, ended his critical biography of Trotsky in a manner quite similar to Arnold Zweig:

[Trotsky] speaks for the power of the people against those who speak for the power of the state. He speaks against privilege to those who speak for the subservience of others. He speaks for the liberation of ideas, to those who speak only for the confinements of theirs. He speaks for the will to resist, regardless of cost, to those who only know to speak for the intimidation of dissent.

It is in the voice of this revolution, too, rejecting and offering, that Trotsky speaks still for humanity.... He speaks to a world where, within particular states, storehouses contain such hoards of surplus food that terms are borrowed from geography to describe them; while, a few jet-hours away, famine crosses the frontiers of sovereignty without recognizing the requirements of a passport. And he will speak for as long as wealth is no more than the obverse of want, in the coinage of a system that proclaims itself the source of personal freedom and that provides instead the imprisonment of property...

Trotsky believed that men only had to recognize the cage around them to find the means of making their escape. And he struck, above all else, at the cage that is within the mind: of an original sin that consigns redemption to the safe-deposit of another world; or of a permanent primal savagery that informs a past of repeated warnings and a future of corresponding restraint. He speaks still for the promise of man's imagination and reason...

In an era of so much separate futility: when so many intellectuals sit whining on the sidelines of events, and so many artists turn their heads to play patience with their sensibilities; when politics is a special form of white-collar employment, and soldiering asks for all the moral investment of warrior ants: Trotsky bears witness to the creative force of that essential revolutionary, the integral man.... In the long aftermath of his fall, Trotsky remained true to himself, answering to so much death around him with his ardour for life, so much despair with his faith. And in this, he speaks for that joy and that defiance in humanity which no defeat can contain.[20]

Following on from the judgements of Arnold Zweig and Ronald Segal, we would sum up Trotsky's historical role in the following way: he incorporated the unbending will to resist everything that is inhuman in today's world, without regard for the effects on his own destiny. This is expressed most clearly in his fight against imperialism, against fascism and against Stalinism. This will to resist, this culture of resistance, is accompanied by a radical rejection of fatalism, resignation or sycophancy. It is based on a scientifically and morally solid conviction that effective collective resistance sometimes can succeed, because the class of wage-earners has the ability, in specific situations, to confront and to overthrow the oppressive relations of domination. To create the necessary organizational preconditions for this is part of the culture of resistance.

After seventy years of lies and slanders, after fifty years of silence: the mill of history grinds slowly, but it grinds, it grinds. In the light of everything that is happening now in Russia and the world, we have no doubt that history will give Trotsky full justice.

Notes

1. *Writings of Leon Trotsky 1939–1940*, New York 1969 and 1973, p. 159.
2. This is expressed in the following way in the Transitional Programme of the Fourth International:

> The strategic task of the next period – a pre-revolutionary period of agitation, propaganda and organization – consists in overcoming the contradiction between the maturity of objective revolutionary conditions and the immaturity of the proletariat and its vanguard (the confusion and disappointment of the older generation, the inexperience of the younger generation) . . .
> The historical crisis of mankind is reduced to the crisis of the revolutionary leadership.
>
> *Documents of the Fourth International*, New York 1973,
> pp. 182 and 181

3. Trotsky and Yoffe became friends during Trotsky's exile in Vienna. Yoffe, an educated and versatile revolutionary socialist, suffered from a nervous disorder and was being treated by Freud's student, Alfred Adler. He made Trotsky aware of the importance of Freudian psychoanalysis, something that fascinated Trotsky for the rest of his life. In spite of his health problems, Yoffe played a key role in the October Revolution and in the peace negotiations of Brest-Litovsk. Later, he became a prominent Soviet ambassador. He committed suicide in 1927. His funeral was the last big demonstration of the Left Opposition in Moscow. He and Christian Rakovsky were Trotsky's closest political and personal friends between 1917 and 1927.

4. Alfred Rosmer was one of the founders of the French Communist Party and was a member of the Comintern executive (ECCI) between 1920 and 1922. He was a member of the Left Opposition until 1930 when he resigned because of political and organizational differences with the majority. He and Trotsky became personally reconciled in 1936.

5. See Lunacharsky's portrait of Trotsky in his *Revolutionary Silhouettes*, London 1967.

6. Trotsky's close friendship with Sneevliet, Comintern leader and co-founder of the Indonesian and Chinese Communist Parties, lasted seven years. They fell out in 1937 over the question of the Spanish Revolution. James Cannon was a leader of the American Communist Party. Léon Lesoil was co-founder and leader of the Belgian Communist

Party. Ch'en Tu-hsiu was the father of Chinese Marxism and founder of the Chinese Communist Party. Raymond Molivier and Pierre Frank were among the closest members of Trotsky's staff between 1930 and 1936, but fell out at that time on questions of different tactics in France.

7. Jean Van Heyenoort, *Sept ans auprès de Leon Trotsky*, Paris 1978, p. 47.

8. Angelica Balabanoff, *Impressions of Lenin*, Michigan 1968, p. 132.

9. Max Eastman, *Great Companions*, New York 1959.

10. Isaac Deutscher, *The Prophet Armed*, Oxford 1970, p. 184.

11. *My Life*, New York 1960, pp. 208–9.

12. H. De Man, *Gegen den Strom. Memoiren eines europäischen Sozialisten*, Stuttgart 1953.

13. On the complex problem of the role of the individual in history, see Ernest Mandel, 'The Role of the Individual in History: The Case of World War Two', in *New Left Review* 157, London 1986, pp. 61–77.

14. 'Introduction to the Critique of Hegel's Philosophy of Right', in *Early Writings*, Harmondsworth 1975, p. 251.

15. In *In Defense of Marxism*, New York 1973, p. 9.

16. Jan Meijer in *The Trotsky Papers*, The Hague 1971, vol. 2, pp. 843–5.

17. The term 'Trotskyism' was first coined by the bourgeois-liberal politician, the Cadet leader, Milyukov.

18. Kurt Mandelbaum, *Sozialdemokratie und Leninismus*, Berlin 1974, p. 75.

19. *Sinn und Form*, March–April 1990, pp. 317, 320.

20. Ronald Segal, *The Tragedy of Leon Trotsky*, Harmondsworth 1983, pp. 404, 405, 406.

Index